A REALISTIC THEORY OF LAW

This book articulates an empirically grounded theory of law applicable throughout history and across different societies. Unlike natural law theory or analytical jurisprudence, which are narrow, abstract, ahistorical, and detached from society, Tamanaha's theory presents a holistic vision of law within society, evolving in connection with social, cultural, economic, political, ecological, and technological factors. He revives a largely forgotten theoretical perspective on law that runs from Montesquieu through the legal realists to the present. This book explains why the classic question "what is law?" has never been resolved, and casts doubt on theorists' claims about necessary and universal truths about law. This book develops a theory of law as a social institution with varying forms and functions, tracing law from hunter-gatherer societies to the modern state and beyond. Tamanaha's theory accounts for social influences on law, legal influences on society, law and domination, multifunctional governmental uses of law, legal pluralism, international law, and other legal aspects largely overlooked in jurisprudence.

Brian Z. Tamanaha is William Gardiner Hammond Professor of Law at Washington University School of Law. He is the author of nine books, including the prize-winning *A General Jurisprudence of Law and Society*.

A Realistic Theory of Law

BRIAN Z. TAMANAHA

Washington University, St. Louis

CAMBRIDGE
UNIVERSITY PRESS

CAMBRIDGE
UNIVERSITY PRESS

University Printing House, Cambridge CB2 8BS, United Kingdom

One Liberty Plaza, 20th Floor, New York, NY 10006, USA

477 Williamstown Road, Port Melbourne, VIC 3207, Australia

314-321, 3rd Floor, Plot 3, Splendor Forum, Jasola District Centre, New Delhi - 110025, India

79 Anson Road, #06-04/06, Singapore 079906

Cambridge University Press is part of the University of Cambridge.

It furthers the University's mission by disseminating knowledge in the pursuit of education, learning and research at the highest international levels of excellence.

www.cambridge.org
Information on this title: www.cambridge.org/9781316638514
DOI : 10.1017/9781316979778

First published 2017

A catalogue record for this publication is available from the British Library

ISBN 978-1-107-18842-6 Hardback
ISBN 978-1-316-63851-4 Paperback

For Happy, Katsugi, Jolijt, Kats, Vinnie, Sava, and Honorata

Contents

Acknowledgments

I owe thanks to many people for assistance in this endeavor. Professor Maks Del Mar organized several workshops and symposia at Queen Mary University Law School on several draft chapters. Professor Marc de Wilde did the same for me at the University of Amsterdam. Professor Kosuke Nasu coordinated workshops and lectures at multiple universities in Japan and edited a collection of responsive papers on my work. This book improved substantially thanks to the critical feedback I received on these occasions. I am deeply indebted to Maks, Marc, and Kosuke for their efforts. For critical comments on various draft chapters, I thank Maks Del Mar, Brian Bix, Michael Giudice, Michael Lobban, Ken Himma, Danny Priel, Gregoire Webber, Frank Lovett, Kosuke Nasu, Jan Klabbers, Richard Nobles, John Gardner, Gregory Shaffer, Melissa Waters, Leila Sadat, and David Law. I also thank people who commented on draft chapters I presented at Queen Mary Law School, University of Amsterdam, William & Mary Law School, Georgetown Law School, Cardozo Law School, Yale Legal History Colloquium, Kansai University, Chukyo University, Doshisha University, Tohoku University, Zhejiang University, Washington University Law School, and at the Kobe Memorial Lecture. I owe special thanks to William Twining for our many discussions about legal theory over the years, as well for his critical comments on draft chapters. I thank Ami Naramor for careful copy-editing with a light touch.

Chapter 1 is a substantially revised version of the George Wythe Lecture (2014) I delivered at William & Mary Law School, published as "The Third Pillar of Jurisprudence" in the *William & Mary Law Review*. Chapter 4 is a substantially revised version of the Kobe Memorial Lecture (2014) I delivered in Tokyo, published as "Insights about the Nature of Law from History" in *Archiv für Rechts- und Sozialphilosophie*. Chapter 3 is a revised version of "Necessary and Universal Truths about Law?" (2017) published in *Ratio Juris*. Though versions of these particular chapters appear in other venues, it was conceived and written as a monograph.

Finally, I thank John Berger for his enthusiasm and support. We have worked together on several books now, and John has always been an ideal editor.

Introduction: A Realistic Perspective

Contemporary jurisprudence suffers from a profound gap. Law is rooted in the history of a society, continuously remade in relation to social factors. Law is an integral aspect of society and society infuses law, their interaction mutually constitutive and bidirectional in cause and effect. Law assumes different forms and functions in connection with levels of social complexity and surrounding economic, political, cultural, technological, ecological, and social factors. Interconnected with society in these and other ways, law must be apprehended holistically. Theories that center on law within social and historical contexts, however, have been all but banished from jurisprudence.

Legal philosophers abstract law from history and from society to present theories of law as timeless and universally true.[1] "Principles of natural law ... have no history," says John Finnis.[2] Joseph Raz declares, "It is easy to explain in what sense legal philosophy is universal. Its theses, if true, apply universally, that is, they speak of all law, of all legal systems; of those that exist, or that will exist, and even of those that can exist though they never will."[3] Natural law theorists concentrate on objective principles of morality and their implications for law. Legal positivist analytical jurisprudents focus on "those few features which all legal systems necessarily possess."[4] Beyond these two main branches of legal theory lies a jumble of schools of thought: legal realism, law and economics, critical legal studies, critical feminism, critical race theory, legal pragmatism, and so on.[5] These various theoretical approaches have particular angles and concerns – none considers law in its social totality.

---

[1] See Joseph Raz, *Between Authority and Interpretation* (Oxford: Oxford University Press 2009) 91.
[2] John Finnis, *Natural Law and Natural Rights* (Oxford: Clarendon Law Series 1980) 24.
[3] Raz, *Between Authority and Interpretation*, supra 91–92.
[4] Joseph Raz, *The Authority of Law*, 2nd ed. (Oxford: Oxford University Press 2009) 105.
[5] For an exhaustive survey, see Brian Bix, *Jurisprudence: Theory and Context*, 6th ed. (Durham, NC: Carolina Academic Press 2012); see also Jeffrie G. Murphy and Jules L. Coleman, *Philosophy of Law: An Introduction to Jurisprudence*, rev. ed. (Boulder, CO: Westview 1990); Robert L. Hayman, Nancy Levitt, and Richard Delgado, *Jurisprudence Classical and Contemporary: From Natural Law to Postmodernism*, 2nd ed. (St. Paul, MN: West 2002).

To observe that holistic theories of law within society are excluded from contemporary jurisprudence is not to say they are nonexistent. An illuminating
account conveyed later in this Introduction was constructed by Adam Smith.
Montesquieu, Henry Maine, Rudolf von Jhering, Eugen Ehrlich, and Max
Weber produced enlightening theories of law in society, discussed in the course
of this book. These major intellectual figures and contemporary theorists working
along similar lines, however, are ignored in jurisprudence texts. Jurisprudence in
recent decades has become increasingly abstract, specialized, and narrow.
Analytical jurisprudence, dominated by legal positivists, has traveled the furthest
in this direction.

The dual objectives of this book are to articulate a realistic theory of law, and more
generally to demonstrate the significance to jurisprudence of theories that center on
law in society (what I call social legal theories). Realism has various meanings, three
of which I invoke. In jurisprudence, legal realism is commonly portrayed as
a skeptical view of judging attributed to Karl Llewellyn and Jerome Frank, among
others. The realistic theory I construct focuses on law more broadly, including but
not limited to judging, and draws on views within historical and sociological
jurisprudence that informed the legal realists, particularly the insight that law is
subject to historical and social influences and must be seen in terms of its functions
and consequences.[6] Social scientific realism – or naturalism – sees humans with
natural traits and requirements who manage collective tasks through culturally
informed intentional actions, collectively giving rise to social practices, institutions,
and structures that are continuously produced and evolve over time.[7] Last, commonsense realism holds that law can best be understood by paying close attention to
what people say about law, what people think about law, and what people do with
law. All three senses of realism require that law be understood empirically. A realistic
theory of law is built on observations about the past and present reality of law rather
than on intuitions, thought experiments, musings about all possible worlds, claims
about self-evident truisms, and other non-empirical modes of analysis frequently
utilized by analytical jurisprudents.

My realistic perspective is informed by the classical pragmatism of William
James, John Dewey, Charles Saunders Peirce, and George Herbert Mead. It builds
on the notion that truths are established through the collective pursuit of projects
in the world. Pragmatism is a method or orientation modeled on scientific inquiry,

---

[6]   The basis for realism and pragmatism applied in this book is laid out in Brian Z. Tamanaha, *Realistic
      Socio-legal Theory: Pragmatism and a Social Theory of Law* (Oxford: Clarendon Press 1997). For
      a study of the legal realists in particular, see Brian Z. Tamanaha, *Beyond the Formalist–Realist Divide:
      The Role of Politics in Judging* (Princeton, NJ: Princeton University Press 2010).

[7]   An account of social scientific realism is elaborated in Peter T. Manicas, *A History & Philosophy of the
      Social Sciences* (Oxford: Blackwell 1987) chapter 13. See Roy Bhaskar, *The Possibility of Naturalism*
      (Atlantic Highlands, NJ: Humanities Press 1979). My epistemological views are grounded in pragma-
      tism, which diverges at certain points from versions of scientific realism. See Cleo H. Cherryholmes,
      "Notes on Pragmatism and Scientific Realism," 21 *Educational Researcher* 13 (1992).

which is continuous with all human inquiry. The pragmatist, James explains, "turns away from abstraction and insufficiency, from verbal solutions, from bad a priori reasons, from fixed principles, closed systems, and pretended absolutes and origins. He turns towards concreteness and adequacy, towards facts, towards action and towards power."[8] Beliefs, theories, and concepts are given meaning by and evaluated in terms of the consequences that follow from actions based thereon. In Dewey's words, "a thing is – is defined as – what it does, 'what-it-does' being stated in terms of specific effects extrinsically wrought in other things."[9] This perspective requires close attention to the empirical reality of law. Another key pragmatic notion reflected in this book is that existence is continuously evolving. Natural and social circumstances are always in the process of being made and remade through the intentional and unintentional consequences of our purposeful actions. "And this taking into consideration of the future takes us to the conception of a universe whose evolution is not finished, of a universe which is still, in James' term, 'in the making,' 'in the process of becoming, of a universe up to a certain point still plastic."[10]

An empirically oriented theoretical approach that portrays law in terms of developing social institutions accounts for important aspects of law that jurisprudents presently overlook. For instance, legal philosophers say little about how law has evolved over time in connection with society. They focus almost exclusively on state law, largely ignoring other forms of law like customary law, religious law, and international law, and overlooking the pervasiveness of legal pluralism. Legal theorists routinely conceptualize law in terms of rule systems engaged in social ordering, although state law has become a multifunctional instrument used for all sorts of tasks, from creating entities like corporations and government agencies to structuring internal operations of government. Legal theorists make no mention of the modern creation of a legal fabric within society, constituting a new stage of law. These and other pivotal aspects of law neglected in jurisprudence are brought to the surface through my realistic theory.

Law is a social historical growth – or, more precisely, a complex variety of growths – tied to social intercourse and complexity. Certain of these legal manifestations develop and evolve, while others whither or are absorbed or supplanted. Law has roots planted in the history of a society, develops in social soil alongside other social and legal growths, tied to and interacting with surrounding conditions. The realistic theory of law I elaborate conveys law in these terms.

---

[8] William James, *Pragmatism and The Meaning of Truth* (Cambridge, MA: Harvard University Press [1907] 1975) 31.

[9] John Dewey, "The Historic Background of Corporate Legal Personality," 35 *Yale Law Journal* 655, 660 (1926).

[10] John Dewey, *Philosophy and Civilization* (New York: Capricorn Books [1931] 1963) 25.

ADAM SMITH'S REALISTIC ACCOUNT OF LAW

A holistic historical theory of law in society is best introduced by way of example. What follows is a brief discursive of Adam Smith's account of law, not a systematic theory, which he announced, though never completed.[11] Smith worked out his ideas in the company of the Scottish Enlightenment philosophers, famously including David Hume, who shared naturalistic assumptions about human social development and were deeply impressed by Montesquieu's perspective.[12] "They discard all speculations regarding man before the beginning of society; man is for them an animal living in certain types of groups."[13] Producing their theories prior to the division of knowledge into separate disciplines, they aspired to achieve a scientifically grounded philosophy of society that ranged across psychology, sociology, history, economics, politics, and law, exhibiting a holistic perspective on law interconnected within society seldom seen today. Central to their perspective was human nature and people living in social groups that develop over time.[14]

Smith builds his accounts of morality and law on natural human traits: anger, hatred, resentment, and jealousy; generosity, kindness, compassion, and friendship; selfish passions, including the desire for wealth, fame, prestige, and the esteem of others; and pursuit of comfort, pleasure, and well-being.[15] His theory of morality combines the human capacity for empathy with desire for the sympathy and admiration of others, filtered through what he calls the "impartial spectator."[16] When evaluating others, people imagine themselves in the position of the actors, sympathizing with or disagreeing with the actors' feelings and motives, rendering judgments on their conduct. Moral sentiments prevailing within society color the

[11] This discussion is based on two detailed sets of student notes from separate classes in the early 1760s, supplemented by discussions of law in his other published works. See Adam Smith, *Lectures on Jurisprudence*, edited by R. L. Meek, D. D. Raphael, and P. G. Stein (Indianapolis, IN: Liberty Fund 1982); Adam Smith, *The Essential Adam Smith*, edited by Robert L. Heilbronner (New York: W.W. Norton & Co. 1986).

[12] A rich introduction to the views of the Scottish philosophers is Christopher J. Berry, *Social Theory of the Scottish Enlightenment* (Edinburgh: Edinburgh University Press 1997). On the connection to Montesquieu, see Peter Stein, "Law and Society in Eighteenth Century Scottish Thought," in *Scotland in the Age of Improvement: Essays in Scottish History in the Eighteenth Century*, edited by N. T. Phillipson and Rosalind Motchison (Edinburgh: Edinburgh University Press 1970) 157.

[13] Roy Pascal, "Property and Society: The Scottish Historical School of the Eighteenth Century," 1 *Modern Quarterly* 167, 170 (1938).

[14] See Arthur Herman, *How the Scots Invented the Modern World* (New York: Broadway Books 2001) 62–107.

[15] Henry J. Bittermann, "Adam Smith's Empiricism and the Law of Nature," 48 *Journal of Political Economy* 487, 509–10 (1940). An informative brief summary of Smith's thought is James R. Ottenson, "Unintended Order Explanations in Adam Smith and the Scottish Enlightenment," in *Liberalism, Conservatism, and Hayek's Idea of Spontaneous Order*, edited by Louis Hunt and Peter McNamara (New York: Palgrave Macmillan 2007).

[16] See D. D. Raphael, *The Impartial Spectator: Adam Smith's Moral Philosophy* (Oxford: Clarendon Press 2007). Glenn R. Morrow, "The Significance of the Doctrine of Sympathy in Hume and Adam Smith," 32 *Philosophical Review* 60 (1923).

judgments of an impartial spectator. "The individual moral consciousness is the result of social intercourse; the individual moral judgments are the expression of the general sentiments of the society to which the individual belongs."[17]

Fundamental natural sentiments become embodied in obligatory general rules of justice enforced by positive law.[18] "Fraud, falsehood, brutality, and violence" excite reactions of "scorn and abhorrence," Smith observed, and murder, theft, and robbery "call loudest for vengeance and punishment."[19] Protections for personal injury, property rights, and contract enforcement, in Smith's account, obtain legal backing when people sympathize (via the impartial spectator) with a victim against a wrongdoer.[20] These sentiments are informed by conventional moral views and involve consideration of perceived benefits and harms to parties, as well as natural responses like resentment at perceived injustice. He identified an innate sense of justice as the "main pillar that upholds" society, without which it would "crumble into atoms."[21] "Nature has implanted in the human breast that consciousness of ill desert, those terrors of merited punishment which attend upon its violation, as the great safeguards of the association of mankind, to protect the weak, to curb the violent, and to chastise the guilty."[22] "Smith does recognize a general framework of legal notions which are found universally in any society: property, contract, punishment for injury, marriage, succession, and so on. These ideas are a part of the nature of man, whatever the state of society he is living in."[23] Although legal rules on these matters exist everywhere, the substance of these notions varies across societies and over time in connection with attendant economic, political, material, and cultural factors. Diverse rules of justice across societies reflect different moral sentiments. Legal regimes also vary because elites in control of legal institutions and powerful groups within society are able to produce laws that serve their interests.[24]

Smith articulated a four-stage theory of law-society revolving around property rights. Hunter-gatherers (first stage) had few property rights because people had few possessions, so theft was not significant. In shepherd or pastoral societies (second stage), when people tended flocks and herds, property rights were treated seriously and theft was harshly sanctioned because herders invested substantial efforts and

[17] Morrow, "The Significance of the Doctrine of Sympathy in Hume and Adam Smith," supra 70. See Bittermann, "Smith's Empiricism and the Law of Nature," supra 510–11.

[18] See Lisa Herzog, "Adam Smith's Account of Justice between Naturalness and Historicity," 52 *Journal of the History of Philosophy* 703, 705–07 (2014).

[19] Smith, *Essential Adam Smith*, supra 116, 94.

[20] See Adam Smith, *Lectures on Jurisprudence*, edited by R. L. Meek, D. D. Raphael, and P. G. Stein (Indianapolis, IN: Liberty Fund 1982) 16–17, 183, 104. Raphael informatively conveys and supplements Smith's account of property rights, contract, and crimes, and the impartial spectator at Raphael, *Impartial Spectator*, supra 105–14. See also Peter G. Stein, *Legal Evolution: The Story of an Idea* (Cambridge: Cambridge University Press 1980) 42.

[21] Smith, *Essential Adam Smith*, supra 97. [22] Id.

[23] Peter G. Stein, "Adam Smith's Theory of Law and Society," in *Classical Influences on Western Legal Thought A.D. 1650–1870*, edited by R. R. Bolgar (Cambridge: Cambridge University Press 1979) 265.

[24] See Herzog, "Adam Smith's Account of Justice between Naturalness and Historicity," supra 708.

resources in raising animals and wealthy people with large herds sought protection of their holdings. In agricultural societies (third stage), property law expanded to account for more forms of moveable and fixed property. In the age of commerce (fourth stage), laws and regulations multiplied to cover new kinds of property and economic exchanges. "It is easy to see that in these severall ages of society, the laws and regulations with regard to property must be very different."[25]

During each stage, laws are commensurate with and suited to the extent of social differentiation and means of subsistence. "The more improved any society is and the greater length the severall means of supporting the inhabitants are carried," Smith observed, "the greater will be the number of their laws and regulations necessary to maintain justice, and prevent infringements of the right of property."[26] In early societies, only the most heinous crimes like murder and robbery were punished; trials "were carried on by the whole people assembled together; and this was not so much to inflict a punishment as to bring about a reconciliation and some recompense for the damage the injured party may have sustained."[27] Laws at this stage are conventions and settled practices.[28] Contracts were not considered binding early on because the value at issue was insufficient to gather the entire community, and ambiguities made it difficult to determine agreements.[29] When trade grew to sizable amounts and spanned greater distances, communities began to enforce contracts to provide security for transactions.[30]

Rejecting the social contract theories of Hobbes and Locke, Smith believed government formed in the age of shepherds "from the natural progress which men make in society."[31] From previously egalitarian circumstances, chieftains emerge as leading figures and use their authority to marshal wealth, which over time is parlayed into hereditary leadership. Government came about with the accumulation of property and resultant disparity between rich and poor. "Laws and government," he said in terms redolent of Marxism, "may be considered in this and indeed in every case as a combination of the rich to oppress the poor, and preserve to themselves the inequality of the goods which would otherwise soon be destroyed by the attacks of the poor, who if not hindered by the government would soon reduce the others to an equality with themselves by open violence."[32] This arrangement is supported by ideological justifications (religious, aristocratic, and caste traditions) and secured by legal force.

At the outset, the state cared little about the private affairs of people beyond keeping disputes from erupting. "Those which immediately affect the state are those which will first be the objects of punishment";[33] threats to state power, including treason and desertions by soldiers, were treated severely.[34] "A government is often maintained, not for the nation's preservation, but its own."[35] The government's primary orientations are to maintain the elite (rulers, aristocracy, high caste, priests,

---

[25]   Smith, *Lectures on Jurisprudence*, supra 16.   [26]   Id.   [27]   Id. 88.
[28]   Stein, *Legal Evolution*, supra 35.   [29]   See Smith, *Lectures on Jurisprudence*, supra 88–94.
[30]   Id.   [31]   Id. 207.   [32]   Id. 208.   [33]   Id. 130.   [34]   Id. 209.   [35]   Id. 547.

wealthy) and the government itself, though the entire community benefits from the security law provides in protecting property, enforcing contracts, punishing murder and personal injuries, and resolving disputes.[36] Smith thus extolled the essential social benefits supplied by law while also matter-of-factly depicting law as coercive power used by political, economic and cultural elites to their advantage as well as by the government itself to dominate others.[37]

A prime example of law's enforcement of domination is slavery. Slavery would not soon disappear, he opined, because "the love of domination and authority over others ... is naturall to mankind."[38] Presaging the American Civil War, he doubted that a democracy would voluntarily relinquish slavery. "In a democraticall government it is hardly possible that it ever should [abolish slavery], as the legislators are here persons who are each masters of slaves; they therefore will never incline to part with so valuable a part of their property ... this love of domination and tyrannizing, I say, will make it impossible for the slaves in a free country ever to recover their liberty."[39]

Smith's views of family law are bluntly realistic. He compares humans to all animals in that "the inclination of the sexes towards each other is precisely proportional to the exigencies of the young and the difficulty of their maintenance."[40] Husbands everywhere have great authority over wives, he explains, because "The laws of most countries being made by men generally are very severe on the women, who can have no remedy for this oppression."[41] In many societies, only the husband had the right of divorce; adultery by a wife was a great offense, sometimes punishable by death, whereas infidelity by husbands was not considered adultery or was treated more leniently. "The real reason is that it is men who make the laws with respect to this; they generally will be inclined to curb the women as much as possible and give themselves the more indulgence."[42] Modern critical feminist theorists would heartily concur.

In Smith's account, as summarized earlier, natural human traits of jealousy, self-interest, and desire for esteem and wealth, as well as sympathy, kindness, and generosity, are filtered through cultural views and ideologies that inform moral sentiments about justice and fairness and become entrenched within law. The legal disabilities of wives are not justified by naked admissions that men benefit from controlling women's property and sexuality; rather, within a paternalistic world view, these legal doctrines are for the protection and benefit of women. Slavery laws

---

[36] Id. 338.

[37] As Jennifer Pitts comments, "Smith makes clear in the Wealth of Nations that the economically and socially powerful will always act politically, using their power to shape law and policy to enhance their wealth and standing, not always successfully but often to the prejudice of public interests." Jennifer Pitts, "Irony in Adam Smith's Critical Global History," *Political Theory* 1, 9–10(2015): 0090591715588352.

[38] Smith, *Lectures on Jurisprudence*, supra 192.   [39] Id. 186.   [40] Id. 141.   [41] Id. 146.

[42] Id. 147.

are not justified in terms of the selfish interests of owners; instead, slaves are painted as naturally inferior, deserving their subjugation, which is for their own good.

Smith presents a slow evolution of judicial institutions in connection with social needs as well as attitudes and incentives of the actors involved. "The judicial power gradually arises from being at first merely an interposition as a friend without any legal authority, which however will be of considerable effect if this third person have a great influence with both parties, to be, 2ndly, a power resembling that of an arbiter to decide the causes referred to them and inflict some gentle penalty."[43] "At the first establishment of judges there are no laws; every one trusts the naturall feeling of justice he has in his own breast and expects to find in others."[44] The strict writ system came about in England, Smith says, because judges were suspected of irregularity, injustice, and corruption. "They were therefore ordered to judge by the strict law, and were to be tried [for bribery] in their proceedings by their own records, which were kept all along with great exactness, and no alteration, explanations, or amendments of any sort would be admitted, and any attempt of this sort would be punishable."[45] Competition between courts for claimants motivated improvements in how judges functioned. "As the whole profits of the courts thus depended on the numbers of civil causes which came before them, they would all naturally endeavor to invite every one to lay his cause before the court, by the precision, accuracy, and expedition (where agreeable) of their proceedings, which emulation made a still greater care and exactness of the judges."[46] The explosive growth of commerce also had an impact on the judicial system because many cases arose that did not fit within existing statutes and writs, "which proved very detrimental, and could not go long without a remedy."[47] The equitable Court of Chancery initially took up these cases, providing remedies that previously were unavailable in law.

Longevity is essential to the functionality of legal institutions. Smith observed that extended duration results in normalization and social fixity. New courts and laws are inevitably uncertain. "It takes time and repeated practice to ascertain the precise meaning of a law or to have precedents enough to determine the practice of a court."[48] After a system is established, its stability is enhanced because people become accustomed to and build arrangements on top of legal regimes despite their known defects.[49] "Everyone would be shocked at any attempt to alter this system," Smith said of the English polity, "and such a change would be attended with the greatest difficulties."[50] The existing system becomes an implicit aspect of the daily lives of citizens. "And indeed," Smith notes, "it will but seldom happen that one will be very sensible of the constitution he has been born and bred under; everything by custom appears to be right or at least one is but very little shocked at it. In this case and in any others the principle of authority is the foundation of that of utility or common interest."[51]

---

[43] Smith, *Lectures on Jurisprudence*, supra 213.   [44] Id. 314.   [45] Id. 279.   [46] Id. 281.
[47] Id. 281.   [48] Id. 287.   [49] Id. 322.   [50] Id. 271.   [51] Id. 322.

ORGANIZATION OF THIS BOOK

My purpose in reciting Smith's views is not to endorse the details, though much of what he says is edifying. Oliver Wendell Holmes likewise grounded the origins of law in primitive opinions of "vengeance," "a feeling of blame," "an opinion ... that a wrong has been done."[52] His impartial spectator resembles George Herbert Mead's "taking the role of the other."[53] His claims about the orientation of early proto-states find some support in the work of anthropologists and political scientists. Aspects of his account of the development of English courts have been echoed by later legal historians Frederic Maitland, Frederick Pollock, and A. W. B. Simpson.[54] And his association between law and domination is confirmed at various points in this study. That said, I make no effort to defend Smith's ideas and do not heavily rely on them. The main value of his account, along with Montesquieu's views conveyed in the next chapter, is its portrayal of law developing over time in connection with natural human tendencies and surrounding social circumstances. Smith's perspective on law is consistent with legal realism, social scientific realism, and commonsense realism.

Chapter 1, "The Third Branch of Jurisprudence," redraws current jurisprudential understandings. Legal philosophers today present natural law and legal positivism as the two main rival theories of the nature of law. A century ago, however, three prominent theoretical perspectives on law were widely recognized: natural law, analytical jurisprudence (mainly legal positivism), and historical-sociological jurisprudence. The latter branch, which I label *social legal theory*, has since been excluded. This chapter fills in the missing branch and explains why it merits an essential place within jurisprudence. At the heart of social legal theory lies Montesquieu's account of law influenced by and interacting with surrounding social, economic, cultural, political, ecological, and technological circumstances. This core insight was central to historical jurisprudence, sociological jurisprudence,

---

[52] Oliver Wendell Holmes, *The Common Law* (Chicago; ABA Publishing: Transaction Publishers [1881] 2009) 2.

[53] Echoing Smith, Mead observed, "in responding to ourselves, we are in the nature of the case taking the attitude of another than the self that is directly acting, and into this reaction there naturally flows the memory images of the responses of those about us, the memory images of those responses of others which were in answer to like actions." George Herbert Mead, "The Social Self," 10 *Journal of Philosophy, Psychology, and Scientific Methods* 374, 377 (1913). On the resemblance, see Dennis H. Wrong, *The Problem of Order: What Unites and Divides Society* (Cambridge, MA: Harvard University Press 1994) 88, 109. On Adam Smith's influence on Mead, see T. V. Smith, "The Social Philosophy of George Herbert Mead," 37 *American Journal of Sociology* 368, 378 (1931).

[54] Competition among courts for cases as a means to obtain fees was identified by Maitland as seminal in the development of the English legal system. Frederic Maitland, *The Constitutional History of England* (Oxford: Oxford University Press, 1919) 135. Maitland and Pollock credited the writ system for imposing checks on incompetent or corrupt judges. Frederic W. Maitland and Frederick Pollock, *The History of English Law*, vol. 2, 2nd ed. (Cambridge: Cambridge University Press 1899) 563. A. W. B. Simpson describes the early development of English courts as a competition for cases between common law courts and the Chancery. A. W. B. Simpson, *The History of The Land Law*, 2nd ed. (Oxford: Oxford University Press 1986) 162, 186–87.

and legal realism, as I show, producing a theoretical perspective that contrasts with as well as complements natural law and legal positivism. The social historical perspective of law articulated in this chapter informs my realistic theory of law.

Chapter 2 takes on the classic question "What is law?" Rather than immediately answer the question – which extends back two and a half millennia to the Platonic dialogue *Minos* – instead I first explain why no answer to this question has proven successful despite theorists' countless attempts. The commonplace assertion that law is an essentially contested concept does not uncover the sources of the theoretical impasse. Concepts or theories of law typically are grounded in intuitions and comprised of various combinations of form and function. For reasons I reveal, all form and function-based accounts inevitably are over- or under-inclusive. I also expose the common error of conflating rule system with legal system. Using Searle's ontology of social institutions, I explain how state law is distinct from other rule systems within society, and I account for multiple, coexisting forms of law.

Chapter 3, "Necessary and Universal Truths about Law?," critically examines often repeated assertions by analytical jurisprudents that they pursue necessary, universal truths about law. I show why these claims are problematic in relation to concepts and social institutions that vary and evolve over time, and I demonstrate that their claims about the nature of law have not been established in *a priori* or *a posteriori* terms. I distinguish universal application from universal truth, indicating why the former is sound but the latter is not. I also question how legal theorists select the central case of law, and I reveal two ways they immunize their theories of law from refutation. Finally, I explain why resort to conventionalism in the identification of law is unavoidable, and provides the starting point to answer "What is law?"

Chapter 4, "A Genealogical View of Law," offers snapshots of different forms and functions law has assumed in the course of history across different societies. Along the way, I juxtapose actual manifestations of law past and present against theories of law propounded by analytical jurisprudents, showing time and again that law is contrary to their accounts. Drawing from anthropology, archeology, sociology, political science, and history, I discuss law in hunter-gatherer societies, chiefdoms, early states, and empires; the consolidation of the law state in the late Middle Ages; the development of legality as a professional culture; and I close with an account of the modern thickening of state law. Across human history flows a recognizable continuity to law as well as fundamental changes in law linked to increases in social interaction and complexity. Old forms of law survive and evolve while new ones develop, resulting in a multiplicity of historically rooted legal forms that coexist today.

Chapter 5, "Law in the Age of Organizations," describes law in the modern age. Theories of law, including those influentially propounded by Lon Fuller and H. L. A. Hart, typically portray law as rule systems that maintain social order. This narrow focus renders them unable to account for a great deal of contemporary legislation and administrative regulation. Governments utilize law as a multifunctional instrument to carry out all sorts of tasks, from securing the power of government, to constructing internal arrangements, to pursuing objectives in the social arena. To bring this out, I distinguish two orientations of law: background rules of social intercourse, and uses of law by government. The former orientation traces back to law in primitive societies, while the latter orientation has become ubiquitous with the modern consolidation of state law, the rise of organizations, and pervasive legal instrumentalism. I describe courts as organizations that process cases. And I show how the aggregate result of instrumental uses of law by government and uses of law by organizations has created a relatively fixed legal fabric within advanced capitalist societies.

Chapter 6, "What Is International Law?," extends this theoretical perspective of law to international law and transnational regulation. I identify confusions that followed from Jeremy Bentham's accidental distortion of international law. I chronicle the historical development of international law within the Roman Christian legal tradition and its subsequent extension through Western imperialism, and I reveal three sources that slant international law. I describe the history of interaction between and across polities leading up to present discussions of transnational law. Using this background, I expose common theoretical confusions relating to the conflation of international law as a system and a category, and I show why international law is unquestionably a form of law. I then clarify that international law is neither a discrete system nor separate from domestic law, but instead involves complexes of discourses and institutions that operate across multiple arenas, and I explain the relationship between international law and transnational regulation.

The first six chapters have critical and explanatory thrusts. Each is constructed in a way that breaks down currently dominant assumptions in jurisprudence, particularly analytical jurisprudence, to create an opening for social legal theories in general and my realistic theory in particular. My realistic theory emerges out of my showing of flaws and gaps in existing theories of law. The final chapter, "A Realistic Theory of Law," draws together the threads of the argument with summary statements of the core propositions of the theory of law I construct.

1

The Third Branch of Jurisprudence

In "The Nature of Law," an essay in a leading encyclopedia of philosophy, legal philosopher Andrei Marmor observes: "In the course of the last few centuries, two main rival philosophical traditions have emerged, providing different answers to these questions. The older one, dating back to late mediaeval Christian scholarship, is called the natural law tradition. Since the early 19th century, natural law theories have been fiercely challenged by the legal positivism tradition promulgated by such scholars as Jeremy Bentham and John Austin."[1]

Legal theorists a century ago would have been surprised by Marmor's identification of only *two* great jurisprudential rivals, and also by the prominence he accords natural law. "Jurisprudence, in its specific sense as the theory or philosophy of law," John Salmond wrote at the turn of the twentieth century, "is divisible into three branches, which may be distinguished as analytical, historical, and ethical."[2] Roscoe Pound likewise remarked, "it has been possible to divide jurists into three principal groups, according to their views of the nature of law and the standpoint from which the science of law should be approached. We may call these groups the Philosophical School [natural law], the Historical School, and the Analytical School."[3]

In the late nineteenth century, the historical school was equal in stature to legal positivism,[4] while natural law theory had long been silent. Writing in 1906, prominent American jurist Melville Bigelow observed, "Two distinct schools have in succession held the field, more or less, of legal education in English and American law, the analytical of Bentham and Austin and the historical school."[5]

[1] Andrei Marmor, "The Nature of Law," *Stanford Encyclopedia of Philosophy*, at http://plato.stanford.edu/entries/lawphil-nature/.

[2] John Salmond, *Jurisprudence*, 7th ed. (London: Sweet & Maxwell 1924) 4.

[3] Roscoe Pound, "The Scope and Purpose of Sociological Jurisprudence," 24 *Harvard L. Rev.* 591, 591 (1911).

[4] Roscoe Pound, "Book Reviews," 35 *Harvard L. Rev.* 774, 774 (1921). See also Melville M. Bigelow, "A Scientific School of Legal Thought," 17 *Green Bag* 1, 1 (1905).

[5] Melville M. Bigelow, *Centralization and the Law: Scientific Legal Education* (Boston, MA: Little, Brown and Company 1906) 165.

Legal historian J. M. Kelly noted, "If we scan the nineteenth century for any trace of the natural-law belief which had survived from the ancient world until well after the Reformation, being eclipsed only by the rational scientific spirit of the Enlightenment, we will find it difficult to locate anywhere outside the teaching of the institutional Catholic Church, which never abandoned the Aristotelian-Thomistic tradition."[6] This statement ignores that natural law thought was taught in the standard school curriculum of this period,[7] but Kelly is right that natural law theory was hardly discussed by jurisprudents. Renowned Oxford Professor James Bryce remarked in *Studies in History and Jurisprudence* (1901) that "we now seldom hear the term Law of Nature. It seems to have vanished from the sphere of politics as well as from positive law."[8] For decades it remained dormant. An article in 1915 noted, "Now and again we are told that a revival of the Law of Nature is in process or impending," but continued, a "new movement of this character . . . can scarcely be seen."[9] Lon Fuller lamented in 1940 that natural law was then widely seen as "cobwebby illusion."[10] "I believe," he wrote, "there is much of great value for the present day in the writings of those thinkers who are classified, and generally dismissed, as belonging to the school of natural law, and I regard it as one of the most unfortunate effects of the positivistic trend still current that it has contributed to bring about the neglect of this important and fruitful body of literature."[11]

Historical jurisprudence was a formidable rival, not just in eclipsing natural law for a time, but in mounting a powerful critique against natural law.[12] "All thinkers in the historicist tradition held that the doctrine of natural law had illegitimately universalized the values of eighteenth-century Europe as if they held for all epochs and cultures."[13] Friedrich von Savigny, the early nineteenth-century progenitor of historical jurisprudence, offered the historical perspective as an antidote to this natural law tendency: "The historical spirit, too, is the only protection against a species of self-delusion, which is ever and anon reviving in particular men, as well as in whole nations and ages; namely, the holding that which is peculiar to ourselves to be common to human nature in general."[14] Henry Maine, another founding figure

---

6   J. M. Kelly, *A Short History of Western Legal Theory* (Oxford: Clarendon Press 1992) 33.
7   See Knud Haakonssen, *Natural Law and Moral Philosophy* (Cambridge: Cambridge University Press 1996) 310–41.
8   James Bryce, *Studies in History and Jurisprudence* (New York: Oxford University Press 1901) 604. Bryce identifies four schools – Metaphysical (natural law), Analytical, Historical, and Comparative – the latter two connected (pp. 607–37). Frederick Pollock also describes the latter two as intimately related, both grounded in Montesquieu and Maine. See Frederick Pollock, "The History of Comparative Jurisprudence," 5 *J. Social and Comparative Legislation* 74, 75–84 (1903).
9   A. W. Spencer, "The Revival of Natural Law," 80 *Central L. J.* 346, 346 (1915).
10   Lon L. Fuller, *Law in Quest of Itself* (1940) 104.   11   Id. 101.
12   See Charles Groves Haines, *The Revival of Natural Law Concepts* (Cambridge, MA: Harvard University Press 1930) 71.
13   Frederick C. Beiser, *The German Historical Tradition* (Oxford: Oxford University Press 2011) 13.
14   Friedrich Carl von Savigny, *The Vocation of Our Age for Legislation and Jurisprudence*, translated by Abraham Hayward (London: Littlewood & Co. 1831) 134.

of historical jurisprudence, attributed this challenge to Montesquieu: "the book of Montesquieu, with all its defects, still proceeded on that Historical Method before which the Law of Nature has never maintained its footing for an instant."[15] By detailing extraordinary variations of law across societies and legal development in connection with society, Maine likewise cast substantial doubt on natural law theory. "Accordingly we cannot but regard Mr. Maine as having conferred a real service upon the philosophy of law, and indeed upon philosophy itself by demolishing in the department of jurisprudence this theory of a law of nature," a jurist remarked at the time.[16]

The conventional jurisprudential narrative fastens on subsequent developments to disregard these details of intellectual history. Historical jurisprudence apparently expired early in the twentieth century while natural law theory revived after mid-century. "In the United States, historical jurisprudence is considered to be dead," writes legal historian and theorist Harold Berman.[17] A leading contemporary jurisprudence text proclaims, similarly, "historical jurisprudence has largely disappeared."[18]

That view, I show in this chapter, while superficially correct, is wrong in substance. Although the label fell into disuse, the core theoretical propositions espoused by historical jurists, propositions that define the third branch of jurisprudence, carried on and spread, descending to the present within a cluster of views now attributed to the legal realists. These theoretical propositions did not originate with the Historical School and are not exclusive to it.

LAW WITHIN SOCIETY

Montesquieu's *The Spirit of the Laws*, published in 1748 to wide acclaim, contains this fecund passage:

> Laws must relate to the nature and the principle of the government that is established or that one wants to establish; whether they form it, as may be said of political laws; or whether they support it, as in the case of civil institutions. They should be related to the physical aspect of the country; to the climate, be it freezing, torrid, or temperate; to the properties of the terrain, its location and extent; to the way of life of the peoples, be they plowmen, hunters, or herdsmen; they should relate to the degree of liberty that the constitution can sustain, to the religion of the inhabitants, their inclinations, their wealth, their number, their commerce, their mores and their manners; finally, the laws are related to one another, to their origin, to the purpose of the legislator, and to the order of things on which they are established. They must be considered from all these points of view.[19]

[15]   Henry Summer Maine, *Ancient Law* (London: John Murray 1920) 91.
[16]   Anonymous, "Maine on Ancient Law," 19 *Westminster Review* 457, 469–70 (1861).
[17]   Harold J. Berman, "The Historical Foundations of Law," 54 *Emory L.J.* 13, 18 (2005)
[18]   Brian Bix, *Jurisprudence: Theory and Context*, 6th ed. (Durham, NC: Carolina Academic Press 2012) 276.
[19]   Montesquieu, *The Spirit of the Laws* (Cambridge: Cambridge University Press 1989) 8–9.

"Law should be so appropriate to the people for whom they are made," he advised, "that it is very unlikely that the laws of one nation can suit another."[20]

Montesquieu set forth a descriptive and prescriptive account of law as a social institution consonant with its surrounding milieu, and that ought to match if the legal system and society are to function well. Law is the product of and reflects the polity, religion, trade, manners, moral views, customs, geography, and everything else within a society. This is a holistic vision of law interconnected with its surroundings. Sociologist Emile Durkheim wrote that Montesquieu "saw quite clearly that all these elements form a whole and that if taken separately, without reference to the others, they cannot be understood."[21] Montesquieu highlighted "the interrelatedness of social phenomena."[22]

He also set an influential example by assuming a naturalistic-scientific perspective of law, in contrast to then current modes of philosophical or religious speculation or idealization. Hobbes's state of nature and social contract theories are myths, he argued. By nature humans are social-sexual beings who live in communities, so no foundational contract was necessary to explain society.[23] Montesquieu demonstrated that law could be understood by gathering a large body of information on historical and current societies, engaging in close observation of facts, applying inductive and deductive reasoning, observing connections and patterns, constructing ideal types, and formulating general propositions about social-legal arrangements.[24] Durkheim credited Montesquieu as the theorist who "first laid down the fundamental principles of social science,"[25] and "instituted a new field of study, which we now call comparative law."[26]

Writing in the heyday of Enlightenment natural law thought,[27] Montesquieu domesticated and diversified natural law (in a manner of speaking); reason is universal, but legal provisions cannot be uniform because what reason requires in law varies owing to variations in surrounding context. Societies with different political-economic-cultural-technological-ecological complexes will have different conditions, and consequently, the law will be different in structure and content.[28] David Hume, who with Adam Smith exhibited a naturalistic perspective of humans as social animals with natural traits, endorsed this seminal insight:

> In general, we may observe, that all questions of property are subordinate to the authority of civil laws, which extend, restrain, modify, and alter the rules of natural

[20] Id. 8.
[21] Emile Durkheim, *Montesquieu and Rousseau: Forerunners of Sociology* (Ann Arbor: University of Michigan Press 1960) 56.
[22] Id. 57.   [23] Montesquieu, *Spirit of the Laws*, supra 6–7.
[24] Isaiah Berlin, "Montesquieu," in *Against the Current*, edited by Henry Hardy (Princeton, NJ: Princeton University Press 2001) 139.
[25] Durkheim, *Montesquieu and Rousseau*, supra 61.   [26] Id. 51.
[27] Previous natural law thought was grounded in religion. Enlightenment natural law thought focused on human nature as a basis for deriving natural laws of social and political organization.
[28] Berlin, "Montesquieu," supra 158.

justice, according to the particular convenience of each society. The laws have, or ought to have, a constant reference to the constitution of government, the manners, the climate, the religion, the commerce, the situation of each society. A late author of genius [Montesquieu], as well as learning, has prosecuted this subject at large, and has established, from these principles, a system of political knowledge, which abounds in ingenious and brilliant thoughts, and is not wanting in solidity.[29]

Montesquieu's perspective not only counters the universalism of natural law theory, but also pushes back against legal positivism. By locating the efficient causes of law in social forces, he displaces *will* of the lawgiver as the primary source of law.[30] In an essay on Montesquieu, philosopher Isaiah Berlin conveyed this thrust: "His whole aim is to show that laws are not born in the void, that they are not the result of positive commands either of God or priest or king; that they are, like everything else in society, the expression of the changing moral habits, beliefs, general attitudes of a particular society, at a particular time, on a particular portion of the earth's surface, played upon by the physical and spiritual influences to which their place and period expose human beings."[31] Montesquieu emphasized that law develops organically in connection with the needs of a changing society.[32]

Having presided as a provincial magistrate for a decade,[33] Montesquieu knew law firsthand. He cautioned that legislative enactments that clash with prevailing moral and social norms may well fail and may require tyrannical force to be effective.[34] "The lesson for legislators is that they must understand law first of all as part of the social whole which they rule, as well as an instrument of deliberate government. The spirit of the laws is thus a mixture of intentional human designs and of the deep circumstances which condition all rules of society."[35] His view of law and society has been criticized as overly deterministic and conservative – a charge regularly leveled at holistic theories of law within society – but, as Berlin noted, it also has been enlisted "by social reformers and radicals as so many demands that the law shall constantly respond to changing social needs and not be tied to some obsolete principle valid only for some epoch dead and gone."[36]

HISTORICAL JURISPRUDENCE

When historical jurisprudence emerged early in the nineteenth century, at its core stood Montesquieu's insight. A rare contemporary scholar who situates his work within historical jurisprudence, Peter Stein, makes this plain: "Nineteenth-century

---

[29]   David Hume, *An Enquiry Concerning the Principles of Morals*, edited by Tom L. Beauchamp (Oxford: Oxford University Press 1998) 93.

[30]   Durkheim, *Montesquieu and Rousseau*, supra 40–44.   [31]   Berlin, "Montesquieu," supra 153–54.

[32]   Id. 156–57.   [33]   See Judith Shklar, *Montesquieu* (Oxford: Oxford University Press 1987) 1–28.

[34]   Montesquieu, *Spirit of the Laws*, supra 308–33; Berlin, "Montesquieu," supra 155. Montesquieu held to a strict view that judges interpreted the laws as written, and thus did not extend the influence of social forces to the realm of judicial interpretation. Id. 154.

[35]   Shklar, *Montesquieu*, supra 69.   [36]   Berlin, "Montesquieu," supra 156.

historical jurisprudence was founded on the connection between law and social and economic circumstances."[37] Another prominent historical jurisprudent, Harold Berman, presents the same thrust: "Historicists emphasize the source of the law that 'is' and the law that 'ought to be' in the customs and traditions of the given society – including both the previous decisions of its courts and the scholarly writings of its jurists – contending that the meaning of legal rules and the meaning of justice are to be found in the character, the culture, and the historical values of the society."[38]

Friedrich von Savigny's *The Vocation of Our Age for Legislation and Jurisprudence*, published in 1814 to challenge the enactment of a civil code for Germany, is the inaugural piece of historical jurisprudence. Savigny criticized the natural law "conviction that there is a practical law of nature or reason, an ideal legislation for all times and all circumstances,"[39] and he criticized the legal positivist postulate that "all law, in its concrete form, is founded upon express enactments of the supreme power."[40] Against these positions, he argued law is the unplanned product of forces within society:

> In the earliest times to which authentic history extends, the law will be found to have already attained a fixed character, peculiar to the people, like their language, manners and constitution. Nay, these phenomena have no separate existence, they are but the particular faculties and tendencies of an individual people, inseparably united in nature, and only wearing the semblance of distinct attributes in our view.[41]

The source or "seat" of the law, he held, is the "common consciousness of the people."[42] Law is "first developed by the customs and popular faith" of the people,[43] then jurists work these into legal doctrine; law is produced "everywhere, therefore, by internal, silently operating powers, not by the arbitrary will of the legislator."[44] Savigny credited Montesquieu with establishing that law is tied to the unique circumstances of the people, and therefore diversity of law among communities is to be expected.[45]

Owing to multifarious connections between law and society, Savigny insisted it is folly to think that one could produce a new code that severs "all historical associations" and begins "an entirely new life."[46] This is delusive because existing law grows out of what came before and also because the thinking of jurists is permeated by preexisting ways. "For it is impossible to annihilate the impressions and modes of thought of the jurists now living, – impossible to change completely the nature of existing legal relations; and on this twofold impossibility rests the indissoluble

---

[37] Peter Stein, "The Tasks of Historical Jurisprudence," in *The Legal Mind: Essays for Tony Honore*, edited by Neil MacCormick and Peter Birks (Oxford: Clarendon Press 1986) 293.
[38] Berman, "The Historical Foundations of Law," supra 14.
[39] Savigny, *The Vocation of Our Age for Legislation and Jurisprudence*, supra 23.   [40] Id.
[41] Id. 24.   [42] Id. 28, 24.   [43] Id. 30, 28.   [44] Id. 30.   [45] Id. 57.   [46] Id. 132.

organic connection of generations and ages; between which, development only, not absolute end and absolute beginning, is conceivable."[47]

This is not a rigidly conservative view. To the contrary, change has a vital place within the historical perspective; it reminds us, however, of "the element of continuity from past to future in the development of the culture of a society, including its legal culture."[48] An aspect of social and legal change also involves absorbing the impact of interaction with other societies, from the reception of ideas to invasion by external powers (Savigny was a Roman law scholar). Society is constantly moving, and law with it, Savigny wrote:

> But this organic connection of law with the being and character of the people is also manifested in the progress of the times; and here, again, it may be compared with language. For law, as for language, there is no moment of absolute cessation; it is subject to the same movement and development as every other popular tendency;
> . . . Law grows with the growth, and strengthens with the strength of the people, and finally dies away as the nation loses its nationality.[49]

Savigny's theory of law has two central planks: law is the product of society and law is constantly evolving in connection with changes in society. Law, therefore, bears the indelible imprint of the history of a society.[50]

Henry Maine, the second great figure of historical jurisprudence, writing in the second half of the nineteenth century, also explicitly acknowledged Montesquieu's influence.[51] Presenting his work as a scientific theory of law grounded in evidence, he criticized natural law and legal positivism for their excessive abstractions and for lacking historical and comparative awareness in their speculations about law.[52]

Maine focused on the organization of society and how this is manifested in law. Primitive society, he observed, revolves around families, which aggregate to form clans and tribes, which in turn aggregate at higher levels of organization, all linked through a common lineage; legal arrangements are determined by status relations within the group. In contrast, modern society revolves around individuals with legal relations determined through voluntary agreement. Thus his famous evolutionary antithesis:

> The movement of the progressive societies has been uniform in one respect. Through all its course it has been distinguished by the gradual dissolution of family dependency and the growth of individual obligations in its place. The individual is

---

[47]   Id. 132.   [48]   Berman, "Historical Foundations of Law," supra 18–19.

[49]   Savigny, *Vocation of our Age*, supra 27.

[50]   This account, focusing on the connection between law and society, leaves out other aspects of Savigny's thought, in particular his assertion that legal concepts could be reduced to a logical or geometrical system.

[51]   Maine, *Ancient Law*, supra 133–34.

[52]   See Maine, *Ancient Law*, supra chapters IV and V. See also Paul Vinogradoff, *The Teaching of Sir Henry Maine* (1904) 4–6; Stein, *Legal Evolution*, supra 89–90. An excellent study of Maine's criticism of these schools is Stephen G. Utz, "Maine's Ancient Law and Legal Theory," 16 *Connecticut L. Rev.* 821 (1984).

steadily substituted for the Family, as the unit of which civil laws take account. The advance has been accomplished at varying rates of celerity. ... But, whatever its pace, the change has not been subject to reaction or recoil. ... Nor is it difficult to see what is the tie between man and man which replaces by degrees those forms of reciprocity in rights and duties which have their origin in the Family. It is Contract. Starting, as from one terminus of history, from a condition of society in which all the relations of Persons are summed up on the relations of Family, we seem to have steadily moved towards a phase of social order in which all these relations arise from the free agreement of individuals. ... We may say that the movement of the progressive societies has hitherto been a movement from Status to Contract.[53]

The evolution of society is the evolution of law, and vice versa, conjoined aspects of one and the same process. The challenge for modern legal systems is that societies change more swiftly than law, constantly generating a gap between them. "Law is stable; the societies we are speaking of are progressive. The greater or less happiness of a people depends on the degree of promptitude with which the gulf is narrowed."[54]

Rudolph von Jhering, a German contemporary of Maine, cast aside Savigny's mystical "common consciousness" and emphasis on custom as the underlying source of law.[55] Jhering instead described legal development in terms of battles between competing individuals and groups seeking legal support to advance their purposes and interests. Law is created and used instrumentally. "In the course of time," Jhering wrote, "the interests of thousands of individuals, and of whole classes, have become bound up with the existing principles of law in such a manner that these cannot be done away with, without doing the greatest injury to the former. ... Hence every such attempt, in natural obedience to the law of self-preservation, calls forth the most violent opposition of the imperiled interests, and with it a struggle in which, as in every struggle, the issue is decided not by the weight of reason, but by the relative strength of opposing forces."[56] Jhering optimistically opined that individual egoism (infused with ethical notions) and social purposes combine in this process to give rise to a legal order that benefits individuals and society generally.

A major legal figure in his day, though seldom mentioned by jurisprudence scholars today, Jhering's seminal contribution was to articulate a thoroughly instrumental view of law, previously introduced by Jeremy Bentham, that reflected the new perceptions of the age, which would take over by the early twentieth century (independent of Jhering).[57] He identified instrumental resort to law as a crucial moving force propelling the evolution of law within society. Jhering rejected social contract theories as fictional, proffering instead a bracing account of law as

---

[53] Maine, *Ancient Law*, supra 163–65.   [54] Id. 29.

[55] "It has been said of Jhering that he was at once the fulfillment and the end of the historical school." Carl Joachim Friedrich, *The Philosophy of Law in Historical Perspective*, 2nd ed. (Chicago, IL: Chicago University Press 1963) 154.

[56] Rudolph von Jhering, *The Struggle for Law* (Westport, CT: Hyperion Press 1979) 10–11.

[57] See Brian Z. Tamanaha, *Law as a Means to an End: Threat to the Rule of Law* (New York: Cambridge University Press 2006).

organized force: "Whoever will trace the legal fabric of a people to its ultimate origins will reach innumerable cases where the force of the stronger has laid down the law for the weaker."[58] "Force produces law immediately out of itself," Jhering contended, "and as a measure of itself, *law evolving as the politics of force*. It does not therefore abdicate to give the place to law, but whilst retaining its place it adds to itself law as an accessory element belonging to it, and becomes legal force."[59] Over time in many places, though not everywhere, law evolves from an instrument of the powerful to also impose limitations on the powerful, gaining legitimacy in the process.

Oliver Wendell Holmes's orientation is closely compatible with historical jurisprudence, though he did not commit himself to any particular school of jurisprudence and seldom credited others as intellectual influences. Holmes took extensive notes on Savigny and Maine. His seminal early work, *The Common Law*, combined history with jurisprudential analysis, tracing out the evolution of law much in the manner that Maine did, as reviewers at the time noted, though the trajectory he emphasized was the shift from subjective to objective standards of legal liability.[60] Holmes expressed a socially infused view of law. "The life of the law has not been logic: it has been experience. The felt necessities of the time, the prevalent moral and political theories, intuitions of public policy, avowed or unconscious, even the prejudices which judges share with their fellow-men, have a good deal more to do than the syllogism in determining the rules by which men should be governed. The law embodies the story of a nation's development through many centuries."[61] More than a decade earlier, Jhering had made a similar observation: "Let us break the charm, the illusion which holds us captive. All this cult of logic that would fain turn jurisprudence into legal mathematics is an error and arises from misunderstanding law. Life does not exist for the sake of concepts, but concepts for the sake of life. It is not logic that is entitled to exist, but what is claimed by life, by social intercourse, by the sense of justice – whether it be logically necessary or logically impossible."[62]

Holmes, much like Jhering, described the process of legal recognition as a struggle between competing individual and social interests (though Jhering has a more optimistic spin). "This tacit assumption of the solidarity of interests of society is very common, but seems to us false . . . in the last resort a man rightly prefers his own interest to that of his neighbors. And this is as true in legislation as in any other form of corporate action,"[63] Holmes wrote. "[W]hatever body may possess the supreme

58 Rudolph von Jhering, *Law as a Means to an End*, translated by Issack Husik (1914) 185.
59 Id. 187.
60 David M. Rabban, *Law's History: American Legal Thought and the Transatlantic Turn to History* (Cambridge: Cambridge University Press 2013) 218–20.
61 Oliver Wendell Holmes, *The Common Law* (New Brunswick, NJ: Transaction Publishers [1881] 2005) 5.
62 Rudolph von Jhering, *Geist des Römischen Rechts*, III, 302., translated and quoted in Paul Vinogradoff, *Introduction to Historical Jurisprudence* (Oxford: Oxford University Press 1920) 142 n. 1.
63 Oliver Wendell Holmes, "The Gas Stoker's Strike," 7 *American L. Rev.* 582, 583 (1873).

power for the moment is certain to have interests inconsistent with others which have competed unsuccessfully. The more powerful interests must be more or less reflected in legislation; which, like every other device of man or beast, must tend in the long run to aid the survival of the fittest."[64] Legislation "is necessarily made a means by which a body, having the power, puts burdens which are disagreeable to them on the shoulders of everyone else."[65] "[I]t is no sufficient condemnation of legislation that it favors one class at the expense of another; for much or all legislation does that, and none the less when the *bona fide* object is the greatest good of the greatest number."[66]

Jhering and Holmes are transitional figures. They took the preexisting consensus perspective of law as a reflection of customs, morals, and collective social views in the direction of a conflict view of law as the product of struggle between contesting individuals and groups within society. Their theoretical accounts reflected the times, when pitched battles between conflicting interests were fought within legal arenas, and legislatures were busily enacting instrumental legislation to achieve social, economic, and political objectives.

CONTINUITY OF SOCIOLOGICAL JURISPRUDENCE

The Historical School faded from the jurisprudential scene around the turn of the twentieth century. Why it suffered this fate is a matter of debate – a confluence of factors contributed. No systematic theory was articulated by its founders. Jhering discredited Savigny. Maine's immediate jurisprudential successors, Frederick Pollock and Paul Vinogradoff, failed to organize its fundamental propositions.[67] The general historicist tradition in Germany also declined in this period, suggesting broader intellectual factors played a role.[68] Several legal theorists and historians argue historical jurisprudence was done in by its association with evolutionary theory, which fell out of favor after the turn of the twentieth century when faith in inevitable human progress was dashed by incessant social strife and the devastating Great War.[69] This period witnessed rapid and sweeping social changes, rendering a

---

[64] Id. [65] Id. [66] Id. 584.
[67] Neil Duxbury suggests that historical jurisprudence did not carry on in English jurisprudence because it lacked a distinctive jurisprudential agenda. "These men [Maine, Vinogradoff, Pollock] may well have been Oxford professors of jurisprudence, but their reflections on the subject were insufficiently well structured and focused to ensure that their own jurisprudential achievements would have lasting appeal." Neil Duxbury, *Frederick Pollock and the English Juristic Tradition* (Oxford: Oxford University Press 2004) 91.
[68] See Frederick C. Beiser, *The German Historicist Tradition* (Oxford: Oxford University Press 2011).
[69] Stein, "The Tasks of Historical Jurisprudence," supra 293. Donald Elliot speculates that the absence of evolutionary theory from jurisprudence between 1920 and 1970 was probably due to the backlash against Social Darwinism. E. Donald Elliott, "The Evolutionary Tradition in Jurisprudence," 85 *Columbia L. Rev.* 38, 59 (1985). Calvin Woodward argues that historical jurisprudence collapsed in Anglo America owing to a combination of three factors: 1) the rejection of evolutionary ideas; 2) the

seemingly backward-looking jurisprudential school less relevant;[70] the explosion of hotly contested economic, labor, and social welfare legislation and the growth of the administrative state made talk about customs and organic growth appear outdated.

Why historical jurisprudence apparently expired, while interesting to contemplate, distracts from the more consequential point that the core theoretical views of law and society it advanced continued to thrive. Austrian jurist Eugen Ehrlich vigorously promoted the selfsame cluster of positions in his 1913 text, *Fundamental Principles of the Sociology of Law.*[71] Identifying with Montesquieu, Ehrlich asserted, "As law is essentially a form of social life, it cannot be explained scientifically otherwise than by the workings of social forces."[72] Ehrlich also credits Savigny, writing, "In forming an estimate of the doctrines of Savigny and Puchta, one must bear in mind that it was they who first introduced the idea of development into the theory of the sources of law and clearly saw the relation between the development of law and the history of a people as a whole."[73]

A prominent theme in *Fundamental Principles* was law's vibrant interaction with social forces subject to ceaseless change. "The center of gravity of legal development therefore from time immemorial has not lain in the state but in society itself, and must be sought there at the present time."[74] Society is constantly transforming and law with it. New legislation alters the law in an overt fashion, but legal change is more extensively accomplished through judicial interpretations using subtle distinctions and fictions that "put a new picture into an old frame."[75] "Transformations of this sort, pregnant with immeasurable consequences, are likely to be at work every moment in affecting legal and social judgments concerning legal relations; yet it might not be necessary on that account to change a single line of written law."[76] The agents on the front lines of legal change, Ehrlich identified, are the multitude of lawyers who modify legal forms or draw up legal documents or construct new legal arrangements to meet novel social and economic demands.[77] Law is never in repose.

Ehrlich brought home the lesson that it is a mistake, commonly committed by jurists, to view law in isolation: "The problem is not simply to know what a rule

---

rejection of Germans ideas after World War I; and 3) the rejection of laissez-faire thought (which Maine was associated with) with the rise of the social welfare state. See Calvin Woodward, "A Wake (Or Awakening?) for Historical Jurisprudence," in *The Victorian Achievement of Sir Henry Maine: A Centennial Reappraisal* (Cambridge 1991) 220–28.

70   Berman, "Historical Foundations of Law," supra 18–19.

71   Eugen Ehrlich, *Fundamental Principles of the Sociology of Law*, translated by Walter Moll (Cambridge, MA: Harvard University Press 1937).

72   Eugen Ehrlich, "Montesquieu and Sociological Jurisprudence," 29 *Harvard L. Rev.* 582 (1916).

73   Ehrlich, *Fundamental Principles of the Sociology of Law*, supra 443.   74   Id. 390.

75   Id. 397, 436–71.

76   Eugen Ehrlich, "Judicial Freedom of Decision: Its Principles and Objects," in *Science of Legal Method: Selected Essays by Various Authors*, translated by Ernest Bruncken (Boston, MA: Boston Book Company 1917) 57. See Benjamin N. Cardozo, *The Paradoxes of Law* (New York: Columbia University Press 1928) 1–30.

77   Ehrlich, *Fundamental Principals of the Sociology of Law*, supra 433, 439, 341–45.

means, but how it lives and works, how it adapts itself to the different relations of life, how it is being circumvented and how it succeeds in frustrating circumvention."[78]

Another prominent theme in the book was his argument that social life is filled with multiple norm-governed orders tied to social associations, which exist independent of the state. This "living law," as he memorably called it, interacts with the official law of the state, is often more efficacious than state law, is a source of state law norms, and can give rise to a plurality of coexisting legal and normative orders.[79] To apprehend the operation and effect of state law, one must attend to the multiple normative orders that saturate social arenas.

Ehrlich was neglected by Continental jurists, but he found a receptive audience in the United States. Oliver Wendell Holmes, Roscoe Pound, and Karl Llewellyn were effusive about the book. In correspondence with Frederick Pollock, Holmes called *Fundamental Principles* "the best book on legal subjects by any living continental jurists."[80] Pound declared (in 1915), "I think it is the best thing that has been written lately."[81] He praised Ehrlich for showing "that it is not enough to be conscious that the law is living and growing, we must rather be conscious that it is a part of human life. It is not merely that it should look upon nothing human as foreign to it, in a sense everything human is a part of it."[82] After reading Ehrlich, Llewellyn confessed he was "somewhat crushed in spirit, because [Ehrlich] had seen so much."[83]

The conventional jurisprudential narrative has historical jurisprudence dying and supplanted by sociological jurisprudence. This is incorrect. They are distinct strains of a broader jurisprudential tradition;[84] rather than expiring, the former morphed into the latter, retaining core ideas while asserting different emphases and adopting new methodologies and perspectives. Paul Vinogradoff's *Introduction to Historical Jurisprudence*, published in 1920, ranges across history, psychology, sociology, economics, and political theory as they bear on social-legal development. Roscoe Pound witnessed this transformation: "At first this wider historical jurisprudence was thought of as a comparative ethnological jurisprudence. But it was not long in assuming the name and something of the character of a sociological jurisprudence."[85] A French legal philosopher at the time also perceived their identity:

---

[78] Id. 78.
[79] See generally Marc Hertogh, ed., *Living Law: Reconsidering Eugen Ehrlich* (Oxford: Hart Publishing 2009).
[80] Quoted in N. E. H. Hull, *Roscoe Pound and Karl Llewellyn: Searching for an American Jurisprudence* (Chicago, IL: Chicago University Press 1997) 110.
[81] Id.   [82] Id. 108–09.   [83] Id. 291.
[84] It is important to note that the historical jurists and sociological jurists differed in several respects. They were of different generations and the former tended to be more conservative, favoring slower, more organic legal change, whereas the latter tended to advocate rapid change through legislation. See Berman, "Historical Foundations of Law," supra 19.
[85] Pound, "The Scope and Purpose of Sociological Jurisprudence," supra 614. Although he is describing the German wing, Pound noted that a similar expansion had occurred in the English branch. 614–15 n. 79.

"Like the historical school, it [the sociological school] considers law in its evolution, in its successive changes, and connects these changes with those which are experienced by society itself."[86] Philosopher Michael Oakeshott likewise remarked, "Both of these interpretations [economic and 'sociological theories of the nature of law'] share, in part, the presuppositions which determine the character of historical jurisprudence, and therefore cannot be distinguished from it absolutely."[87]

The connection between historical and sociological theories of law extends back to Montesquieu. He saw law as a product of the history and conditions of a society and he combined history and sociology in his methodology. He surveyed "the ideas, customs, and institutions of all peoples at all times and all places, to put them side by side";[88] he plumbed historical knowledge to construct ideal types of basic social arrangements, then analyzed what he found in sociological terms.[89] Isaiah Berlin noted that Montesquieu's account of law as the product of society "is the foundation of the great German School of historical jurisprudence" *and* "various modern sociological theories of law."[90]

THROUGH LEGAL REALISM TO THE PRESENT

More than any other American jurist, Pound is identified with sociological jurisprudence, owing to his explanatory advocacy piece in the *Harvard Law Review*, "The Scope and Purpose of Sociological Jurisprudence."[91] Pound presented law in functionalist terms: "I am content to think of law as a social institution to satisfy social wants – the claims and demands and expectations involved in the existence of civilized society – by giving effect to as much as we may with the least sacrifice, so far as such wants may be satisfied or such claims given effect by an ordering of human conduct through politically organized society."[92] Observing law over the arc of history, Pound saw "a continually more efficacious social engineering."[93]

---

[86] Joseph Charmont, "Recent Phases of French Legal Philosophy," in *Modern French Legal Philosophy*, edited by Arthur W. Spencer (Boston, MA: Boston Book Company 1916) 65. They also share opposition to natural law theory. Id. 69–70.

[87] Michael Oakeshott, *The Concept of a Philosophical Jurisprudence: Essays and Reviews, 1926–1951* (Exeter, UK: Imprint Academic 2007) 161.

[88] Carl L. Becker, *The Heavenly City of the Eighteenth Century Philosophers* (New Haven, CT: Yale University Press 1932) 100.

[89] See Ernst Cassirer, *The Philosophy of the Enlightenment* (Princeton, NJ: Princeton University Press 1951) 209–16; Alan Baum, *Montesquieu and Social Theory* (Oxford: Pergamon Press 1979) 97–119.

[90] Isaiah Berlin, "Montesquieu," in *Against the Current*, edited by Henry Hardy (Princeton, NJ: Princeton University Press 2001) 154.

[91] Roscoe Pound, "The Scope and Purpose of Sociological Jurisprudence," 24 *Harvard L. Rev.* 591 (1911) (Part I); 25 *Harvard L. Rev.* 140 (1912)(Part II).

[92] Roscoe Pound, *An Introduction to the Philosophy of Law*, rev. ed. (New Haven, CT: Yale University Press 1953) 47.

[93] Id.

Legal philosopher Morris Cohen (father of legal realist Felix Cohen) wrote in 1915 that judges are constantly modifying the law (common law, statutes, and Constitution) through creative interpretation that amounts to judicial legislation. "These changes have been necessitated by the changed conditions of industry and commercial life and the courts have consciously or unconsciously changed the law accordingly."[94] Cohen was critical of "two contradictory absolutistic conceptions of what law is. One is that the law is the will of the sovereign and the other is that law is eternal reason or immutable justice."[95] Although both notions are informative when softened and not framed as opposites, in practice law must be apprehended and evaluated as an instrument to achieve social ends. "The issue, therefore, is not between a fixed law on the one hand, and social theories on the other, but between social theories unconsciously assumed and social theories carefully examined and scientifically studied."[96]

Benjamin Cardozo likewise emphasized that law is continually engaging with social developments, writing that law's constant task is to manage "permanence with flux, stability with progress."[97] "We live in a world of change. If a body of law were in existence adequate for the civilization of today, it could not meet the demands of the civilization of tomorrow. Society is inconstant. So long as it is inconstant, and to the extent of such inconstancy, there can be no constancy in law. The kinetic forces are too strong for us."[98] A great deal of legal change necessarily and legitimately is accomplished by judges, he affirmed.[99] When business customs change such "that a rule of law which corresponded to previously existing norms or standards of behavior, corresponds no longer to the present norms or standards . . . then those same forces or tendencies of development that brought the law into adaptation to the old norms and standards are effective, without legislation, but by the inherent energies of the judicial process, to restore the equilibrium."[100] The same is true of social mores. "The moral code of each generation, this amalgam of custom and philosophy and many an intermediate grade of conduct and belief, supplies a norm or standard of behavior which struggles to make itself articulate in law."[101] The "pressure of society on the individual mind," he observed, "is ever at work in the making of the law declared by courts."[102] "The standards or patterns of utility and morals will be found by the judge in the life of the community."[103]

Legal realists espoused the same views. On his list of legal realist propositions, Karl Llewellyn declared 1) "the conception of law in flux, of moving law, and of judicial creation of law"; 2) "the conception of law as a means to social ends and not as an end in itself"; and 3) "the conception of society in flux, and typically in flux faster than

---

94   Morris R. Cohen, "Legal Theories and Social Science," 25 *International J. of Legal Ethics* 469, 476 (1915). See Morris R. Cohen, "The Process of Judicial Legislation," 48 *American L. Rev.* 161 (1915).
95   Cohen, "Legal Theories and Social Science," supra 482.   96   Id. 485.
97   Cardozo, *Paradoxes of Legal Science*, supra 6.   98   Id. 10–11.   99   Id. 7–8.   100   Id. 14–15.
101   Id. 17.   102   Id. 17.
103   Benjamin Cardozo, *The Nature of the Judicial Process* (New Haven, CT: Yale University Press 1921) 105.

law."[104] Llewellyn named Ehrlich as an early exemplar of realist jurisprudence.[105] Both accorded primacy to judges as vehicles through which law is altered to keep up with social changes. Llewellyn wrote:

> It is society and not the courts which gives rise to, which shapes in the first instance the emerging institution; which kicks the courts into action. It is only from observation of society that the courts can pick their notions of what needs the new institution serves, what needs it baffles. ... In any event, if the needs press and recur, sooner or later recognition of them will work into the law. Either they will induce the courts to break through and depart from earlier molds, or the bar will find some way to put new wine in old bottles and to induce in the bottles that elasticity and change of shape which, in the long run, marks all social institutions.[106]

Though today jurisprudents credit these ideas to the legal realists, sociological and historical jurisprudents had articulated them decades earlier.[107]

Common to all these depictions of law is that society oozes through law directly and indirectly through multiple pores – legislative, judicial, executive, administrative, and the daily activities of lawyers serving the causes of clients.[108] "What is certain," Cardozo proclaimed in 1928, "is that the gaps in the [legal] system will be filled, and filled with ever-growing consciousness of the implications of the process, by a balancing of social interests, an estimate of social values, a reading of the social mind."[109]

A modern rendering of law–society clusters was presented in *Law in Modern Society* by Robert Unger. "A society's law constitutes the chief bond between its culture and its organization; it is the external manifestation of the embeddedness of the former in the latter."[110]

> Each of the forms of social life discussed in this book – tribal, aristocratic, and liberal society, or the post liberal, the traditionalistic, and the revolutionary socialist variant of modernity – is a meaningful whole of the most comprehensive kind. Each embodies an entire mode of human existence. And for each the law plays a crucial role in revealing and determining the relationship of belief to organization.[111]

Unger would later back away from this ideal-type presentation, eschewing the conservative connotation that attaches to the notion of society-law as coherent wholes,

---

[104]   Karl Llewellyn, "Some Realism about Realism – Responding to Dean Pound," 44 *Harvard L. Rev.* 1222, 1236 (1931).

[105]   Karl Llewellyn, "A Realistic Jurisprudence – The Next Step," 30 *Columbia L. Rev.* 431 453 (1930).

[106]   Karl Llewellyn, *The Bramble Bush: On Our Law and Its Study* (New York: Oceana [1930] 1960) 63–64.

[107]   See Brian Z. Tamanaha, "Understanding Legal Realism," 87 *Texas L. Rev.* 731 (2009).

[108]   Not all theorists who saw law in social terms extended this insight to judicial decision making. Montesquieu in particular described judging as if the judge was strictly interpreting the law. See Shklar, *Montesquieu*, supra 88.

[109]   Cardozo, *Paradoxes of Legal Science*, supra 77.

[110]   Roberto M. Unger, *Law in Modern Society* (New York: Free Press 1976) 259.   [111] Id. 252.

preferring instead to emphasize the mutability of legal-social arrangements.[112] But his vision of law as enmeshed in social forces remained. "The law is the product of real collective conflict," he wrote, "carried on over a long time, among many different wills and imaginations, interests and visions."[113]

Many legal theorists today would assent to this statement, which harkens to Jhering and Holmes. A range of contemporary theoretical approaches implicitly presumes that law is an instrument to achieve individual and social purposes infused with and buffeted by social forces.[114] Law and economics posits law as a means to maximize social wealth. Critical theorists argue that beneath a façade of neutrality law serves and enforces social hierarchies of power (whether economic, gender-based, or racial). Legal pragmatism connotes "a rejection of the idea that law is something grounded in permanent principles and realized in logical manipulation of those principles, and the determination to use law as an instrument for social ends."[115]

Major elements of the view of law espoused by historical and sociological jurisprudence, as this chronicle shows, are nigh taken for granted within the legal culture today. Donald Elliott observed three decades ago that the notion that law evolves in connection with society is "deeply ingrained," though its original theoretical provenance has been forgotten. "We speak of the law 'adapting' to its social, cultural, and technological environment without the slightest awareness of the jurisprudential tradition we are invoking."[116] Legal historian Robert Gordon recently remarked that evolutionary-functionalist "theory and its accompanying narrative [has] dominated Western thinking about the relation between law and social change for the last two centuries, although in strictly legal writing the theory is usually inexplicit: it lurks as a set of background assumptions rather than being explicitly set forth and argued for."[117]

A BRANCH OF JURISPRUDENCE

As we have seen, views of the interconnectedness of law within society that extend back to Montesquieu were central to historical and sociological jurisprudence and have become widespread independent of the theories that initially promoted them. Theories that revolve around this insight constitute a branch of jurisprudence I call social legal theory. It is essential to clarify that a social-historical "perspective" or "orientation" toward law or widely held "background assumptions" do not amount

---

[112]   See Roberto M. Unger, *What Should Legal Analysis Become?* (New York: Verso 1996) 126–28.
[113]   Id. 65.   [114]   See Tamanaha, *Law as a Means to an End,* supra 118–32.
[115]   Richard A. Posner, *Overcoming Law* (Cambridge, MA: Harvard University Press 1995) 405.
[116]   Elliott, "The Evolutionary Tradition in Jurisprudence," supra 38.
[117]   Robert W. Gordon, "Critical Legal Histories Revisited: A Response," 37 *Law & Soc. Inquiry* 200, 202 (2012).

to a *theory of law*. A theory of law consists of explicitly formulated propositions about what law is and what law does.

While not theories in themselves, widely held background assumptions lie behind all theories of law. Legal positivism embodies the commonsense recognition that law is whatever legal officials enforce as law regardless of whether it is bad in content or consequence. Natural law theory is built on common beliefs that law is (or should be) just and that morality is objective (in some sense). Social legal theory is grounded on the obvious points that law is a social institution that develops in connection with society and has social consequences.

The connection between background beliefs and theories is large because theories themselves are social products linked to existing views, practices, and circumstances. "For jurists and philosophers do not make these theories as simple matters of logic by inexorable development of philosophical fundamentals," Pound observed. "Having something to explain or to expound they endeavor to understand it and to state it rationally and in so doing work out a theory of what it is. The theory necessarily reflects the institution which it was devised to rationalize, even though stated universally."[118] Theories of law wax and wane and have shifting emphases subject to social, economic, and political developments at the time and place of their formulation (more on this shortly).

A jurist (or citizen) can adhere to *all three* sets of background beliefs simultaneously without inconsistency – she can believe that legal rules are legally valid even when immoral; that law should be just and certain moral norms are objectively right; and that law is a social institution utilized to achieve ends. Only when these beliefs are framed at higher levels of abstraction and counter-posed as opposing theoretical positions do incompatibilities arise.

The failure to mark the distinction between theories of law and background assumptions has been a fertile source of confusion. Citing adherence to the background assumption underlying legal positivism, for example, Lon Fuller lumped together Oliver Wendell Holmes, the legal realists, and sociologists of law (including Ehrlich), as legal positivists, even though they did not explicitly align themselves with legal positivism.[119] Theorists still debate whether Holmes was a legal positivist[120] and whether the legal realists can be seen as legal positivists.[121] Assertions like these are prone to commit the error of thinking that a jurist who holds the background assumption contained within a theory also, therefore, holds the higher-level theory. This promotes confusion, as just

---

[118]   Pound, *An Introduction to the Philosophy of Law*, supra 30.
[119]   See Fuller, *Law in Quest of Itself*, supra 45–59.
[120]   See Frederic R. Kellogg, *Oliver Wendell Holmes, Jr., Legal Theory, and Judicial Restraint* (New York: Cambridge University Press 2007) (challenging the notion that Holmes was a positivist).
[121]   See, e.g., Danny Priel, "Were the Legal Realists Legal Positivists?" 27 *Law and Philosophy* 309 (2007); Anthony Sebok, "Misunderstanding Positivism," 93 *Michigan L. Rev.* 2054 (1995).

explained, because a jurist can accept one or more background assumption without necessarily committing to the theory that centers on that assumption.

Another clarification is that social legal theory is a *branch* of jurisprudence. Multiple social theories of law exist. In addition to theorists mentioned earlier, examples include accounts produced by Adam Smith, Max Weber, and Julius Stone,[122] and among contemporary jurisprudents, William Twining, Roger Cotterrell, Lawrence Friedman, and Neil MacCormick.[123] Social legal theories proffer concepts of law, theories about the origins of law and functions of law, about the institutional nature of law, about social forces that enable, condition, and shape law, and much more.[124] The realistic theory of law I elaborate in the course of this book is one version of social legal theory among others. Because social legal theorists disagree among themselves on fundamental points, it is not possible to present a detailed list of shared theoretical propositions beyond that law is a social institution with manifold consequences that must be apprehended holistically and empirically. The broad range and sheer diversity of social legal theories obscures that they fall within a single jurisprudential branch. And Montesquieu, Maine, and Weber are major figures outside jurisprudence in fields like sociology and anthropology.[125] (Weber gained fame as a sociologist, but was trained in law, worked for several years as a lawyer, and initially taught law.[126]) This diversity makes it easy to lose sight of the overlapping aspects that place them under a single jurisprudential umbrella.

The natural law tradition also contains radically diverse approaches, including the Catholic branch of Aquinas and John Finnis, Lon Fuller's proceduralism, Michael Moore's metaphysical realism, and Ronald Dworkin's law as integrity, to mention a few natural law theories that have little in common.[127] Natural law theory is developed in philosophy, law, political theory, and theology departments.[128]

---

[122] See Julius Stone, *The Province and Function of Law: Law as Logic, Justice, and Social Control* (Cambridge, MA: Harvard University Press 1959); Niklas Luhmann, "Operational Closure and Structural Coupling: The Differentiation of the Legal System," 13 *Cardozo L. Rev.* 1419 (1992).

[123] See, e.g., William Twining, *General Jurisprudence: Understanding Law from a Global Perspective* (Cambridge: Cambridge University Press 2009); Roger Cotterrell, *The Politics of Jurisprudence* (Oxford: Oxford University Press 2003); Lawrence M. Friedman, *Impact: How Law Affects Behavior* (Cambridge, MA: Harvard University Press 2016); Neil MacCormick, *Institutions of Law: An Essay in Legal Theory* (Oxford: Oxford University Press 2007).

[124] See generally, Brian Z. Tamanaha, *A General Jurisprudence of Law and Society* (Oxford: Oxford University Press 2001).

[125] Some of the most interesting current theorizing about law as a social institution is coming out of evolutionary thought in political science and anthropology. See, e.g., Francis Fukuyama, *The Origins of Political Order: From Prehuman Times to the French Revolution* (New York: Farrar, Straus and Giroux 2011).

[126] See Stephen P. Turner and Regis A. Factor, *Max Weber, the Lawyer as Social Thinker* (London: Routledge 2001).

[127] An overview of this diversity is provided in Jonathan Crowe, "Natural Law beyond Finnis," 2 *Jurisprudence* 293 (2011); see also West, *Normative Jurisprudence*, supra 12–59 (discussing a range of existing theories and advocating the addition of progressive versions).

[128] See Crowe, "Natural Law beyond Finnis," supra 297 ("contemporary natural law scholarship has become splintered between distinct academic fields").

Legal positivism is likewise internally riven by disputes among competing positivist theories – a gulf separates Hartian and Kelsenian positivists – though the range of disagreement among positivists is much narrower. The limited diversity within legal positivism is perhaps explained by the fact that questions that occupy analytical jurisprudents hold little interest for outsiders. Natural law and social legal theory, in contrast, entertain issues taken up by an assortment of theorists from other disciplines.

THREE CONTRASTING-COMPLEMENTARY ANGLES ON LAW

These three jurisprudential branches represent long-standing theoretical alternatives. Each branch fixes on a different aspect of law and brings a different perspective to bear. Natural law takes a *normative* angle. Analytical jurisprudence takes a *conceptual* or *analytical* angle. Social legal theory takes an *empirically* oriented angle. Natural law is grounded in moral philosophy, legal positivism in analytical philosophy, and social legal theory in social science. (I invoke "science" expansively to encompass history, economics, sociology, anthropology, psychology, political science – any approach with an empirical focus using observation, evidence, verification, falsification, induction, deduction, abduction, data gathering, and other such methods.) The term "angle" denotes that, while each stream has its own distinctive center, they are not mutually exclusive compartments. When not pushed to antagonistic extremes, these three orientations balance one another, prompting Morris Cohen to declare, "No great individual jurist ever belonged exclusively to the analytic, historical, or philosophical school."[129] All three have normative implications; all three engage in conceptual analysis; all three accept that law is a social institution.

A century ago, this tripartite division was well known. John Salmond noted that most jurisprudence texts dealt primarily with analytical, historical, or ethical branches of thought, but insisted, "These three aspects of the law … are so involved with each other that the isolated treatment of any one of them is necessarily inadequate."[130] In the mid-twentieth century, Julius Stone divided jurisprudence into three main branches: "Analytical Jurisprudence"; "Sociological (or Functional) Jurisprudence"; and "Theories of Justice (or Critical or Censorial or Ethical Jurisprudence)."[131] Legal philosopher Hans Kelsen presented the same triangulation. "The limits of this subject [analytical jurisprudence] and its cognition must be clearly fixed in two directions: the specific science of law, the discipline usually called jurisprudence, must be distinguished from the philosophy of justice, on the one hand, and from sociology,

---

[129]   Morris R. Cohen, *Law and the Social Order: Essays in Legal Philosophy* (New York: Harcourt Brace & Co. 1933) 347.
[130]   Id. 5.   [131]   Stone, *The Province and Function of Law,* supra 31–32.

or cognition of social reality, on the other."[132] In Kelsen's breakdown, analytical jurisprudence focuses on law as a normative system with its own criteria of validity; natural law is about principles of justice or morality; sociological jurisprudence, which he associated with the "American legal realists,"[133] looks at what law actually does. Kelsen considered natural law theory a delusion,[134] but he was not hostile to sociological jurisprudence, though it had no place in his theory of law. "The pure theory of law by no means denies the validity of such sociological jurisprudence, but it declines to see in it, as many of its exponents do, the only science of law. Sociological jurisprudence stands side by side with normative [analytical] jurisprudence, and neither can replace the other because each deals with completely different problems."[135]

In the absence of social legal theory, theoretical discussions about the nature of law are missing an essential perspective.[136] Analytical jurisprudence and natural law have large blind spots owing to their lack of attention to social context and their failure to attend to the historical dimension of law. For example, analytical jurisprudents can parse elements of the rule of law, but they say nothing about how the rule of law develops within a society. The rule of law is not itself a legal rule or a rule system, but a political and cultural ideal that emerges over time and provides essential support for the proper functioning of law.[137] Analytical jurisprudents and natural lawyers, moreover, pay limited attention to the myriad ways in which "pressures in society" course through legislation and judge-made law, informing legal interpretation and application; and they do not examine legal consequences, which can only be discerned empirically.[138] Many jurists, to cite yet another example, have highlighted the enduring challenge law faces to reconcile legal stability with social change, which natural law theory and analytical jurisprudence seldom mention. These latter two jurisprudential branches cannot address the

---

[132]   Hans Kelsen, "The Pure Theory of Law and Analytical Jurisprudence," 55 *Harvard L. Rev.* 44, 44 (194).

[133]   Id. 52 n. 2.

[134]   Id. 45–49. See Hans Kelsen, "The Natural-Law Doctrine before the Tribunal of Science," 2 *The Western Political Science Quarterly* 481 (1949).

[135]   Kelsen, "The Pure Theory of Law and Analytical Jurisprudence," supra 52. Although he identified his theory with analytical jurisprudence, Kelsen uses the term "normative jurisprudence" to label his "pure theory of law" because his theory focuses on law as a system of norms. As Hart observed, this choice of labels is a source of confusion. H. L. A. Hart, "Kelsen Visited," 10 *UCLA L. Rev.* 709, 712–13 (1965).

[136]   Oakeshott argued that each of these positions was incomplete in different respects, and he hoped that they could be superseded by a more comprehensive theory of law. He specifically faulted analytical jurisprudence for its overly abstract bent: "It is clear, I think, that a philosophical enquiry into the nature of law would very soon apprehend the incompleteness of the explanation of the nature of law offered in an analytical jurisprudence and would make the best of its way to something less abstract." Oakeshott, *The Concept of a Philosophical Jurisprudence*, supra 177.

[137]   See Brian Z. Tamanaha, *On the Rule of Law: History, Politics, Theory* (Cambridge: Cambridge University Press 2004).

[138]   See Edwin W. Patterson, "Hans Kelsen and His Pure Theory of Law," 40 *California L. Rev.* 5, 7 (1952) (these comments are directed at Kelsen, but apply to analytical jurisprudents generally).

dynamic engagement of law within society over time.[139] Natural law theory is silent about these features of law because universal natural principles are timeless and unchanging. Analytical jurisprudence neglects them because social forces are outside the positivist focus on legally recognized mechanisms of legal change, and social influences and consequences are too messy, context sensitive, and variable to be amenable to analytical treatment. Social legal theory answers these weaknesses.

REALISTIC PERSPECTIVE OF LEGAL THEORIES THEMSELVES

Another noteworthy difference is that social legal theories can illuminate aspects of analytical jurisprudence and natural law theory that they are unable to account for because they lack reflexivity, that is, they do not examine themselves as objects of inquiry. My realistic theory of law brings out two particularly significant aspects of this: 1) theories of law are themselves subject to surrounding social-legal influences, and 2) theories of law are involved in the social construction of law.

The first point is a reminder that theories are not formulated in intellectual or cultural vacuums. They bear the marks of social influences like a period of social turmoil or rapid social change that affect legal developments, as well as influences within intellectual settings in which legal theories are produced, like institutionalized support and scholarly norms or fads. John Dewey noted, "there never has been a philosopher who has not seized upon certain aspects of the life of his time and idealized them."[140] Similarly, George Herbert Mead observed that the meaning of natural rights (a cognate of natural law thought) is not fixed but rather is filled in through social battles. And "we never fight the same battles over again," with new questions emerging owing to new situations, so the content of rights continually changes.[141]

The Thomist version of natural law theory, for example, bears unmistakable religious influences and owes its continuous presence to sustained institutionalized support from the Catholic Church. John Finnis elaborates an account of natural law grounded in self-evidence that purportedly holds without religious groundings. Not coincidentally, the basic forms of human flourishing he identifies and the conclusions he draws therefrom align with the Catholic position. He and fellow natural law theorist Robert George, for instance, recently argued gay marriage must be prohibited because same-sex acts "involve disrespect for the basic good of marriage."[142]

[139]   Harold Berman argues each branch "has isolated a single important dimension of law, and it is both possible and important to bring the several dimensions together into a common focus." Harold J. Berman, "Toward an Integrative Jurisprudence: Politics, Morality, History," 76 *California L. Rev.* 779, 779 (1988).

[140]   John Dewey, *Philosophy and Civilization* (New York: Capricorn Books [1931] 1963) 16.

[141]   George Herbert Mead, "Natural Rights and the Theory of the Political Institution," 12 *Journal of Philosophy, Psychology, and Scientific Methods* 141, 147 (1915).

[142]   John Finnis and Robert George, "Natural Law and the Unity and Truth of Sexual Ethics: A Reply to Gary Gutting, Public Discourse," March 17, 2015, www.thepublicdiscourse.com/2015/03/14635/?utm_source=The+Witherspoon+Institute&utm_campaign=7523d98a78-RSS_EMAIL_CAMPAIGN&utm_medium=email&utm_term=0_15ce6af37b-7523d98a78-84094917.

Legal positivism ascended in the nineteenth century at the same time that state legislation substantially increased in number and scope to deal with modern conditions and social pressures. The positivist will theory matched the reality of assertive legislative interventions in society and the economy and the structuring of government. Analytical jurisprudence today is more philosophically oriented than preceding generations thanks to greater training and commitment of legal theorists to philosophical disciplines; its continuing intellectual prominence is bolstered by having secured institutional strongholds in elite institutions like Oxford and Yale.

Social legal theories reflect the rise of science with the Enlightenment. This is why leading contributors like Montesquieu, Adam Smith, Maine, and Weber are considered founding figures in the social sciences. The empirical orientation of social legal theories manifests the modern scientific mindset. The virtual absence of social legal theory in contemporary jurisprudence is in part attributable to scant institutionalized support within legal academia – few courses in social legal theory are taught and few advanced degrees are issued.

In these and other ways, theories of law are influenced by surrounding factors. They, too, are products of history and social influences. Their soundness must be evaluated on their merits, but included in this evaluation is awareness and consideration of their social and historical conditions and contingency.

The second point is that jurisprudential theories themselves have social and legal consequences as aspects of the overall legal tradition within society. When laying out his natural law theory, Finnis makes a threshold distinction between natural law principles, which he claims exist outside of history, versus natural law discourse, which has a long history with good and bad consequences.[143] He asserts natural law "could not have historical achievements to its credit. It could not be held responsible for disasters of the human spirit or atrocities of human practice."[144] This contrast is sound only if natural law principles indeed exist as objective truths outside of history as he claims. If this claim is false – an illusion in the minds of proponents[145] – there is nothing other than its social historical manifestations.

A realistic theory brackets questions about the truth of natural law to focus on its actual social realizations. Natural law theory is a complex of beliefs about law acted on in ways that affect the world.[146] As Max Weber observed, natural law is "sociologically relevant only when practical legal life is materially affected by the

Their position is based on self-evidence and practical reasonableness. See John Finnis, *Natural Law and Natural Rights* (Oxford: Clarendon Press 1980).

[143] John Finnis, *Natural Law and Natural Rights*, 2nd ed. (Oxford: Oxford University Press 2011) 24–25.

[144] Id.

[145] This was Hans Kelsen's view. Kelsen, "The Natural-Law Doctrine before the Tribunal of Science," supra.

[146] For a recent example of this perspective on human rights, see Lawrence Friedman, *The Human Rights Culture: A Study in History and Context* (New Orleans, LA: Quid Pro Quo Books 2011). Another example is George Herbert Mead, "Natural Rights and the Theory of the Political Institution," supra.

conviction of the particular 'legitimacy' of certain legal maxims, and of the directly binding force of certain principles which are not to be disrupted by any concessions to positive law imposed by mere power."[147]

From the late Middle Ages up through the nineteenth century, natural law ideas were taught in schools, discussed in treatises, and invoked in court decisions – alongside statutes, precedents, and other legal sources – in both civil law and common law traditions.[148] A court in the mid-nineteenth century declared, "The common law adopts the principles of natural law."[149] Natural law was also invoked to lend legitimacy to law. A judge exclaimed in 1789 that the "common law was derived from the law of nature and of revelation; those rules and maxims of immutable truth and justice, which arise from the eternal fitness of things, which need only to be understood, to be submitted to; as they are themselves the highest authority; together with certain customs and usages, which had been universally assented to and adopted in practice, as reasonable and beneficial."[150] Natural law theory also played an essential role in the establishment of international law, conveyed in Chapter 6.

Natural law remains consequential today. The 2016 Republican Platform declares:

> that man-made law must be consistent with God-given, natural rights; and that if God-given, natural, inalienable rights come in conflict with government, court, or human-granted rights, God-given, natural, inalienable rights always prevail; that there is a moral law recognized as "the laws of nature and of Nature's God."[151]

Opponents of abortion assert that laws permitting abortion are invalid because killing a fetus violates natural law.

Natural law can be conservative when invoked to bolster existing law, or critical when invoked to challenge it. Critics have fastened on it conservative uses.[152] "One of the chief offices of the idea of nature [natural law and justice] in political and judicial practice," John Dewey observed, "has been to consecrate the existent state of affairs, whatever its distribution of advantages and disadvantages, of benefits and losses; and to idealize, moralize, the physically given."[153] In the nineteenth century,

---

[147]   Max Weber, *Economy and Society*, vol. 2, edited by Guenther Roth and Claus Wittich (Berkeley: University of California Press 1978) 866. For a presentation of natural law as a social phenomenon, see Tamanaha, *A General Jurisprudence of Law and Society*, supra, chapters 6 and 7.

[148]   See Richard H. Helmholz, *Natural Law in Court: A History of Legal Theory in Practice* (Cambridge, MA: Harvard University Press 2015).

[149]   Surocco v. Geary, 3 Cal. 69 (1853).

[150]   Jesse Root, "The Origin of Government and Laws in Connecticut," Preface to Volume 1, *Root's Reports* (1798), http://lonang.com/library/reference/1798-olc/.

[151]   Republican Platform 2016, Republican National Convention, https://prod-static-ngop-pbl.s3.amazonaws.com/media/documents/DRAFT_12_FINAL[1]-ben_1468872234.pdf.

[152]   See Kelsen, "The Natural-Law Doctrine before the Tribunal of Science," supra 493–94 (1949); John Dewey, "Nature and Reason in Law," 25 *International Journal of Ethics* 25, 30–31 (1914).

[153]   Dewey, "Nature and Reason in Law," supra 30–31.

advocates of laissez-faire like Hebert Spencer and apologists for slavery cited natural law in support.[154] When ruling that women can be denied entry to the practice of law, the U.S. Supreme Court cited "the law of the Creator" that the "paramount destiny and mission of women are to fulfil the noble and benign offices of wife and mother."[155] "What were natural rights," Roscoe Pound commented, "was determined chiefly by ideas drawn from the existing social order and presently the natural rights of men became as tyrannous as the divine rights of states and rulers."[156] Even prominent advocates of natural law acknowledge that it has been employed to justify bad ends.[157]

Legal positivist theories also have social and legal consequences. Legal positivists like H. L. A. Hart, for instance, have argued that recognition of the separation of law and morality makes it easier to resist immoral law by detaching moral authority from law.[158] This is countered by critics, like Gustav Radbruch, who blame legal positivist beliefs for the complicity of German legal professionals in carrying out morally abhorrent Nazi laws.[159] Whichever side one finds convincing, both positions accept that legal positivist theories of law affect beliefs and actions of jurists in the construction of law.

Social legal theories have effects on law as well. Savigny effectively employed his historical theory to argue against the enactment of a code. American historical jurisprudents conservatively enlisted their theory of law to resist the enactment of instrumental legislation and interference with the common law; sociological jurisprudents writing a generation later invoked the argument that law is out of sync with a rapidly changing society to advocate reformist legislation. It is possible, though speculative, that legal realist arguments that judges should explicitly consider the social consequences of their decisions affected how subsequent generations of judges decide cases and structure judicial decisions.

As these examples demonstrate, a realistic theory of law can consider social influences on and consequences of natural law and analytical theories of law in ways the theories themselves are not capable of addressing. A realistic theory folds all theories of law, including itself, into the broader environment of beliefs and actions about law within society.

---

[154] In an infamous example, the vice president of the Confederacy justified slavery on natural law grounds. Alexander H. Stephens, "'Corner Stone' Speech, Savannah, Georgia, March 21, 1861," Teaching American History.org., http://web.archive.org/web/20130822142313/http:/teachingamerican history.org/library/document/cornerstone-speech/.

[155] *Bradwell v. Illinois*, 83 U.S. (16 Wall.) 130, 142 (1876).

[156] Roscoe Pound, "The End of Law as Developed in Juristic Thought," 27 *Harvard L. Rev.* 605, 610 (1914).

[157] Jacque Maritain, *Man and the State* (Chicago, IL: University of Chicago Press 1951) 81.

[158] H. L. A. Hart, "The Separation of Law and Morals," 71 *Harvard L. Rev.* 593, 617–18 (1958).

[159] See Stanley L. Paulsen, "Lon L. Fuller, Gustav Radbruch, and the 'Positivist' Thesis," 13 *Law and Philosophy* 259 (1994).

VIRTUALLY ERASED FROM JURISPRUDENCE

The empirical-scientific orientation of social legal theory prompts an objection. Natural law and legal positivism are entitled to their elevated status as theoretical approaches to the nature of law, it might be said, because only they are truly theoretical. A legal philosopher urged Ramond Wacks to "eliminate altogether" the chapters on historical and sociological jurisprudence from his *Jurisprudence* book "because they were 'mainly empirical' – and insufficiently intellectual."[160]

Brian Bix exemplifies this erasure in his exhaustive *Jurisprudence* text. He travels expansively across the jurisprudential terrain, exploring many theoretical nooks and crannies, mounting sophisticated discussions of civic republicanism and game theory, among a multitude of other well-known and obscure theory topics, even spending a chapter on law and literature. Bix does not discuss sociological jurisprudence at all, however, referring to it once in passing in connection with Pound. He allocates page-length treatment to historical jurisprudence in the "Other Approaches" chapter, noting its demise, with a few quick words about Savigny and Maine.[161] No mention is made of Jhering or Ehrlich in the text. Weber shows up in a handful of footnotes. Cicero gets greater coverage from Bix than all of them combined.[162] He does not discuss law as a social institution or holistic views of law within society. Bix engages with legal realism, but with no mention of the rich theoretical veins that lie untapped beneath the realists' understanding of law.

The contemporary exclusion of social legal theories from jurisprudence is the product of artificially narrow, self-imposed strictures on what qualifies as "theoretical." "Social sciences cannot tell us what the law is because it studies human society," declares analytical jurisprudent Scott Shapiro. "Its deliverances have no relevance for the legal philosopher because it is a truism that nonhumans could have law."[163] His point is that only legal philosophy is capable of identifying universal truths about law (for aliens as well), a dubious assertion, as I show in Chapter 3. Earlier generations of legal theorists were not so dismissive. Salmond, an analytical jurisprudent, considered analytical, historical, and ethical jurisprudence informative "branches" within the "philosophy of law."[164] Oakeshott described historical and sociological jurisprudence as full-fledged versions of "philosophical jurisprudence" alongside analytical jurisprudence and natural law. He recognized that they undertook the same basic task, albeit

---

[160] Raymond Wacks, *Understanding Jurisprudence: An Introduction to Legal Theory* (Oxford: Oxford University Press 2012) 317.

[161] Bix, *Jurisprudence*, supra 275–76.   [162]   Id. 68.

[163] Scott Shapiro, *Legality* (Cambridge, MA: Harvard University Press 2011) 406–07. Ironically, just as legal philosophers declare the irrelevance of social science, we witness the opposite of the tendency of scientists denying the relevance of philosophy. See Austin L. Hughes, "The Folly of Scientism," 37 *The New Atlantis* 32 (2012), www.thenewatlantis.com/publications/the-folly-of-scientism. On all sides, this has the feel of intellectual border patrolling and one-upmanship.

[164] Salmond, *Jurisprudence*, supra 4.

from different perspectives: "Neither analytical jurisprudence nor historical jurisprudence accept law in the character in which it first appears to them; both are attempts to expound the nature of law by relating law as it first appears to some general principle and in this way transforming and making fuller our view of the nature of law."[165]

The self-proclaimed detachment of contemporary analytical jurisprudents from social scientific understandings of law stumbles over the root reality that law is a *social* institution.[166] Theories of law constructed by legal philosophers look much the same as theories of law produced by social legal theorists because they are working from the same material. Whether one is an analytical jurisprudent or a social legal theorist, the starting point is the same: positing a paradigm of law then identifying core elements, functions, structures, consequences, and so forth.

The expulsion of social legal theories impoverishes jurisprudence. Legal theory discussions revolve around schools of thought defined by characteristic propositions clashing with opposing schools espousing contrary sets of propositions. Theories have intellectual identities that position them "vis-a-vis various competitors."[167] Absent an acknowledged identity and seat at the table, a theoretical perspective virtually does not exist. Historical jurisprudence is all but forgotten. Sociological jurisprudence is occasionally mentioned though seldom engaged. Theoretical work on law and society is relegated to the nethermost region at the border of the social sciences, cabined off from jurisprudence. This leaves no accepted space within jurisprudence for major aspects of law articulated in this book. The realistic theory of law I construct incorporates historical and sociological insights about law conveyed in this chapter, applying this perspective and the knowledge it generates to describe and explain law.

---

[165] Oakeshott, *The Concept of a Philosophical Jurisprudence*, supra 165–66.

[166] Not all analytical jurisprudents reject social science. See Keith Culver and Michael Giudice, *Legality's Borders: An Essay in General Jurisprudence* (Oxford: Oxford University Press 2010). Jules Coleman suggests that sociological findings provide material for theoretical work. Jules Coleman, "Methodology," in *The Oxford Handbook of Jurisprudence and Philosophy of Law*, edited by Jules L. Coleman and Scott Shapiro (Oxford: Oxford University Press 2002).

[167] Scott Frickel and Neil Gross, "A General Theory of Scientific/Intellectual Movements," 70 *American Sociological Review* 204, 224 (2004).

2

What Is Law?

A Platonic dialogue written nearly two and a half millennia ago, *Minos*, has been called "the foundational document in the history of legal philosophy."[1] Socrates begins: "I ask you, what is law?"[2] This question has beguiled and perplexed legal philosophers ever since. H. L. A. Hart observed, "Few questions concerning human society have been asked with such persistence and answered by serious thinkers in so many diverse, strange, and even paradoxical ways as the question 'What is law?'"[3] Though none of the multitude of proposed answers to this question has achieved a consensus, legal theorists remain undeterred in their quest for this ultimate prize.

Theorists who tackle "What is law?" usually acknowledge the difficulty of the question, then, with hardly a pause, launch into their proposed answer. Instead, focusing on three main categories of concepts of law, I explain why previous attempts have failed to achieve a consensus. To put it concisely, law involves multiple social-historical phenomena that have taken on different forms and functions in different times and places and therefore cannot be captured by a singular definition of law. Theories of law based on form and function, I show, are inevitably over-inclusive or under-inclusive. They also lead to an erroneous conflation of legal systems with rule systems. Unwinding these conceptual puzzles prepares the basis for a conventionalist understanding of law, developed in this and the following chapter, that accounts for the reality of multiple legal forms.

---

[1] V. Bradley Lewis, "Plato's Minos: The Political and Philosophical Context of the Problem of Natural Right," 60 *Review of Metaphysics* 17, 17 (2006); see also Huntington Cairns, "What Is Law?" 2 *Washington and Lee L. Rev.* 193, 201–02 (1970). Scholars disagree over whether *Minos* was actually written by Plato, though all accept that it was written at the time. See William S. Cobb, "Plato's Minos," 8 *Ancient Philosophy* 187 (1988).
[2] Cairns, "What Is Law?" supra 211.
[3] H. L. A. Hart, *The Concept of Law* (Oxford: Clarendon Press 1961) 1.

THREE CATEGORIES OF THE CONCEPT OF LAW

Although law has been defined in numerous ways, "three general types of concepts have predominated,"[4] as eminent jurist Harold Berman explained. One type "sees both the ultimate origin of law and the ultimate sanction of law in 'tradition,' 'custom' and 'national character.'"[5] The second type "sees both the ultimate origin of law and the ultimate sanction of law in 'the will of the state.'"[6] A third type "emphasizes the relationship between law and moral justice; it sees both the ultimate origin of law and the ultimate sanction of law in 'right reason.'"[7] Remarkably, these same three alternatives were considered in *Minos*: 1) law is "the body of settled rules and customs"; 2) "all law is a decision of the state"; and 3) "we must then hold law to be excellent [consistent with justice] and to pursue it as a good."[8] The three main branches of jurisprudence outlined in the preceding chapter broadly align with these types, respectively, historical-sociological jurisprudence, legal positivism, and natural law.

Answers in the first category hold that law is a matter of custom, usages, and ordered social relations. This is perhaps the oldest view of law. *Nomos*, the Greek term for law, in its broadest sense meant "what is usual, customary, normal."[9] The identification of law with custom has a rich history. Customary law was a major form of law in primitive societies, in Greek and Roman law, and throughout the medieval period, and remains an important body of law in rural areas of the Global South today.[10] In terms that have been echoed many times, Friedrich von Savigny asserted law is "first developed by the customs and popular faith of the people," which jurists work into legal doctrine.[11] "That to which we give the name of Law has always been, still is, and will forever continue to be Custom,"[12] declared American historical jurisprudent James Carter in 1907. Custom descended from time immemorial is the classical self-understanding of the common law, with theorists asserting that judges do not make law, but merely declare already imma-nent law of the community. Roscoe Pound described the common law as derived from "the custom of the people, the expression of their habits of thought and action as to the relations of men with each other."[13] "Law, then, is custom transformed,"

---

[4] Harold J. Berman, *The Nature and Functions of Law* (Brooklyn, NY: Foundation Press 1958) 20. See also Brian Z. Tamanaha, *A General Jurisprudence of Law and Society* (Oxford: Oxford University Press 2001) chapter 1.

[5] Berman, *The Nature and Functions of Law*, supra 21. To reduce confusion, I have reordered Berman's three types to match the ordering in *Minos*.

[6] Id.   [7] Id.

[8] Translation from Cairns, "What Is Law?" supra 211, 212, 217. Translations differ in their wording.

[9] Cobb, "Plato's Minos," supra 191.

[10] See David J. Bederman, *Custom as a Source of Law* (New York: Cambridge University Press 2010) 1–26.

[11] Friedrich Carl von Savigny, *The Vocation of Our Age for Legislation and Jurisprudence*, translated by Abraham Hayward (London: Littlewood & Co.: 1831) 30, 28.

[12] James C. Carter, *Law: Its Origin, Growth, and Function* (New York: De Capo Press 1907).

[13] Roscoe Pound, "The Need of a Sociological Jurisprudence," 19 *Green Bag* 607, 615 (1907).

Berman asserted, "and not merely the will or reason of the lawmaker. Law spread upward from the bottom and not only downward from the top."[14]

Prominent legal sociologists and anthropologists have also espoused versions of this view of law. Eugen Ehrlich identified law with concrete usages and social practices. "The living law," he wrote, "is the law which dominates life itself even though it has not been posited in legal propositions."[15]

> It is not an essential element of the concept of law that it be created by the State, nor that it constitute the basis for the decisions of courts or other tribunals, nor that it be the basis of a legal compulsion consequent upon such a decision. A fourth element remains, and that will have to be the point of departure, i.e. the law is an ordering.[16]

Law, in this view, can be found in ongoing patterns of rule-governed behavior in fundamental aspects of social life. Conceptions of law in this category assert that law exists in all societies, primitive and modern, because all societies have rule-governed order.[17]

Because multiple forms of rule-based social ordering exist, however, this approach to law proves too expansive. "Under Ehrlich's terminology," Felix Cohen objected, "law itself merges with religion, ethical custom, morality, decorum, tact, fashion, and etiquette."[18] Similarly, in *Minos*, Socrates and his companion concluded law is more distinctive than settled rules and customs, involving the capacity to recognize or declare law.[19]

The second answer explored in *Minos* is that law involves rules and decisions issued by the state. Most concepts of law point to the state or are abstractions from the institutionalized structure of state law. There are numerous variations of this category. Law is the command of the sovereign. Law is governmental social control. Law is a coercive rule system. Law is social norms backed by institutional enforcement. Law involves obligatory rules administered within a system that identifies what counts as valid laws, how to change them, and how to apply them. And so on.

These concepts of law share with the first category the view that the function of law is to maintain social order, to which they add the structure of law as an institutionalized system. Law thus is defined by a characteristic *form* (organized institutions) and *function* (maintain social order). "Many, if not all, legal philosophers have been agreed that one of the defining features of law is that it is an institutional normative system,"[20] Joseph Raz asserts. Hans Kelsen identified the

[14] Harold J. Berman, *Law and Revolution: The Formation of the Western Legal Tradition* (Cambridge, MA: Harvard University Press 1983) 556.

[15] Eugen Ehrlich, *The Fundamental Principles of the Sociology of Law* (New York: Arno Press 1975) 497.

[16] Id. 24.

[17] See Friederich A. Hayek, *Law, Legislation, and Liberty*, vol. 1 (Chicago, IL: University of Chicago Press 1973) 46.

[18] Felix Cohen, *The Legal Conscience* (New Haven: Yale University Press 1960) 187.

[19] Cairns, "What Is Law?" supra 211; see also Mark J. Lutz, "The Minos and the Socratic Examination of Law," 54 *American Journal of Political Science* 988, 993 (2010).

[20] Joseph Raz, *The Authority of Law* (Oxford: Oxford University Press 1979) 105.

presence of an organized coercive system as what makes law distinct from morality: "The reaction of law consists in a measure of coercion enacted by the [legal] order, and socially organized, whereas the moral reaction against immoral conduct is neither provided by the moral order, nor, if provided, socially organized."[21] Max Weber offered a frequently cited formulation: "The term 'guaranteed law' shall be understood to mean that there exists a 'coercive apparatus,' i.e., that there are one or more persons whose special task is to hold themselves ready to apply specially provided means of coercion (legal coercion) for the purposes of norm enforcement."[22]

In contrast to the first category, these concepts of law deny that law exists in all societies: rudimentary societies with low social complexity, like hunter-gatherers, lacked institutionalized systems. Requiring systematic institutional enforcement as a necessary feature of law entails that customary law and international law, and other manifestations of law that are not fully systematized, do not count as law.[23] For this reason, H. L. A. Hart deemed primitive law and international law prelegal, not fully fledged "law."

Many anthropologists and international lawyers have vehemently disagreed. Anthropologist Bronislaw Malinowski insisted that "'law' and 'legal phenomena' . . . do not consist in any independent institutions."[24] Law can exist as binding obligations on fundamental matters without "a definite machinery of enactment, administration, and enforcement of law."[25] The primary mechanisms of legal enforcement, Malinowski argued, are social relations and recognition of binding obligations. International lawyers repeatedly insist international law has been an effective form of law for centuries, pointing out that most international laws are followed most of the time.[26] "In practice International Law is constantly recognized as law,"[27] observed Lassa Oppenheim. "The fact is that States, in breaking the Law of Nations, never deny its existence, but recognize its existence through the endeavor to interpret the Law of Nations as justifying their conduct."[28]

Socrates raised a different objection in *Minos*: it is inadequate to identify law with the state, for state law sometimes is unjust, unworthy of law.[29] "[Royal law] which is not true is not law," Socrates asserted, "and even though it appears to be law to the ignorant, it is, on the contrary, unlawful."[30] "Nomos is also objective," in his view, "in the sense that it is true and right and a proper basis for adjudicating disputes,

21 Hans Kelsen, *General Theory of Law and State* (Cambridge, MA: Harvard University Press 1945) 20.
22 Max Weber, *Max Weber on Law in Economy and Society*, edited by Max Rheinstein (New York: Clarion Book 1954) 13.
23 Glanville L. Williams, "International Law and the Controversy Concerning the Word 'Law,'" 22 *British Yearbook of International Law* 146 (1945).
24 Bronislaw Malinowski, *Crime and Custom in Savage Society* (London: Routledge and Kegan Paul 1926) 59, 14.
25 Id. 14.   26 See Louis Henkin, *How Nations Behave: Law and Foreign Policy*, 2nd ed. (1979).
27 Lassa Oppenheim, *International Law: A Treatise*, 7th ed., edited by H. Lauterpacht (London: Longmans, Green and Co. 1948) 15.
28 Id.   29 Cairns, "What Is Law?" supra 213, 217.   30 Id. 217.

while not denying that it is essentially connected with custom and 'subjective' acknowledgement and 'recognition.'"[31] This is the third category of the concept of law, the natural law position.[32] Conceptions of law in this vein insist that law comports with objectively true universal moral principles, law is right reason reflected in a just social order, law furthers the common good, or law inherently includes an element of justice and right. Without justice and right, according to this position, coercive enforcement of norms is raw power or tyranny, the antithesis of law.

Citing various laws permitting and prohibiting human sacrifice, Socrates's Companion in *Minos* countered with the skeptical objection that different societies or the same society at different times have contrasting laws, and opinions differ on what is just and right.[33] Incorporating justice as a requirement injects irresolvable normative controversies into what counts as law. Legal positivists raise yet another objection: there have been many examples of legal systems with evil laws or that were immoral or contrary to the common good, which nonetheless have the form and function of law and are recognized as law. Denying that slavery laws in the United States or apartheid laws in South Africa count as law, for example, is belied by reality.

CONTRASTING INTUITIONS ABOUT LAW

Behind all theoretical conceptions of law lie common beliefs and intuitions. Law is a folk concept held in the community, which theorists work with when formulating theories of law. To begin his analysis, H. L. A Hart posited "municipal law" as the paradigm because "most educated people" see that as law.[34] Joseph Raz invokes "our" concept of law – state law – as the basis for his exploration of the nature of law.[35] "Conceptual analysis proceeds on the basis of our intuitions,"[36] Scott Shapiro asserts, "identifying those truths that those who have a good understanding of how legal institutions operate (lawyers, judges, legislators, legal scholars, and so on) take to be self-evident, or at least would take to be so on due reflection."[37]

The debate over what law is has never been resolved because different folk concepts circulate and theorists hold contrary intuitions about what is fundamental to law. A conception abstracted from state law is persuasive to many theorists because state law has become a dominant form of law. But it also makes sense that customary law and international law count as law in the intuitions of other theorists because the rules they enforce and the functions they serve are paradigmatically

---

[31]   Cobb, "Plato's *Minos*," supra 191.   [32]   See Lewis, "Plato's Minos," supra.

[33]   Cairns, "What Is Law?" supra 213–14.   [34]   Hart, *Concept of Law*, supra 2–3.

[35]   Joseph Raz, "Can There Be a Theory of Law?," in *The Blackwell Guide to Philosophy of Law and Legal Theory*, edited by Martin P. Golding and William A. Edmundson (Oxford: Blackwell Publishing 2005) 331.

[36]   Scott Shapiro, *Legality* (Cambridge, MA: Harvard University Press 2011) 17.   [37]   Id. 15.

legal; although lacking the unified structure of state law, they have been considered law by many people in many societies historically and today. And it makes sense that some theorists insist justice is inherent to law because law carries connotations of right, normativity, and legitimacy.

Each of the three categories of the concept of law reflects a different intuition about law. The first category sees law in terms of fundamental rules that order social life. The second sees law as an institutionalized system that declares and enforces norms. The third posits justice and right as integral to law. *Minos* tells us that all three intuitions about law go back millennia. Etymology provides further evidence of their long-standing association. The Greek term *nomos* first referred to "custom," then later to "law" as well as custom.[38] In Athens, "*nomoi* did not differentiate legal from moral concepts and therefore they encompassed customs and 'a way of life' as well as actionable misdeeds which were, at the same time, moral misdeeds."[39] A single term in a number of languages refers to both "law" and "ethically right," including *ius* (Latin), *recht* (German, Dutch), *droit* (French), *diritto* (Italian), *derecho* (Spanish), and *prawo* (Polish), among others.[40] Thus embedded in the vernacular, the tripartite association reflects and feeds intuitions about law.

The "What is law?" debate continues because different intuitions about law at the folk level and at the theoretical level cannot be resolved by reason or empirical evidence. A crucial stumbling block is that theories of law are built on functional analysis, which suffers from insurmountable shortcomings.

OVER-INCLUSIVENESS OF FUNCTIONALISM

Function-based concepts of law produce two versions of over-inclusiveness. The phrases *functional equivalents* or *functional alternatives*,[41] or the "multiple realizability of function,"[42] denote that in social life, multiple phenomena can fulfill the same function. This is the source of one version of over-inclusiveness. When function-based criteria are used to identify or define something, all functional alternatives that fulfill said function are drawn in as well.

Another aspect of functional analysis, what I call the *repetition of functional arrangements*, leads to a different version of over-inclusiveness. The same functional needs exist in many different social settings – i.e., solving disputes, enforcing rules, coordinating behavior – and they are commonly dealt with through similar institutional arrangements, often spread through copying. When the institutional response

---

[38] M. Ostwald, *From Popular Sovereignty to Sovereignty of Law: Law, Society, and Politics in Fifth-Century Athens* (Berkeley: University of California Press 1987) 84–136.

[39] Janet Coleman, *A History of Political Thought: From Ancient Greece to Early Christianity* (Malden, MA: Blackwell Publishers 2000) 24.

[40] See Roscoe Pound, *Jurisprudence*, vol. 2 (St. Paul: West Publishing 1959) 14–18.

[41] R. K. Merton, *Social Theory and Social Structure* (New York: Free Press 1968) 86–91.

[42] Beth Preston, "Philosophical Theories of Artifact Functions," *Philosophy of Technology and Engineering Sciences*, vol. 9, edited by Anthonie Meijers (Amsterdam: Elsevier 2009) 213–33, 215.

to a functional need is used to identify or define something, usually through a combination of form and function, all manifestations of this arrangement are drawn in as well.

Both aspects of functional analysis have created persistent problems for concepts of law. Over-inclusiveness caused by functional equivalents affects concepts of law in the first category; over-inclusiveness caused by the repetition of functional arrangements affects those in the second category.

With respect to the first category, the over-inclusiveness problem was evident in Cohen's criticism, quoted earlier, that Ehrlich's concept merges morality, custom, and etiquette with law. All concepts of law in the first category suffer from this. Malinowski, like Ehrlich, saw law in concrete usages in important aspects of social life. "The rules of law stand out from the rest in that they are felt and regarded as the obligations of one person and the rightful claims of another," he wrote, adding "that reciprocity, systematic incidence, publicity, and ambition, will be found to be the main factors in the finding machinery of primitive law."[43] And tellingly, Malinowski's concept of law has been criticized on grounds identical to Ehrlich's. "The conception of law that Malinowski propounded was so broad that it was virtually indistinguishable from the study of the obligatory aspects of all social relationships,"[44] complained a critic. Social theorist Niklas Luhmann also produced a concept in the first category; he identified law's function as coordinating actions, but conceded that under his account it is "difficult to establish a clear delineation between law, language and its accessories (e.g. rules of spelling). Although it may be intuitively clear that law is not identical with language, it takes some reflection to find the crucial point of difference."[45]

What generates this debilitating over-inclusiveness is that several sources contribute to social order: socialization, customs, morality, habits, language, institutions, and more. These are functional equivalents with respect to social ordering. When social phenomena like law are defined solely in terms of the function they fulfill, all functional equivalents are encompassed. This over-inclusiveness led most theorists to reject Ehrlich's and Malinowski's concepts of law as hopelessly confused.

Theorists believed the over-inclusiveness of the first category was solved by concepts of law in the second category, which supplements the ordering function of law with an institutionalized or organized system of norm enforcement. Owing to the repetition of functional arrangements, however, this approach suffers from its own type of over-inclusiveness.

Consider Hart's concept of law as the union of primary rules of obligation and secondary rules that recognize, change, and apply the primary rules; the function of

---

[43] Malinowski, *Crime and Custom in Savage Society*, supra 55, 68.
[44] Sally Falk Moore, *Law as Process: An Anthropological Approach* (London: Routledge & Kegan Paul 1978) 220.
[45] Niklas Luhmann, *A Sociological Theory of Law* (London: Routledge & Kegan Paul 1985) 81. Luhmann attempted to solve the problem by resorting to a version of the second category.

law, in his view, is to guide conduct and exercise social control.[46] Hart failed to realize that numerous organizations in society guide conduct through a combination of primary and secondary rules. As analytical jurisprudent John Gardner observes, "The features [Hart] enumerates do not yet suffice to distinguish legal systems from many other institutionalized normative systems, such as those regulating universities and trade associations and some competitive games and sports."[47] Legal sociologist Marc Galanter enlisted Hart's concept of law to assert law can "be found in a variety of institutional settings – universities, sports leagues, housing developments, hospitals, etc."[48] This understanding of law underlies the legal pluralist perspective in anthropology and sociology of law, discussed shortly, which is beset with over-inclusiveness.[49]

Legal philosopher Scott Shapiro's theory of law likewise combines form and function and consequently has the same problem. He conceptualizes law as "a self-certifying compulsory planning organization [its form] whose aim is to solve those moral problems that cannot be solved, or solved as well, through alternative forms of social ordering [its function]."[50] Like Hart's and Galanter's concepts of law, Shapiro's version draws in all social phenomena that share the same form and function. The "United States Golf Association [USGA] ... straddles the line between law and nonlaw," he concludes. "The best we can say about the USGA ... is that it is like a legal system in some senses, but not in others, and leave it at that."[51] Even the activities of criminal gangs can count as law in his account: "if a criminal organization presents itself as dedicated to solving serious moral problems (think of Robin Hood and his Merry Men), it too might be eligible to be a legal system. The fact that others consider it to be mere organized crime does not change the reality of the situation."[52] A form-and-function-based concept of law will irresistibly draw in all social phenomena with the same characteristics.

A point must be made about *why* a concept of law is subject to the criticism of over-inclusiveness or under-inclusiveness (taken up next). The answer lies in intuitions about law. In conventional views, morality, customs, and etiquette are not law (over-inclusiveness of first category). It also offends commonsense intuitions to assert that organized crime gangs and the rules of USGA or FIFA (world soccer association) constitute law (over-inclusiveness of second category).

Remember that theoretical concepts of law are grounded in common intuitions. To start with intuitions about law yet end up with a concept of law that violates these very intuitions suggests something went wrong in the course of theoretical

[46] Hart, *Concept of Law*, supra 39, 165, 188, 208.

[47] John Gardner, *Law as a Leap of Faith* (Oxford: Oxford University Press 2010) 278. For a detailed explanation of this issue, see Tamanaha, *A General Jurisprudence of Law and Society*, supra 137–42.

[48] Marc Galanter, "Justice in Many Rooms: Courts, Private Ordering, and Indigenous Law," 19 *Journal of Legal Pluralism* 1, 17–18 (1981).

[49] See Brian Z. Tamanaha, "Understanding Legal Pluralism: Past to Present, Local to Global," 30 *Sydney Law Review* 375 (2008).

[50] Shapiro, *Legality*, supra 225. [51] Id. 224. [52] Id. 424.

abstraction. The culprit is functional analysis itself. Functionalism narrows a given social phenomenon to one dimension – the defining function – and sticks with that dimension as far as it extends; adding form to the function narrows the category, but still extends as far in the dimension as the selected combination goes. Following a dimension to its full extension takes the concept of law beyond the boundaries of conventional understandings of law – encompassing customs and manners, or universities and sports leagues – resulting in over-inclusiveness.

UNDER-INCLUSIVENESS OF FUNCTIONALISM

The flip side of the one-dimensionality of functionalism is under-inclusiveness, which appears here in two manifestations, one owing to function and the second owing to the system requirement for carrying out said function. The first type of under-inclusiveness results because state legal systems are multifunctional. This is an outgrowth of the capacity of organized complexes of action to undertake different activities. Social artifacts are "multiply utilizable." A table can be used to serve dinner on, to have a meeting around, to have sexual intercourse on, to take shelter under during an earthquake, to block a door from intruders, to be a display in a museum, and to stand on to change a light bulb, among other uses. Some uses of social artifacts and institutions exist from the outset while other uses develop over time as people realize they can serve more purposes than originally intended; some might be latent functions that users do not consciously recognize yet are served nonetheless.

Concepts of law that identify a single function – provide social control, coordinate behavior, solve complex moral problems, enforce norms, etc. – will inevitably leave out a great deal of what law does, particularly state law. To offer one example, think of enabling acts. One type of enabling act – the basis of the administrative system – sets out goals and standards, creates an agency to carry them out, and grants the agency the power to exercise rule-making, enforcement, and adjudicative functions to achieve its purposes. Another type of enabling act creates corporations. Enabling laws of these sorts – producing two leviathans of modern society, government agencies and corporations – cannot be shoehorned into any of the standard function-based ways of conceptualizing law. These laws give birth to organizations and imbue them with powers that they utilize in innumerable ways. To characterize this as enforcing rules of social order or as a planning system that solves moral problems entirely misses the point.

There are many other examples of what law does that cannot be captured by singular functional definitions. To offer one multisided example, law is used in various ways to create valid money (legal tender act), to issue money (through empowerment of the Federal Reserve), to acquire money (taxation), to borrow money (authorize bond issues and raise debt ceiling), to establish spending para-meters (budgets), and to allocate money (appropriations). A single set of laws can do multiple things. Tax laws have several functions beyond generating revenues: they pay for things (tax breaks), they provide incentives (tax credits) and disincentives (sin taxes and gas taxes) for social action, and they create employment for tax lawyers and accountants who manipulate tax laws to their clients' advantage. Entities and individuals use law in a multitude of ways, not just to make contracts, possess and transfer property, and seek recovery for harms suffered – which can be captured in functional terms – but also to harass and intimidate others, to obtain money or exact revenge, to fight corporations or government, to try to change society.[53] Functional conceptions that present law in terms of resolving disputes, enforcing norms, coordinating behavior, solving moral problems, or the like, wash out much of what law does and is used to do.

Another manifestation of under-inclusiveness arises when form-and-function conceptions of law exclude conventionally recognized versions of law that lack the required form or function. Examples of this mentioned earlier are Hart's assertion that primitive law and international law are prelegal because they lack fully organized secondary rules. Any theory of law that requires a comprehensive system for the creation, application, and adjudication of rules would exclude many versions of customary law, religious law, and natural law, past and present. Never mind that people in a given social arena might view these legal forms as more immediately binding and legitimate than the state law regime.

WHY FUNCTIONALISM CANNOT ANSWER "WHAT IS LAW?"

Each function-based concept of law in effect creates a *function-based category* that includes phenomena not recognized as law while also excluding recognized forms of law. This can be made plain by simply deleting the words "Law *is* . . . " from the front of each proffered concept of law – what is left is a function-based category. "Institutionalized norm enforcement" includes sports leagues, universities, and state law, among others. "Institutionalized dispute resolution" includes community mediation, business arbitration, state law, and so forth. "Organized compulsory planning system to solve moral problems" includes churches, social organizations with moral objectives, and state law, among others. "Coordinate behavioral expectations" or "maintain social order" or "social control" include habits, language, socialization, education, customs, morality, and state law, and more.

Each functional category includes law, but none contains law alone (over-inclusive), and no category exhausts what law is or what law does (under-inclusive). The existence of functional alternatives (different things that satisfy the same function) and the repetition of functional arrangements (multiple settings utilize the same institutionalized arrangement to fill needs) make it impossible to

[53] See Robert A Kagan, *Adversarial Legalism: The American Way of Law* (Cambridge, MA: Harvard University Press 2003).

isolate law using functional criteria; and multiple utilizations of social artifacts will overrun any singular functional account. Consequently, no attempt to conceptualize law in functional terms can be constructed in a fashion that refers only to law and that fully captures law.

The distinction between *folk concepts* (ideas and concepts social groups hold) and *analytical concepts* (concepts social scientists and philosophers formulate to study folk concepts and social phenomena) helps crystallize the point. Law in the first instance is a folk concept because law *is* what people see as "law." Legal theorists abstract from folk concepts of law – the source of their intuitions about law – to construct theoretical concepts of law. Form-and-function-based analytical concepts of law inevitably clash with folk concepts because how people perceive law cannot be captured by functional analysis for reasons detailed previously. An additional twist arises because in many social groups multiple folk concepts of law exist (state law, customary law, religious law, international law, etc.), which various theorists, themselves members of the folk, differentially internalize as intuitions about law. Consequently, a clash arises not only between analytical concepts and folk concepts, but also between competing analytical concepts that theorists produce by abstracting from different or multiple folk concepts of law.

ERROR OF CONFLATING LEGAL SYSTEM AND RULE SYSTEM

Theorists who attempt to identify what law is by paring it down to a basic form and function commonly make the mistake of conflating legal systems with rule systems. Shapiro commits a version of this when he says a criminal gang can count as law, as does Joseph Raz in a recent essay, "Why the State?" Raz is "critical of jurisprudential theories that focus more or less exclusively on the state."[54] Owing to changes in the wake of globalization, he urges legal philosophers to break out of this narrow view to examine "other kinds of law," including "international law, or the law of organizations like the European Union, but also Canon Law, Sharia Law, Scottish Law, the law of native nations, the rules and regulations governing the activities of voluntary associations, or those of legally recognized corporations, and more, including many transient phenomena, like neighborhood gangs."[55] This openness to other types of law is a welcome turnaround for Raz, who himself has been criticized for exclusively focusing on state law.[56] The expanded focus he advocates portends a fundamental shift in legal philosophy, with unsettling implications for long-held positions, which

---

[54] Joseph Raz, "Why the State?" (2014) 1 (unpublished essay on file with author), available at http://papers.ssrn.com/sol3/papers.cfm?abstract_id=2339522.

[55] Raz, "Why the State?" supra 3.

[56] See Brian Z. Tamanaha, *A General Jurisprudence of Law and Society* (Oxford: Oxford University Press 2001) 138–48, 151. See generally William Twining, "A Post-Westphalian Conception of Law," 37 *Law & Society Review* 199 (2003); William Twining, *General Jurisprudence: Understanding Law from a Global Perspective* (Cambridge: Cambridge University Press 2009).

I discuss in the next chapter. In Chapter 6, I answer his call, articulating a theory of international law as a specific social historical tradition.

For immediate purposes, it is essential to clarify that Raz's list of kinds of law crosses over two qualitatively distinct categories: 1) international law, Canon Law, Sharia, EU law, etc.; and 2) the rules and regulations of voluntary associations and corporations, etc. As their names reflect, the first category consists of conventionally recognized manifestations of "law." Members of the second category, in contrast, are not conventionally perceived as law, but nonetheless have been included by Raz because they involve institutionalized rule systems that resemble the form and function of state law. He is correct to think of the former as law because they are collectively recognized as such, but it is a mistake to call the second category "law" because it is plagued by over- and under-inclusiveness for the reasons just explained.[57]

In treating the second group as law, Raz is headed down the same fraught trail legal pluralists followed for decades. "The [legal] institutions I have in mind are themselves rule governed," he elaborates, "ultimately governed by practice-based rules that determine if not all at least the most important aspects of their constitution, powers, and mode of operation. Perhaps the most elementary powers legal institutions have are enforcement and adjudicative powers, namely the powers to take measures to enforce other rules and to adjudicate disputes about their applicability."[58] Based on this understanding, Raz concludes, "the rules of the U.S. and of Columbia University *are legal systems*."[59] "There can be *law-based* systems governing members of a profession, co-religionists, inhabitances of a certain territory, and so on . . . *law-like* systems apply to groups, united by the rules, such as members of a university, a sports club, a profession, or a locality."[60]

To call them "law-like" is an analogy, which is unproblematic insofar as the analogy holds. But to call them "law-based," "kinds of law," or "legal systems," as Raz does in these passages, is to assert they *are* law.[61] Before accepting these characterizations, we must determine what the most sensible general category is. Social institutions can be categorized along different dimensions, so the category one selects should be based on what best facilitates analysis and understanding. Are these better understood as *law*-based systems or *rule*-based systems? Are all rule systems types of law or is law just one type of rule system? Many social organizations have rule-making and judicial-type bodies, like universities and sports leagues. Though he purports to identify the institutional features of *law*, Raz's statement

---

[57]   Citing examples similar to Raz's, another legal theorist who crosses over these two categories is Neil MacCormick, "Institutions and Laws Again," 77 *Texas Law Review* 1429, 1431–32 (1999).

[58]   Raz, "Why the State?" supra 6.   [59]   Id. 7 (emphasis added).   [60]   Id. 8.

[61]   Leslie Green is correct to emphasize the difference between "things being *like* law and things *counting as* law." Leslie Green, "The Forces of Law: Duty, Coercion, and Power," 29 *Ratio Juris* 164, 178 (2016). In an earlier work, Raz declared, "We know that the regulations of a golf club are not a legal system." Raz, *Between Authority and Interpretation*, supra 28. The recent essay indicates a change in position.

can be read as a generic description of complex rule systems, which are ubiquitous. If those characteristics define legal systems, then society is overflowing with a profusion of "law."

Anthropologists and sociologists who identify themselves as legal pluralists arrived at precisely this conclusion several decades ago. As mentioned earlier, Galanter asserted law can "be found in a variety of institutional settings – universities, sports leagues, housing developments, hospitals, etc."[62] John Griffiths, who penned the most influential theoretical elaboration of legal pluralism, declared, "all social control is *more* or *less* legal."[63] Another leading theorist, Boaventura de Sousa Santos, offered this defense: "It may be asked: why should these competing or complementary forms of social ordering be designated as *law* and not rather as 'rule systems,' 'private governments,' and so on? Posed in these terms, this question can only be answered by another question: Why not?"[64]

To call these social institutions "legal systems," one might respond, is confusing and lacks theoretical justification. It amounts to a massive relabeling of rule systems as "legal" with no real conceptual gain. After a quarter century of insisting that all rule systems are forms of law, Griffiths, an outspoken champion of the notion of legal pluralism, late in his career repudiated this position. Owing to irresolvable conceptual problems with isolating distinctively legal phenomena (owing to the functionalist problems identified earlier), he became convinced "that the expression 'legal pluralism' can and should be reconceptualised as 'normative pluralism' or 'pluralism in social control.'"[65]

This version of legal pluralism went wrong by fastening on features common among social institutions, which cannot serve to distinguish law. John Searle's ontology of social institutions helps reveal why. "Human institutions vary enormously, all the way from religions to nation-states to sports teams to corporations," Searle observed, but beneath the surface lie "purely formal features they have in common that enable them to function in human life."[66]

Notice that Searle identifies the very same examples as Raz and legal pluralists: religions, nation-states, sports teams, and corporations. Significantly, however, when invoking these examples, Searle is not talking about *law* per se – but about social institutions that share underlying features. When Raz asserts that universities, sports clubs, and professions have "legal systems" (or are "law-based" or "law-like"), he is picking up on the fact that they are constituted through rules and regulate the conduct of their members by rules that must be promulgated, enforced, and applied.

---

[62] Galanter, "Justice in Many Rooms," supra 17–18.

[63] John Griffiths, "What Is Legal Pluralism?" (1981) 24 *Journal of Legal Pluralism* 1, 38.

[64] Boaventura de Sousa Santos, *Toward a New Common Sense: Law, Science in Paradigmatic Transition* (London: Routledge & Kegan Paul 1995) 115 (emphasis added).

[65] John Griffiths, "The Idea of Sociology of Law and Its Relation to Law and to Sociology" 8 *Current Legal Issues* 49, 63–64 (2005)

[66] John R. Searle, *Making the Social World: The Structure of Human Civilization* (Oxford: Oxford University Press 2010) 123.

These cannot be distinguishing features of "law" because a multitude of institutions have the same elements. Searle recognizes this: "The ontology I have given [for government or state] so far might also fit nonpolitical structures such as religions, corporations, universities, and organized sports."[67]

The feature that "distinguishes governments from churches, universities, ski clubs, and marching bands," says Searle (who subsumes law within government), is a monopoly over armed violence within a territory: "it maintains a constant threat of physical force."[68] He echoes Max Weber's assertion, "we have to say that a state is a human community that (successfully) claims the monopoly of the legitimate use of physical force within a given territory."[69] Searle does not address "What is law?," but his analysis shows it cannot be answered by referring to the formal features legal institutions share with all rule systems.

STATE LAW AS ONE TYPE OF RULE SYSTEM

Sociologists and philosophers of society accept that social life is suffused with institutions that structure, enable, constrain, and channel social interaction.[70] Institutions exist, in Searle's account, when people collectively recognize statuses to which specified rights and obligations are attached.[71] He formalizes institutions thusly: X *counts as* Y *in context* C. X is an object, person, or entity; "counts as" is collective recognition; Y is a status with deontic powers (which he defines as carrying "rights, duties, obligations, requirements, permissions, authorizations, entitlements, and so on"[72]); context C specifies the circumstances under which the powers attach. A cut of paper with certain dyed markings (X) counts as money (Y) when it is printed by the Bureau of Engraving and Printing and circulated (C).[73] It counts as money because we collectively accept it as money. To serve as a means of exchange is the primary power of money.

Institutions consist of constitutive and regulative rules. Constitutive rules are fundamental in Searle's account because they construct the institution, creating

---

[67] Id. 170. Searle treats "government" and "states" equivalently for the purposes of his analysis. Id. 161 n. 12. As I later elaborate, what distinguishes law from other rule systems is the conventional identification of law.

[68] Id. 171.

[69] H. H. Gerth and C. Wrights Mills, eds., *From Max Weber: Essays in Sociology* (New York: Oxford University Press 1946) 78; Max Weber, *Economy and Society*, edited by Guenther Roth and Claus Wittich (Berkeley: University of California Press 1978) 904.

[70] For an informative summary, see Frank Hindriks, "Constitutive Rules, Language, and Ontology," 71 *Erkenn* 253 (2009).

[71] John R. Searle, *Making the Social World: The Structure of Human Civilization* (Oxford: Oxford University Press 2010); John R. Searle, "What Is an Institution?" 1 *Journal of Institutional Economics* 1, 11 (2005).

[72] Searle, *Making the Social World*, supra 8–9.

[73] There are other forms of money, including money that has no corresponding object, like electronic money. This raises a question about the adequacy of Searle's formulation because it is not a "thing" as required by his X.

the possibility of institutional actions and facts. Regulative rules specify norms of conduct. Both types of rules are matters of convention and can be set forth formally or informally observed, and frequently involve both. Under the constitutive rules of football across much of North America, for example, a "touchdown" worth six points is scored when a pointy-ended ball gets past the goal line in the possession of a player; a regulative rule (among many) prohibits striking an opposing player from behind. In South America, under the constitutive rules of football, a "goal" worth one point is scored when a round ball crosses the goal line between two posts below the crossbar; a regulative rule (among many) prohibits deliberately tripping an opposing player. The constitutive and regulative rules for these two types of football vary greatly depending on context, from professional leagues, to street games with make-shift balls and goals and rules made for the occasion. And the constitutive and regulative rules of football have histories, evolving over time.

Legal phenomena can be usefully seen in terms of this formal structure.[74] Property and marriage consist of constitutive and regulative rules (which vary widely and have evolved over time). Property exists when people collectively recognize that a person or group has the right to possess, to use, to exclude others, or to transfer something. Marriage exists when people collectively recognize clusters of rights and obligations in connection with family unions. The same analysis can be applied to state legal organizations. Courts and legislatures are organizations composed of people holding offices with collectively accepted statuses carrying legal deontic powers operating through constitutive and regulative rules. Certain people (X) are collectively recognized as possessing legal authority (as police, prosecutors, legislators, judges, etc.) (Y) when duly appointed and acting in their official capacities (context C). People recognize that police have the power to arrest, prosecutors to prosecute, legislators to legislate, judges to judge, and jailors to jail.

What defines a legal status is not the function or task itself – private security officers also engage in policing, private rule systems have rule makers and enforcers, and private arbitrators engage in judging, none of which is legal per se – but rather it is "legal" because these tasks are carried out within a system of institutions collectively recognized as a *legal* system. People acting as state legal officials have legal powers not conferred by statuses in other institutions, with organized physical force standing behind their official legal actions, often justified by claims of justice and right. Possessing "legal" powers is a defining component of how they are socially perceived.

A network of organizations comprised of positions that exercise collectively recognized statuses with legal powers constitutes the legal system. Recognition, Searle emphasizes, does not entail that people normatively endorse or approve of

---

[74] Searle's account has been criticized by many theorists (see, e.g., Hindriks, "Constitutive Rules, Language, and Ontology," supra) and aspects of his analysis are questionable. In particular, the line between constitutive rules and regulative rules is sometimes difficult to draw. I invoke Searle's formula here as a useful way to think about institutions, without committing to his entire theory.

the institutions – only that they recognize the statuses and attached deontic powers.[75] In Searle's scheme, "The system, once accepted by participants, commits them to acceptance of facts within the system."[76] Collective recognition of particular substantive laws and regulations is not required once people collectively recognize the broader system of law creation and application.[77] People in society can be and often are ignorant of the vast bulk of laws and official legal actions, yet they exist as social (legal) facts via collective recognition and actions of legal officials.

This perspective on social institutions facilitates a more nuanced view of what differentiates law from other social institutions, and helps expose multiple forms of law. Contrary to Raz and Shapiro, universities, sports leagues, and criminal gangs are not law because they are not collectively recognized as exercising "legal" deontic powers. On the other hand, customary law, religious law, and international law, among other legal forms, do constitute collectively recognized forms of law with legal deontic powers (as elaborated shortly).

WHAT AND WHO STATE LAW ADDRESSES

Let us continue with universities and sports leagues to draw out further ways in which state law is distinct. Most universities and sports leagues are organized as legal creations, that is, constituted as corporations or limited liability companies (LLCs) under state law. Their existence and powers are granted by state law. Their internal and external activities operate within state laws regarding contract, property, torts, employment, safety, taxes, and more. The rule systems of universities and sports leagues apply only to their members, who participate by choice, whereas a state legal system promulgates regulative rules that apply to all people and entities present on its territory (and extraterritorially on some matters). Members dissatisfied with the actions of these rule systems can go to state law to seek relief. University and sports league officials – and their legal counsel – are keenly aware that their constitutive and regulative rules and operations are built on and subject to the requirements and authority of a state legal system. While people can petition the state legal system to seek recourse from an organization's actions, the only recourse from law, if any recourse is available, must be to a higher or alternative form of law.

The obvious explanation for these differences is the claimed supremacy of state law above other organizations. But the claim of supremacy alone does not get at the heart of what sets law apart – what and who it addresses are distinct from rule systems in organizations. To see this, distinguish two orientations of state law: 1) law establishing fundamental rules of social intercourse, and 2) law as an instrument to

---

[75] Searle, *Making the Social World*, supra 8, 56–58. Group recognition, not private recognition by an individual, is necessary to create a social institution. Id. 60.

[76] Id. 102–03.

[77] See Amie Thomasson, "Foundations for a Social Ontology," 18 *Protosociology* 269, 283 (2003).

advance the activities of government organizations.[78] The latter orientation, discussed more fully in Chapter 5, exhibits certain similarities with rule systems in organizations. The main difference in this second orientation is that state law constructs and enables the polity, which sets it apart from other rule systems.

The former orientation is what primarily distinguishes state law from most rule systems. The claimed function of state law in the social arena is to maintain fundamental legal rules governing social and economic intercourse: individuals and entities carry on their daily activities, engaging in transactions, coordinating with others, satisfying their needs and desires, and pursuing their purposes, undergirded by a framework of laws relating to property, contract, personal injuries, and family unions.[79] Organizations operating in the social arena – universities, sports leagues, etc. – are not themselves legal systems, but rather are subject to the state legal system in this respect. Rule systems within organizations apply only to the operation of the organization itself and its members on a narrow set of matters related to the particular purposes of the organization.

The state legal system today claims to trump other rule systems in establishing the basic rules of social intercourse (first orientation), the legal system backs its edicts with coercive force (its trumping power), and this claim is grounded on the asserted right to rule (normative justification). Notice that these three claims are echoed in the three meanings of law discussed in *Minos*. (Keep in mind that state law does not always make good on these claims and, as discussed next, does not exclusively make these claims.) Universities and sports leagues are not collectively recognized as "legal" systems and do not have the legal deontic powers exercised by legal officials. The members of these very organizations do not typically view their own rule systems as "law," which they recognize they are subject to. Their rule systems do not establish basic rules of social intercourse, are not backed by organized physical force, and make no general claims of justice and right. Hence rule systems in general are not legal systems per se.

COEXISTING MULTIPLE LEGAL FORMS

Collective recognition, as we have seen, is a crucial existence condition for institutions. While the preceding section isolated on the state law paradigm, additional wrinkles arise for "What is law?" because more than one form of law has been collectively recognized historically and today, including customary law, religious law, natural law, international law, and bodies of transnational law. Legal philosophers, as Raz acknowledged, heretofore have focused almost exclusively on state law, failing to examine other manifestations of law.

---

[78] For a discussion of this distinction, see Hayek, *Law, Legislation, and Liberty*, supra 35–54.

[79] A similar point is made in Leslie Green, "The Morality in Law," 5–7, http://papers.ssrn.com/sol3/ papers.cfm?abstract_id=2223760, published in L. Duarte d' Almeida, J. Edwards, and A. Dolcetti, eds., *Reading HLA Hart's The Concept of Law* (Oxford: Hart Publishing 2013), 177–207.

Property and marriage again serve as examples. Property and marriage exist, as mentioned, when people within a group recognize legal rights and obligations (deontic powers) in connection, respectively, with things and family unions. A legal *system* is not necessarily required. People in hunter-gatherer groups, as elaborated in Chapter 4, collectively recognized possession and use rights over tools, game, and land, as well as various rights in childbearing unions and sexual relations; these rights were enforced by the group without standing police and courts. Forms of property and marriage thus existed in these societies, notwithstanding the absence of formal legal systems.

Now consider more complex societies with established state legal systems. For a standing legal system to exist, people within the social group must collectively recognize that legal officials possess various deontic powers in connection with the making, enforcement, and application of law. When this recognition holds, state legal officials – not laypeople – determine who owns property or is married and what their respective legal rights and obligations are in accordance with rules of the legal system. What legal officials collectively recognize becomes institutional legal actions and facts.[80]

Collective recognition has three distinct foci across these examples: first, people collectively recognize property and marriage; second, people collectively recognize the official legal system and the legal powers held by officeholders; third, legal officials collectively recognize legal actions and facts. Legal theorists typically posit an idealized image of law in which the first, second, and third foci fit seamlessly together on the assumption that what legal officials recognize as property and marriage comport with what people in the community recognize. In Hart's account, law consists of a combination of primary rules that govern social behavior, and secondary rules that legal officials follow to recognize, change, and apply primary rules.[81] In his presentation, while occasional inconsistencies arise, primary rules carried out by the legal system generally correspond with the rules recognized by the public – thus official law mirrors socially recognized norms.[82]

Many legal situations past and present have deviated from the model Hart and most legal theorists assume. In colonial and postcolonial contexts, it is often the case that religious and customary law recognized by the community on basic matters of social intercourse – including property, marital rights, inheritance, binding agreements, and personal injury remedies – do not match legal rights recognized by transplanted state legal systems (often not conducted in the local vernacular). Members of the community in these situations know the state legal system exists

---

[80] An elaborate account of legal institutional facts is provided in Neil MacCormick, "Norms, Institutions, and Institutional Fact," 17 *Law and Philosophy* 301 (1998). My version is stripped to the basics.

[81] Hart, *Concept of Law*, supra 77–96.

[82] Hart recognizes the necessity for general acceptance, but he assumes concordance, and does not entertain the implications of substantial divergence. See Hart, *Concept of Law*, supra 59–60, 107.

and exerts legal powers, but many lack knowledge about and do not support the rules carried out by state legal officials. It cannot be said (contra Searle) that they "accept" the institutional legal facts produced by officials. They live by and resort to their own religious or customary laws and tribunals. Today, in rural areas of countries across Africa, the Middle East, Asia, and the Pacific, 80 percent to 90 percent of people take their disputes to customary tribunals for resolution under their own collectively recognized (frequently unwritten) laws rather than to state law courts.[83]

More than a billion people around the globe claim property rights and conduct property transactions on terms inconsistent with official state law, ranging from urban settlements where families have lived for generations to rural areas operating under customary land tenure.[84] Property rights are fragmented across separate coexisting systems as well as in hybrid legal forms. "Some property claimants may resist or ignore [state] law simply because it is the product of a distant centralist state, or a state they perceive as lacking in reliability, legitimacy or probity. Others may prefer local mechanisms for coordinating property relations that are embedded in long-standing mechanisms of social organization. Their expectations may be shaped by self-identification as members of a community, tribe or group rather than citizens of a constitutional state."[85]

In many of these circumstances, inconsistent legal regimes have coexisted for well over a century – one collectively recognized by the social group and its informal or formal tribunals, and another set collectively recognized by state legal officials. State law faces a powerful *legal* rival with respect to basic rules of social intercourse. (State laws in these situations are frequently also at odds with prevailing customs, beliefs, and moral views.) This coexistence of clashing legal institutions is an ongoing source of legal uncertainty in many communities around the world, raising issues from whether customary land rights or state property rights control in disputes, to whether Muslim marriage and divorce rights among immigrants will be recognized by state legal systems in the West. An adequate answer to "What is law?" must account for this plurality of law. How this issue is dealt with depends on how one conceives of the nature of law.

---

[83] See, e.g., L. Chirayath, Caroline Sage, and Michael Woolcock, *Customary Law and Policy Reform: Engaging with the Plurality of Justice Systems* (Washington, DC: World Bank Legal Department 2005); Debbie Isser, *Customary Justice and the Rule of Law in War-Torn Societies* (Washington, DC: U.S. Institute for Peace Press 2011).

[84] A superb account is Daniel Fitzpatrick, "Fragmented Property Systems," 38 *University of Pennsylvania Journal of International Law* (forthcoming), available SSRN http://papers.ssrn.com/sol3/papers.cfm?abstract_id=2773387.

[85] Id. 18.

3

Necessary and Universal Truths about Law?

"A theory consists of necessary truths," Joseph Raz asserts, "for only necessary truths about the law reveal the nature of law. We talk of the 'nature of law,' or the nature of anything else, to refer to those of the law's characteristics which are of the essence of law, which make law what it is."[1] A true theory of law holds for all places and all times. "Naturally, the essential properties of the law are universal characteristics of law. . . . When surveying the different forms of social organization in different societies throughout the ages we will find many which resemble law in various ways. Yet if they lack the essential features of the law, they are not legal systems."[2]

Other analytical jurisprudents have made similar statements. Jules Coleman asserts, "The descriptive project of jurisprudence is to identify the essential or necessary features of our concept of law."[3] A theory of law must "consist of propositions about the law which are necessarily true, as opposed to merely contingently true," writes Julie Dickson, because "only necessarily true propositions about law will be capable of explaining the nature of law."[4] "To discover the law's nature," says Scott Shapiro, "would be in part to discover its necessary properties, that is, those properties that law could not fail to have."[5] Robert Alexy similarly observes, "Thus, for the question, 'What is the nature of law?' one may substitute the question 'What are the necessary properties of law?' . . . Essential or necessary properties of law are those properties without which law would not be law."[6] About the "nature of law," John Gardner writes, "They are things which must be true of something if it is to qualify as law, and hence if it is properly to be included in the data set when making either empirical or evaluative observations about law."[7]

---

[1] Joseph Raz, *Between Authority and Interpretation* (Oxford: Oxford University Press 2009) 24, 17.
[2] Id. 25.
[3] Jules Coleman, "Incorporationism, Conventionality, and the Practical Difference Thesis," 4 *Legal Theory* 381, 393 n. 24 (1998).
[4] Julie Dickson, *Evaluation and Legal Theory* (Oxford: Hart Publishing Company 2001) 18.
[5] Scott Shapiro, *Legality* (Cambridge: Oxford University Press 2011) 9.
[6] Robert Alexy, "On the Concept and the Nature of Law," 21 *Ratio Juris* 281, 290 (2008).
[7] John Gardner, *Law as a Leap of Faith* (Oxford: Oxford University Press 2012) 270.

This chapter critically examines the claim that there are necessary, universal truths about law. First I discuss the differences between natural kinds and social artifacts. Philosophers of society have grappled with the challenges involved in grounding necessary features in social artifacts, engaging issues analytical jurisprudents have not begun to address. The main difficulty for claims about necessary features is that law is a social construction that varies and changes over time. Then I inquire whether assertions about law's necessary features are *a priori* or *a posteriori* knowledge, showing that analytical jurisprudents do not agree among themselves on the basis for their assertions, and most have not explained their position at all. Next, I turn to universal truth claims about necessary features of law, in particular Joseph Raz's effort to straddle parochial conceptual origins with universalistic claims, demonstrating that universal application is sound but universal truth is not. Then I expose that analytical jurisprudents presuppose the paradigm of state law without justification and without considering alternatives that would produce theories of law with different features. I also show they have not provided criteria by which to test the correctness of theories of law, and they resort to two ways to shield their theories of law from refutation.

Replacing their reliance on intuitions and assumptions, I explain why theorists must begin with conventionalist identifications of law (which includes multiple forms of law), and should draw on empirical studies of law to inform their analytical work. Finally, eschewing claims about necessary features and universal truths, I close by indicating how the nature of law can be understood as complexes of social institutions that have evolved over time in connection with society.

SOCIAL INSTITUTIONS AND NECESSARY FEATURES

Talk about essential and necessary features is puzzling in relation to social constructions like law – based on ideas, beliefs, and actions – which come in a multitude of variations and change over time. "Legal systems are not natural kinds ... that have essences," Ronald Dworkin objected. "They are social kinds: to suppose that law has an essence is as much a mistake as supposing that marriage or community has an essence."[8]

When setting out their positions, Raz and Shapiro both cite H_2O as an example. "If being made of H_2O is of the nature of water," Raz writes, "then this is so whether or not people believe that it is so, and whether or not they believe water has essential properties."[9] "Being H_2O is what makes water *water*," Shapiro asserts. "With respect to law, accordingly, to answer the question 'What is law?' on this interpretation is to discover what makes all and only instances of law instances of law and not something else."[10]

---

[8] Ronald Dworkin, "Hart and the Concepts of Law," 119 *Harvard L. Rev.* 95, 95 (2006). See also Brian Bix, "Conceptual Questions and Jurisprudence," 1 *Legal Theory* 465, 468 (1995).
[9] Raz, *Between Authority and Interpretation*, supra 27, 23 n. 7.   [10] Shapiro, *Legality*, supra 9.

Neither Raz nor Shapiro address the manifest ontological differences between water and law. Water has a fixed chemical structure independent of what humans think, whereas law is constructed through the meaningful actions of humans; the features of law are contingent on and shaped by human subjectivity and purposes while the essential properties of water are not. Philosophers generally agree the essential properties of water are mind-independent internal properties: "we are accustomed to thinking of essentialness as fixed by the laws of nature."[11] Law is neither mind independent nor fixed by the laws of nature, but rather is a folk concept with multiple versions and variations. As psychologists who study concepts have found, "it may indeed be the case that for any one type of artifact, there exist an almost infinite number of variations in ontogeny, form, and function."[12]

A few philosophers of society have argued that a limited class of social artifacts can be understood in terms of necessary features. A well-known proponent is Amie Thomasson, who recognizes that a convincing account "will require a substantively different ontology, epistemology, and semantics."[13] Mind dependence, variation, and historical change render essentialist claims about social institutions problematic in ways that cannot be built on the same terms as natural kinds. Functional analysis cannot identify essential properties, Thomasson recognizes, because social phenomena are marked by contingency and variation owing to material, cultural, and historical circumstances.[14] She accepts that features of social artifacts "may be functional, structural, aesthetic, historical, or of various other sorts of combinations";[15] they do not have natural boundaries; and they can be categorized according to various criteria depending on specific purposes or contexts. Moreover, Thomasson acknowledges, "artifactual kinds are notoriously malleable and historical in nature."[16] "Over a long period of time the concept (and corresponding kind) can gradually change so much that it is unclear whether or not we should really count items at the beginning and end of the series as being of the same artifactual kind."[17] Trying to overcome these hurdles, Thomasson grounds essential properties of social artifacts in the intentions of human makers: "the specific natures of

---

[11] Crawford L. Elder, "On the Place of Artifacts in Ontology," in *Creations of the Mind: Theories of Artifacts and Their Representation*, edited by Eric Margolis and Stephen Laurence (Oxford: Oxford University Press 2007) 37.

[12] Frank C. Keil, Marissa L. Greif, and Rebekkah S. Kerner, "A World Apart: How Concepts of the Constructed World Are Different in Representation and Development," in *Creations of the Mind*, supra 233.

[13] Amie L. Thomasson, "Realism and Human Kinds," 67 *Philosophy and Phenomenological Research* 580 581 (2003). A collection of arguments on the issues can be found in Margolis and Laurence, *Creations of the Mind*, supra.

[14] Amie L. Thomasson, "Artifacts and Human Concepts," in *Creations of the Mind*, supra 71. She notes there is "recurrent evidence against the idea that a common function is sufficient to yield a predictable cluster of properties definitive of an artifact type." On the problems with functions, see also 56–57.

[15] Thomasson, "Realism and Human Kinds," supra 598.

[16] Thomasson, "Artifact Concepts and Human Concepts," supra 62.

[17] Thomasson, "Realism and Human Kinds," supra 601.

artifactual kinds are determined (often gradually and collectively) by makers' concepts about what features are relevant to kind membership."[18] Her core point is we cannot be wrong about the features of artifacts we intentionally create according to our design.

This argument, which specifically applies to efforts to copy or reproduce artifacts, in itself does not make the case for essential and necessary features rather than typical features and family resemblances. Thomasson's account, moreover, is different from the position taken by analytical jurisprudents. She locates essential features in the intentions and designs of makers to create said artifact, whereas for Raz, "it is possible that no one has a completely correct understanding or knowledge of a concept."[19] "While the law has many essential features," he asserts, "we are not aware of all of them."[20] His analogy of law to water is that both have essential features even if people do not recognize what they might be.[21] Raz's stance presupposes that essential features of law exist in some sense to be discovered, independent of individual and collective knowledge, whereas Thomasson argues we are intentional creators and therefore essential features of social artifacts are determined by us. Furthermore, she limits the correctness of the concept to the "time and tradition" that uses it because essential features are intention-dependent.[22] Legal philosophers, in contrast, suggest their theories are universally true, transgressing her limitation (more on this shortly).

Further complicating matters, psychological studies of categorization find that people do not place artifacts in fixed groupings with discrete boundaries.[23]

> Any given artifact can participate in more than one grouping. The same rubber ball may, at different times, be grouped with other spherical, bouncy objects, with other things called ball (including non-bouncy beanbag balls and non-spherical footballs), with other toys such as dolls and board games, or with other things to take to the playground such as a tricycle and a snack.[24]

Our notions of artifacts "extend in various directions on different dimensions."[25] There is no unique way to categorize social artifacts, so we should not expect there to be a single correct concept or set of characteristics.[26] The inability to fix groupings shows up in the fact that each theory of law fastens on a different set of features, i.e., governmental social control, institutionalized norm enforcement, union of primary and secondary rules.

Arguments that social artifacts have essential natures have not won over many philosophers. On his part, John Searle, who has written extensively about the ontology of social institutions, eschews "any kind of essentialism": "There is no set

---

[18]   Thomasson, "Artifacts and Human Concepts," supra 73.
[19]   Raz, *Between Authority and Interpretation*, supra 23.   [20]   Id. 97.   [21]   Id. 23 n. 7.   [22]   Id. 63.
[23]   Barbara C. Malt and Steven A. Sloman, "Artifact Categorization: The Good, the Bad, and the Ugly," in *Creations of the Mind*, supra 120.
[24]   Id. 86.   [25]   Id. 122.   [26]   Id. 122.

of necessary and sufficient conditions that define the essence of the political."[27] Types of social institutions, he asserts, can be distinguished in terms of family resemblances with typical features.

Among analytical jurisprudents who make essentialist claims, Joseph Raz has engaged these issues most extensively, albeit with a series of tantalizing declarations rather than systematic analysis. A threshold uncertainty arises because Raz is not straightforward about whether essential and necessary features are located in the *concept* or in the *thing* the concept refers to. Sometimes he says the former and sometimes the latter. In the latter vein, he writes, "knowledge involved in the complete mastery of the concept, which is the knowledge of all the essential features of the *thing* it is a concept of."[28] "What then is an account of the nature of law, of its essential properties? We are trying, I have suggested, to explain the nature of a certain kind of social institution."[29] "Let us accept that what we are really studying is the nature of institutions of the type designated by the concept of law."[30] These statements locate essential properties in the social institution the concept of law identifies, though one might object that the concept must be already specified in detail if the correct thing is to be picked out at the outset.

In other passages, Raz appears to suggest that essential features are derived from the *concept* itself. "Reference to a concept need not employ any of *its* necessary features."[31] Concepts are cultural products, Raz observes, and philosophers abstract from cultural concepts to determine their core content. "The conditions fixing the identity of particular concepts are idealizations constructed out of our conceptual practices, i.e. out of the use of those concepts in general."[32] "In large measure what we study when we study the nature of law is the nature of our own self-understanding."[33]

So are essential and necessary features located in the *concept* or in the *thing* it refers to? On this critical issue Raz waffles:

> Is it not our aim to study the nature of law, rather than our culture and concept of law? *Yes and no.* We aim to improve our understanding of the nature of law. The law is a type of social institution, the type that is picked up – designated – by the concept of law. Hence in improving our understanding of the nature of law we assume an understanding of the concept of law, and improve it.[34]

"Yes and no" is not a model of analytical clarity. Reflecting this ambiguity, certain analytical jurisprudents locate necessary features in the concept, but others in the entity.[35]

---

[27]   Searle, *Making the Social World*, supra 171.
[28]   Raz, *Between Authority and Interpretation*, 21 (emphasis added).   [29]   Id. 31.   [30]   Id. 32.
[31]   Id. 23 (emphasis added).   [32]   Id. 23.   [33]   Id.   [34]   Id 31 (emphasis added).
[35]   Shapiro specifies that the object of analysis is the *entity* that falls under the concept rather than the concept itself. Shapiro, *Legality*, supra 405 n. 9. Jules Coleman, in contrast, appears to locate the necessary features of law in the concept, writing, "there is a difference between the claim that a particular concept is necessary and the claim that there are necessary features of an admittedly

To reconstruct what appears to be Raz's argument, let us distinguish two assertions: 1) "Water is H2O"; and 2) "The essential features of the *thing* designated by the *concept* water today are H2O." The meaning and concept of water (or law) can change over time, so while the first proposition is true now, it might not be true in the future if water comes to designate some other substance. But the essential features of the *thing* identified by water (or law) today, the second proposition, are necessarily true and will not change. By uncovering information about the essential features of the thing, he says, that helps us understand our concept of the thing.

If this is indeed Raz's argument, it holds for water, but not for law. The first proposition is problematic because, unlike water, there are multiple concepts of law and they apply to different phenomena. The second proposition is problematic because natural properties fix the essential features of water, while nothing equivalent fixes features of social institutions like law. As discussed previously, moreover, actual legal institutions come in numerous variations of form and function (which analytical jurisprudents idealize as a uniform "thing"), and theorists can take multiple angles on social institutions, each producing different core features.

A PRIORI OR A POSTERIORI?

Aware that the basis for claims about necessary and essential features of law is obscure, a few analytical jurisprudents have recently taken up these issues more systematically. The starting point for their analysis is a distinction between *a priori* and *a posteriori* knowledge.[36] *A priori* propositions can be known simply through the meaning or definition of the terms; for example, "all bachelors are unmarried" or "cubes have six sides." These are analytic *a priori* propositions because being unmarried is part of the concept of bachelor and having six sides is part of the concept of cube. *A posteriori* propositions, in contrast, have an empirical component that is known through experience; for example, the propositions "water is H2O" or "it is presently raining" can be confirmed as true only through investigation.

Assertions about the nature or essence of law, according to Kenneth Himma, are commonly thought to be *a priori* grounded in our concept of law.[37] The difficulty with this position is that the concept of law is not suitable for *a priori* claims. No one disputes that bachelors are unmarried or that cubes have six sides. The concept of law, in contrast, is deeply disputed. One might argue an equivalent to "bachelors are unmarried" is "law involves systems of norms," but that is too minimalist to distinguish law from other normative systems, and saying anything more goes beyond

---

contingent concept." Coleman, "Incorporationism, Conventionality, and the Practical Difference Thesis," supra 393 n. 24.

[36] These examples are taken from "A Priori and A Posteriori," *Internet Encyclopedia of Philosophy*, www.iep.utm.edu/apriori/#H3.

[37] Himma elaborates this position without specifically endorsing it. See Kenneth Einar Himma, "Conceptual Jurisprudence: An Introduction to Conceptual Analysis and Methodology in Legal Theory," http://papers.ssrn.com/sol3/papers.cfm?abstract_id=2616916.

a priori. That is why every legal philosopher who takes up the issue presents a markedly different theory of law from others.

When legal philosophers produce theories of law, furthermore, they are not simply examining the meaning or concept of law. First they make a threshold pre-theoretical determination about what counts as law, which has significant consequences, as I later elaborate; then they engage in analytical work to identify essential features. At each step, this process involves choices based on criteria and information that are not contained within the concept of law itself.[38] Hart's union of primary and secondary rules was an abstraction he devised after stripping away what he considered nonessential to the concept of state law. His dual-rule system theory of law is not a purely logical implication or deduction from the concept. Hart acknowledged, for example, it is possible to reduce law to solely rules directed at legal officials dictating what must be done when situation [X] occurs; he rejected this reduction because it obscures too much about law.[39] He also recognized that concepts of law can be formulated in alternative ways. "If we are to make a reasoned choice between these concepts, it must be because one is superior to the other in the way in which it will assist our theoretical inquiries, or advance and clarify our moral deliberations, or both."[40] This is not *a priori.*

Another analytical jurisprudent who makes essentialist assertions about law, Michael Giudice, denies essential features of law can be known *a priori.*[41] When Hart articulates the separation thesis and the union of primary and secondary rules, Giudice notes, "neither thesis receives nor is supported by any kind of semantic analysis or argument."[42] Raz explicitly denies the nature of law can be discerned by inquiring into the meaning of law.[43] "The essential properties of law of which legal theory is trying to give an account are not invoked to account for the meaning of any term or class of terms," Raz emphasizes. "We are inquiring into the typology of social institutions."[44] Since the term "law" is used in all sorts of ways by jurists and others, he says, "while in the course of giving an account of the nature of law one may well engage in explaining the meaning of certain terms, the explanation of the nature of law cannot be equated with the analysis of the meaning of any term."[45] Raz backs his

---

[38] This discussion focuses on analytic *a priori* knowledge. Synthetic *a priori* knowledge goes beyond the meaning of a concept to include information about the world (Kant's example, "all bodies are heavy") to produce knowledge through reason. For the reasons set forth in the text, the features of law are not the type of knowledge about the world discernable through reason in conjunction with meaning, so it also cannot be synthetic *a priori* knowledge.

[39] See Hart, *Concept of Law*, supra 238–39; H. L. A. Hart, "The Separation of Law and Morals," 71 *Harvard Law Review* 593, 605 (1958). See also Danny Priel, "Jurisprudence and Necessity," 20 *Canadian Journal of Law and Jurisprudence* 173, 173–74 (2007) (noting Raz's recognition of evaluative aspects of the analysis).

[40] Id. 204–05.

[41] Michael Giudice, *Understanding the Nature of Law: A Case for Constructive Conceptual Explanation* (Cheltenham, UK: Edward Elgar 2015) 93–96.

[42] Id. 95.   [43] Raz, *Between Authority and Interpretation*, supra 29–30; see also 19–20.   [44] Id. 29.

[45] Id. 30.

assertion that an essential feature of law is a claim to legitimate authority by pointing to claims made by legal officials, which refers to experience.[46] And Raz compares law to H2O, which is known *a posteriori*. Based on these considerations, Giudice concludes that if law has necessary or essential elements, they must be known and established by *a posteriori* means.

The conclusion that law's essential features can be known *a posteriori* brings us back to the initial objection that law is not like water. Without offering an answer, Giudice acknowledges this is *the* challenge for analytical jurisprudents: "to show how *a posteriori* necessity arguments regarding natural kinds (or identities) can be extended to social kinds or practices such as law."[47] It is indeed conceivable that rules of natural necessity might exist for human social groups involving, for example, rules protecting property and persons,[48] as Hart suggested in his discussion of the minimum content of natural law. My later discussion of fundamental rules of social intercourse covers the same ground. But if true, this must be established on empirical grounds, not by reasoning from intuitions and concepts, and it would relate to only one among several concepts of law.

An additional complication analytical jurisprudents must address is that *a posteriori* claims typically involve truths about the actual world,[49] whereas necessary truths are about all possible worlds real and imaginary. Analytical jurisprudents often speak in metaphysical terms. The necessary features of law are "found not only in all existing and historical legal systems, but in all possible ones – or all humanly possible ones," asserts Leslie Green.[50] They must explain how a contingent concept and set of features is true across all possible worlds.

Pointing to variation and change of concepts and social institutions, Frederick Schauer has repeatedly challenged claims that law has essential and necessary properties.[51] He is especially critical of their conclusion that because it is possible to imagine forms of law not backed by force (in a society of angels or purely rational beings[52]), coercive force is not an essential feature of law. (An essential feature, in

---

[46]   The passage Giudice quotes showing his reliance on empirical evidence is Joseph Raz, *Ethics in the Public Domain*, rev. ed. (Oxford: Clarendon Press 1995) 215–16; and Raz, *Between Authority and Interpretation*, supra 38–39.

[47]   Id. 102.   [48]   Giudice makes this suggestion, at id. 99.

[49]   The *a priori/a posteriori* distinction is epistemological, whereas necessity claims are metaphysical, so although they coincide at points, they are not the same. See www.iep.utm.edu/apriori/#H3.

[50]   Leslie Green, "The Morality in Law," 33, http://papers.ssrn.com/sol3/papers.cfm?abstract _id=2223760, published in L. Duarte d' Almeida, J. Edwards, and A. Dolcetti, eds., *Reading HLA Hart's The Concept of Law* (Oxford: Hart Publishing 2013) 177–207.

[51]   See Frederick Schauer, *The Force of Law* (Cambridge, MA: Harvard University Press 2015) 35–41; Frederick Schauer, "On the Nature of the Nature of Law" (2011), at http://papers.ssrn.com/sol3/ papers.cfm?abstract_id=1836494; Frederick Schauer, "The Best Laid Plans," 120 *Yale Law Journal* 586, 613–19 (2013); Frederick Schauer, "The Social Construction of the Concept of Law: A Reply to Julie Dickson," 25 *Oxford Journal of Legal Studies* 493 (2005). Another critique is presented by Dennis Patterson, "Alexy on Necessity in Law and Morals," 25 *Ratio Juris* 47 (2012).

[52]   A critique of this mode of analysis is presented in Kenneth Einar Himma, "Can There Really Be Law in a Society of Angels?", available at http://papers.ssrn.com/sol3/papers.cfm?abstract_id=2839942.

their view, must hold in all possible worlds, real and imagined, and they can imagine legal systems that do not rely on coercive force.[53]) Law is more aptly captured by Wittgenstein's notion of family resemblances, Schauer argues, and is better thought of as a cluster concept. "Maybe both the word 'law' and our concept of law consist of a series of intertwined properties, no one of which is necessary for the correct understanding and application of the concept or the word, and no one set of which is sufficient for their correct application and understanding."[54]

Analytical jurisprudents have repeated for several decades now that their task is to identify essential and necessary features of the nature of law. Yet most jurists who repeat these claims do not explain their basis, leaving it shrouded in obscurity, and theorists who do address it disagree among themselves on basic points. Until the doubts raised earlier are answered, talk about essential and necessary properties of the nature of law will remain mysterious and unconvincing.

UNIVERSAL APPLICATION VERSUS UNIVERSAL TRUTH

The basis for universal truth claims is likewise obscure and leads to a paradox. Raz repeatedly issues unconditional declarations of universality. "It is easy to explain in what sense legal philosophy is universal. Its theses, if true, apply universally, that is they speak of all law, of all legal systems, of those that exist, or that will exist, and even of those that can exist though they never will. Moreover, its theses are advanced as necessarily universal."[55]

Raz then tacks in the opposite direction. "While the general theory of law is universal, it is also parochial."[56] What makes it parochial "is that the concept of law is itself a product of a specific culture."[57] "Talk of *the* concept of law really means *our* concept of law. As has already been mentioned, the concept of law changes over time. Different cultures have different concepts of law. There is no one concept of law, and when we refer to the concept of law we just mean our concept of law."[58] "It follows that in working out a theory of law we are explicating our own self-understanding of the nature of society and politics[.]"[59] Furthermore, change is incorporated within the concept itself. "It is part of our common understanding of the law that its nature (when that word is understood as it usually is) changes over

---

[53]   In his argument denying that coercion is a necessary feature of law, Leslie Green makes numerous assertions about a society of angels. For example: "We all know that even a 'society of angels' would need rules, if only to help them coordinate their altruistic activities." Leslie Green, "The Forces of Law"; Leslie Green, "The Forces of Law: Duty, Coercion, and Power" 29 *Ratio Juris* 164, 165 (2016). To the contrary, we know nothing about a society of angels, which is a fantasy. As such, it is whatever a given theorist projects onto it. Green's angels are like humans (disagreements, conflicting views and desires, etc.), only nicer. His analytical conclusion that coercion is not necessary to law is prefigured by his starting assumptions.

[54]   Schauer, "On the Nature of the Nature of Law," supra 15.

[55]   Raz, *Between Authority and Interpretation*, supra 91.   [56]   Id. 92.   [57]   Id. 95.   [58]   Id. 32.

[59]   Id. 97.

time," he says, "both with changes in social and political practices, and with changes in culture, in philosophy, or more generally, in ways of understanding ourselves and our societies."[60] Raz recognizes "our concept [of law] is liable to be forever in flux."[61]

Setting to the side questions about who Raz speaks for with his royal "our" (discussed later), these assertions prompt an obvious objection: a parochial concept of law that changes over time cannot be the foundation for necessary and universal truths.[62] How does Raz square this circle? In effect, he holds time and space constant, identifying the essential features of law as determined by "our" concept of law in the here and now.[63] "What counts is the nature of the institution which the concept of law (i.e., the one we currently have and use) designates."[64] If other societies past, present, and future lack institutions with the essential features of law, they do not have law according to our current concept of law.

This argument works as long as Raz restricts his assertion to the claim that our parochial concept of law can be *applied* to examine and evaluate other contexts past, present, and future. Most any concept can be applied to examine other times and places (with appropriate caveats). We can, for instance, use our concept of recession to study historical recessions that occurred prior to the invention of this concept in economics. Weber's concept of law as a public staff prepared to exert coercion to enforce norms (which he formulated as an ideal type) can be applied to analyze any context past, present, and future as well. If that is what Raz means, it is uncontroversial.[65]

Raz gets into trouble when he makes the stronger and wholly different claim that his account of the nature of law is not just universally applicable, but also universally *true* for all times and places.

It is easy to explain in what sense legal philosophy is universal. Its theses, *if true, apply universally*, that is they speak of all law, of all legal systems; of those that exist, or that will exist, and even of those that can exist though they never will. Moreover, its theses are advanced as necessarily universal. ... The general theory of law is universal for it consists of claims about the nature of all law, and of all legal systems, and about the nature of adjudication, legislation, and legal reasoning, wherever they may be, and whatever they may be. Moreover, its claims, *if true, are necessarily true*. Suffice it to say that *the truth of the theses of the general theory of law is not*

---

[60]   Id. 27.   [61]   Raz, *Between Authority and Interpretation*, supra 98.

[62]   For a forceful critique of Raz on this point, see Allan C. Hutchinson, "Razzle-Dazzle," 1 *Jurisprudence* 39 (2010).

[63]   Raz states that when we talk about law in other times and places, it is still "our concept of law which calls the shots." *Between Authority and Interpretation*, supra 32. He is correct that when we study other arrangements in other societies past and present, we see them as "law" from the perspective of our own concept of law. This does not make our concept of law universal, but merely confirms that we see things from our own perspective.

[64]   Id. 25.

[65]   I make the same move when I assert in the next chapter that primitive societies that recognized property rights had law; my argument is not that *they* saw it as "law," but that *we* see property rights as legal, and hence it is appropriate to consider this a form of law from our standpoint.

contingent on existing political, social, economic, or cultural conditions, institutions,
or practices. . . .
   The universality of the theses of the general theory of law is a result of the fact that
they claim to be necessary truths, and there is nothing less that they can claim. . . .
A claim to necessity is in the nature of the enterprise.[66]

The first italicized phrase focuses on universal application (contingent on truth).
The subsequent italicized passages tie universality to truth.

A flaw exists at the heart of his assertions. His contention that "the truth of the
theses of the general theory of law is not contingent on existing" institutions and
practices is falsified by the fact that the theory is admittedly derived from *our* concept
of law. He states, "we are explicating our own self-understanding."[67] This contingent
origin is not erased in the abstracting process of theory formation, but rather
becomes entrenched in the theory of law produced, its parochial source concealed
in elaborate philosophical clothing. Legal philosophers living in medieval Europe –
when a multiplicity of legal regimes coexisted, customary law and religious law were
dominant manifestations of law, and the state system had not yet coalesced – would
see law quite differently from how people and jurists view it today.

Parochial origin and conceptual and institutional change give rise to a paradox
when combined with a claim of universal truth. Imagine a legal philosopher
a millennium hence, whom we call Raz 3000. Let us assume that the prevailing
concept of law evolves in the intervening 1,000 years to gain a new essential feature.
To offer one concrete possibility: assume that, unlike today, in year 3000, the prevailing concept sees law as inherently morally right (label this "D"). Like Raz today, let us
assume, Raz 3000 devises a general theory of law using the cultural concept of law
prevailing at his time and place, correctly identifying law's essential and necessary
features. Raz today says the essential features of law are A, B, and C, whereas Raz 3000
says the essential features of law are A, B, C, and D. Although both theories are
necessarily and universally true (per Raz's argument), when evaluated by the criteria of
the other, each theory provides an incorrect account of the nature of law. Each theory
of the nature of law is universally true on its own terms and yet false according to the
other. These nonsensical results follow from the logic of Raz's analysis.

Raz might respond that the concept of law in this scenario has transformed so
much it has become a new concept. We have concept of "law" (Time 1) and concept
of "law" (Time 2), and both can be true despite their inconsistency because they are
different concepts of law in different societies. This response circumvents an out-
right contradiction, but it entails that a true theory of law is true only insofar as it
actually holds, emptying of meaning his declaration that it is true for all times and
places.

---

[66]   Raz, *Between Authority and Interpretation*, supra 91–92 (emphasis added), see also 97 (universal truth
       claim).
[67]   Id. 97.

The paradox can be avoided only if one stipulates the concept of law and the social institution it is a concept of cannot evolve to an extent that alters the composition of essential features. But Raz has affirmed cultural concepts of law are "liable to be forever in flux," and he presents no grounds for a limiting stipulation. And we know that multiple forms of law have undergone a great deal of change over time.

Already unpersuasive on its own terms, Raz's universal truth claim falls apart in light of his recent assertion that legal philosophers must take account of "other kinds of law" beyond state law, including international law, canon law, Sharia, etc.[68] For decades, his theory of law has been based exclusively on state law, which underlies his assertions about *a* universally true theory of law.[69] The various manifestations of law he now wants jurisprudents to consider do not all share the same core features.[70] Certain instances of customary law, to cite one example, are backed by systems, while others are not; and customary law takes different forms in communities prior to the presence of the state, when incorporated within the state, when independent of the state, and in the context of colonization.[71] Manifestations of religious law also come in multiple variations prior to, within, and separate from the state. Both forms of law resemble state law in some respects, but not others. Recognition of multiple forms of law eliminates the singularity that heretofore undergirded his position. Multiple forms of law, consistent with his argument, potentially give rise to multiple universally true concepts of law that conflict with one another.

This critique focuses on Raz's argument because other analytical jurisprudents have followed his lead and he has extensively wrestled with these issues.[72] All legal philosophers who speak about universally true, essential, and necessary features of law are caught on the horns of the same paradox owing to the fact that concepts and social institutions vary and change over time. It shows up in the words of John Gardner: "Philosophers study, *inter alia*, the timeless necessity of all this contingency – the invariant and universal truth, for instance, that law and the idea of law are both equally contingent and variable features of human civilization, features that might one day, perhaps, be lost and even forgotten."[73] "They are universal truths about a decidedly non-universal thing."[74] The enigmatic haze of these passages bespeaks their dilemma.

---

[68] See Joseph Raz, "Why the State?" http://papers.ssrn.com/sol3/papers.cfm?abstract_id=2339522.

[69] See Brian Bix, "Raz, Authority, and Conceptual Analysis," 50 *American J. Jurisprudence* 311 (2006).

[70] See generally William Twining, *General Jurisprudence: Understanding Law from a Global Perspective* (Cambridge: Cambridge University Press 2009); Brian Z. Tamanaha, *A General Jurisprudence of Law and Society* (Oxford: Oxford University Press 2001) 166, supra; William Twining, "A Post-Westphalian Conception of Law," 37 Law & Society Review 199 (2003).

[71] See generally Leopold Pospisil, *Anthropology of Law: A Comparative Theory* (1971); Sally Falk Moore, *Law as Process: An Anthropological Approach* (London: Routledge & Kegan Paul 1978); Anthony Allott, "The Judicial Ascertainment of Customary Law in British Africa," 20 *Modern Law Review* 244 (1957).

[72] See also Julie Dickson, "Methodology in Jurisprudence: A Critical Survey," 10 *Legal Theory* (2004).

[73] Gardner, *Law as a Leap of Faith*, supra 300–01.   [74] Id. 301.

Universal truth claims cannot be grounded on contingent social historical forms, and cannot be proclaimed when there are multiple forms of law that do not share the same core features. The most analytical jurisprudents can say is the features they have identified are true of "our" concept of law and other societies and institutions can be examined through the lens of this concept. This is not universal truth.

MODEST INTERPRETATIONS OF "NECESSARY" AND "UNIVERSAL"

Raz, as suggested previously, might be interpreted more modestly to not really claim universal truth, only application. If that is his position, he should remove any doubt, and correct statements that go beyond what universal application licenses. Raz declares:

> Naturally, the essential properties of the law are universal characteristics of law. They are to be found in law wherever and whenever it exists. Moreover, these properties are universal properties of the law not accidentally, and not because of any prevailing economic or social circumstances, but because there is no law without them. ... When surveying the different forms of social organization in different societies throughout the ages we will find many which resemble the law in various ways. Yet if they lack the essential features of the law, they are not legal systems.[75]

This is not a modest claim that we can examine other manifestations of law past and present in terms of essential characteristics of "our" concept of law. He unreservedly declares that other manifestations of law that lack these features "are not legal systems," invoking his theory of law as an authoritative standard for what truly counts as law for all times and places.

Leslie Green's account of essential and necessary features might also be interpreted modestly. "Legal philosophers try to understand what is necessary and sufficient to some feature of law; they assemble examples and arguments; they strive for a deeper understanding of our concepts; they sharpen them in ways that are meant to be useful or illuminating."[76] The careful analysis of concepts, Green asserts, amounts to "attempts to state necessary and sufficient conditions."[77] A modest reading of Green is that "necessary and sufficient" are technical terms analytical jurisprudents like to apply to their chosen tasks, terms on which outsiders put too much weight. Their talk of all possible worlds is a stylized presentation used for emphasis and to signal rigor. Giudice defends what he calls "pragmatic necessity," which "is still a metaphysical conception of necessity" about "what law really is," but he rejects the notion that these necessary features are "somehow out there,

---

[75]   Joseph Raz, "Can There Be Theory of Law?" in *The Blackwell Guide to the Philosophy of Law and Legal Theory*, edited by Martin P. Golding and William A. Edmundson (Oxford: Blackwell 2005) 328.
[76]   Green, "The Forces of Law," supra 178.   [77]   Id. 179.

existing independently of any conceptual view of law and always serving as truth conditions of all actual and possible conceptual explanations."[78]

If that is their position, perhaps there is no deep issue at stake. But this passage from Green appears to go further:

> Necessity poses problems for any empiricist. Sense experience, with or without the help of instruments, will fail to turn up what is strictly necessary. It must fail, because our experience, individual and collective, is finite while the features necessary to law are those found *not only in all existing and historical legal systems, but in all possible ones – or all humanly possible ones –* and those are numberless and unobservable. So how to proceed? The only way we can. We begin with the most reliable knowledge we have of actual legal systems, then we test conjectures about which of their universal features are necessary features by seeing whether they can resist contrived but intelligible counter-examples.[79]

Green appears to assert, like Raz, that the claim of necessity is tied to universality, identifying what law truly is for all places and times.

Green does not show that law is the sort of concept or thing about which necessity claims can be made, as Thomasson, mentioned earlier, is attempting to elaborate in the philosophy of society – and she explicitly disavows universality. Green recognizes, as Thomasson does, that "many social kinds are multi-criterial; they are made up of various features and properties."[80] "There is no function common to all legal systems that explains why legal systems have the structural features they have, and no function unique to legal systems."[81] These acknowledgments appear to deprive Green of any firm ground in which to anchor necessary, universal truths about law.

If Raz and Green and other analytical jurisprudents do not really mean to claim universal truth for theories of law, only universal application, they should state so plainly because it is essential to their position – particularly since the self-proclaimed objective of their enterprise is to bring conceptual clarity to jurisprudence. This would require more than merely clarification. It would require that they carefully qualify and trim back on what currently come across as bold declarations of truths about the nature of law for everyone now and forever. Until they correct this impression, it is necessary to show why universal truth claims do not hold up.

Oliver Wendell Holmes once skeptically remarked, "The jurists who believe in natural law seem to me to be in that naïve state of mind that accepts what has been familiar and accepted by them and their neighbors as something that must be accepted by all men everywhere."[82] Raz's effort to hoist an admittedly parochial concept of law into a universal standard for the nature of law invites the same skepticism. Assertions by analytical jurisprudents about purportedly universal

---

[78] Giudice, *Understanding the Nature of Law*, supra 108–09.
[79] Green, "The Morality in Law," supra 33 (emphasis added).   [80] Id. 3.   [81] Id. 31.
[82] Oliver Wendell Holmes, "Natural Law," 32 *Harvard Law Review* 40, 41 (1918).

theories of law also bring to mind Holmes's comment that natural law is a manifestation of "a demand for the superlative" that men crave. "It seems to me," he wrote, "that this demand is at the bottom of the philosopher's effort to prove that truth is absolute and of the jurist's search for criteria of universal validity which he collects under the head of natural law."[83] Ironically, the demand for the superlative in this instance is exhibited by legal positivists, erstwhile opponents of natural law theory, revealing that both aspire to universal validity, though in different ways. The similarities in their respective stances, and the critical scrutiny they demand, is compelling when one notices that legal positivist analytical jurisprudents like Scott Shapiro and natural lawyers like John Finnis both ground their analyses in claims about self-evidence – transforming their assumptions of self-evidence into necessary, universal truths for all.[84]

IDENTIFYING AND JUSTIFYING THE CENTRAL CASE OF LAW

Another critical issue is ably laid out by Gregoire Webber. The key issues are what data set represents the standard case of law and how it is chosen or who chooses it. These choices determine what ultimately is identified as law's essential features. "The question is important," Webber writes, "for it is clear that claims of 'invariability' and 'prevalence' depend on what is being identified *pre-theoretically* – that is, *before* a general theory of law is developed – as a part of the data set of law."[85] A theorist can make truth claims on this basis, but universalistic claims are a different matter: "They would be true *about the data set* and so particular to it; at best, they would be true as *generalities* within this data set. But in the study of human affairs, what is true about *one* data set makes no claim about a datum not included within it."[86] Different data sets would produce different accounts of the features of law, and consequently the "resulting descriptive-explanatory truth about law will be contingent on the data set from which it emerges."[87]

This exposes an essential gap in their argument: analytical jurisprudents do not justify what they decide pre-theoretically to include within the data set.[88] When identifying the paradigm of law (filling the data set), they simply make assertions about what lawyers or educated people think law is – invariably state law – without considering that people might hold other concepts of law as well.[89] This method is

---

[83]　Id. 40.

[84]　See Shapiro, *Legality*, supra 13; John Finnis, *Natural Law and Natural Rights* (Oxford: Clarendon Press 1980) 64–69.

[85]　Gregoire Webber, "Asking Why in the Study of Human Affairs," 60 *American Journal of Jurisprudence* 51, 63 (2015).

[86]　Id. 12.　　[87]　Id.

[88]　This argument was made in Danny Priel, "Evaluating Descriptive Jurisprudence," 52 *American Journal of Jurisprudence* 139, 145–47 (2007); Bix, "Raz, Authority, and Conceptual Analysis," supra.

[89]　As Danny Priel argues, if "different people consider different things to be part of the things that count as law, then the theorist does not even have a starting point from which the inquiry can begin. Priel, "Jurisprudence and Necessity," supra 181.

circular: their assumptions about what is the paradigm of law determines the resulting theory of what law is, which is then applied to dictate what does and does not qualify as law for all places and times. It follows from this method that if a given form of law is initially included in the pre-theoretical data set of what counts as law, the theorist will construct her theory of law to account for its features, but if that type of law is excluded at this initial stage, the theory of law produced will not account for its features and consequently it will be deemed *not* law according to the theory.[90]

A concrete example will show the determinative significance of this point. Hart justified his focus on state law with the assertion that "educated people" see this as law.[91] That is true enough. But let us say Hart had asked a follow up question: "Do you believe international law is law?" Many educated people would likely affirm that international law is, of course, "law;" after all, that is what we call it, and the news is filled with references to international law treaties and violations. Had Hart included international law alongside state law within his pre-theoretical data set of what counts as law, he would have modified his theory of secondary rules to accommodate its features, and he would have loosened the systematicity he deemed necessary to law.[92] International law would then have qualified as "law" under the theory he produced, in contrast to the prelegal status he originally accorded it. Jeremy Waldron sharply criticized Hart on these grounds:

> The agenda set out at the beginning of *The Concept of Law* was "to advance legal theory by providing an improved analysis of the distinctive structure of a municipal legal system." Analysis of issues involving international law was always going to be a distraction from this task, and Hart did not venture in the chapter to consider the possibility that we would regard international law as a paradigm of law along with the law of a familiar municipal system; he was unwilling to raise that possibility and unwilling to consider how different our philosophical analysis would have to be if both of these were treated as paradigms instead of only one. So international law was treated from the outset as a borderline case.[93]

Take this scenario one step further. Had Hart asked people in rural Africa or on a Western Pacific island "What is law?" they would likely identify customary law *first*, then state law, and perhaps international law as well. Hart would then have an even more expansive pre-theoretical data set, again affecting the contours of the theory of law produced. Alternatively, had he treated these as different forms of law, Hart would have produced concepts suitable to each, coming up with multiple concepts of law instead of just one.

---

[90] See Webber, "Asking Why in the Study of Human Affairs," supra 62–65.

[91] Hart, *Concept of Law*, supra 2–3.

[92] See Jeremy Waldron, "International Law: 'A Relatively Small and Unimportant' Part of Jurisprudence?" (2013), http://papers.ssrn.com/sol3/papers.cfm?abstract_id=2326758.

[93] Id. 210.

Analytical jurisprudents who ground their position on bald assertions about "our" concept of law have yet to explain why these other choices are not equally or more appropriate ways to proceed.[94] Since they purport to be after necessary truths and universality, it is inadequate to say those are not *our* concepts of law so they do not matter for philosophical purposes, particularly when at least international law counts as law for many people in "our" societies.[95] Another indication that this is a crucial threshold issue is Raz's own essay "Why the State?," which rebukes legal philosophers for heretofore focusing only on state law to the exclusion of customary law, religious law, international law, and other forms of law.[96] His statements implicitly confirm that legal philosophers have all along failed to undertake the preliminary task of justifying their pre-theoretical identification of the central case of law.

THE CONVENTIONALIST IDENTIFICATION OF LAW

Leslie Green asserts that in his skepticism about essential and necessary features of law, Frederick Schauer is guilty of a "downshift to naïve empiricism."[97] "Concept-blind empiricism" goes "nowhere fast," Green says, because theorists and scientists cannot know what to examine without first having a concept of the object: "Before anyone starts counting anything we need to know what counts as what."[98]

Concept-blind empiricism is indeed useless, as Green says. That is why no theorist is guilty of this sin. Nothing can be said about law theoretically or empirically if one does not first have some way to identify what law is.

To answer this threshold requirement, in a previous work I offered: *"law is whatever people identify and treat through their social practices as 'law' (or droit, recht, etc.)."*[99] This formulation is not itself a concept of law, but a conventionalist criterion for the identification of law. Conventional identifications of law typically attach to specific manifestations, like the law of New York State, Sharia in Iran, customary law in Liberia, European Union law, etc. These forms of law are regularly grouped into broader categories, commonly, state law, customary law, natural law, religious law, international law, various bodies of transnational law, and human rights law.[100]

This approach works in several stages. First, the theorist must discern what people in given contexts conventionally recognize as law. This initial identification stage

---

[94] As Brian Bix observes, Raz does not seriously consider alternative conceptions of law. See Bix, "Raz, Authority, and Conceptual Analysis," supra.

[95] By taking this stance, contemporary legal philosophers have produced another version of John Austin's general jurisprudence based on "ampler and maturer systems" of law. See John Austin, *The Uses of the Study of Jurisprudence*, edited by H. L. Hart (London: Weidenfeld & Nicolson 1954) 367.

[96] See Raz, "Why the State?" supra.   [97] Green, "Forces of Law," supra 179.   [98] Id. 179.

[99] Tamanaha, *A General Jurisprudence of Law and Society*, supra 166, 194.

[100] Id. 224–30. In Chapter 6, I question the treatment of international law as a category.

fills in the pre-theoretical data set of law; they can all be included in a single set, or separate data sets can be constructed of different types. Second, the theorist must try to understand how people conceive of each conventionally recognized form of law. This entails grasping the folk concept of each form of law. Third, the theorist must obtain empirical information on how that form of law is structured, what its functions are, how people perceive it, what people do with it, and so forth. The second and third stages require theorists to delve into available sociological, anthropological, and political science studies of the respective forms of law. Fourth, the theorist must engage in conceptual work. Theorists can consider a host of questions, including (but not limited to) whether each has characteristic features, whether certain features are common across forms of law, and whether certain features are common to, or distinct from, other types of social institutions.

All legal theorists partake of stage one, relying on conventionalism even when they do not realize or acknowledge it, unthinkingly presupposing a single conventionalist version, as I explain in a moment. Analytical jurisprudents typically take shortcuts through stages two and three. They posit assumptions about what "educated people" or "lawyers" think about law without making an effort to find out what people actually think about law – which stage two requires. And analytical jurisprudents rely heavily on their intuitions – which Scott Shapiro ratchets up as "self-evident truisms" – to provide the basis for analytical work,[101] whereas stage three requires them to consult studies to learn about these forms of law rather than depend on their own assumptions. Legal philosophers might object that they are engaged in analytical work, not sociology. But stages two and three ask them only to conduct their analysis informed with the best available knowledge, which does not make them sociologists. Their analytical work – at stage four – would then proceed with a more empirically based grasp of legal forms.

A conventionalist approach to the identification of law raises several possible objections. "Law" is a term used in all sorts of fields, like the laws of physics, as Raz points out, so the label alone does not narrow the candidates.[102] The quick answer is that potential ambiguities in reference can be solved by the context of the inquiry. A theorist can determine whether something conventionally labeled "law" is the sense relevant to jurists.

Webber articulated another possible objection: "there is no non-arbitrary reason for a general theory of law to limit itself to how English-language speakers employ the term 'law' and . . . some languages have not one word for 'law' but two: they track the Latin vocabulary of *ius* an *lex*. Should both terms be attended to?"[103]

---

[101] To begin his analysis of the essential features of law, Scott Shapiro assembles a list of "truisms" about law that "are not merely true, but self-evidently so." Shapiro, *Legality*, supra 13. These truisms are common assumptions among Western jurists, which do not hold in many contexts.

[102] Raz, *Between Authority and Interpretation*, supra 28–29.

[103] Webber, "Asking Why in the Study of Human Affairs," supra 61.

My conventionalist approach explicitly includes phenomena conventionally labeled "law" in other languages – *droit, recht,* and so on. If multiple terms in a local vernacular are translated as "law," and multiple phenomena are conventionally labeled with these terms, then yes, they all count as law.

This prompts another objection. John Gardner correctly observes, "To have translated 'law' as 'droit' or 'recht' or anything else, one must already have mapped word to idea; one must already know that there is a common something to which these diverse words and their cognates refer."[104] The conventionalist approach is "mysterious," he says, because "what Tamanaha wants us to search for . . . are presumably *various indigenous ideas (aka concepts) of law.*" "How can we possibly identify them as concepts of law before we know what counts as law?" he objects.[105] There is nothing mysterious about this. An idea of what law means, not a full-blown concept, is enough to complete a translation into other languages.[106] We know this can be done because the cluster of ideas the term "law" represents has been translated from classical languages to contemporary languages across the globe. Gardner's objection applies to all translations, not law alone. Translations, it is true, inevitably face ambiguities and indeterminacies, but that is not a barrier to their achievement. To identify law using a conventionalist method, one should look at what people in a given community consider "law" in their own language, which a theorist can find using common translations.

The historical diffusion of the notion of law and its institutional forms has made this translation process easier. One effect of European colonization and of globalization has been to spread notions of (and names for) "state law," "customary law," "international law," and "human rights" across the globe. "State law" is ubiquitous today – though not three centuries ago – owing to imperialism and local state-building efforts in response.[107] Versions of "customary law," tagged with that very label, were created by colonial regimes and continue to exist today in many developing countries. Manifestations of and aspects of customary law, natural law, religious law, international law, human rights law, and transnational commercial law are known and have been translated around the world.

There are limits to how far conventionalism and translations can take us. This does not work to identify law in early hunter-gatherer societies because we lack access to their ideas and their social life was radically different. When studying contexts like that, a genealogical approach can be applied that starts with what is perceived as "law" and "legal system" today, then traces backward in human

---

[104] Gardner, *Law as a Leap of Faith,* supra 298 (emphasis in original). [105] Id.

[106] The answer is different when we examine prehistoric societies. There, as I discuss in the next chapter in connection with hunter-gatherer societies, we have no alternative but to use our conception of law directly to examine their social forms.

[107] See C. A. Bayly, *The Birth of the Modern World, 1780–1914* (Oxford: Blackwell Publishing 2004).

history to see if early precursors existed, as demonstrated in the next chapter. Such precursors may be counted as "law" for our purposes not because they were conventionally identified as such by people in those societies (we simply don't know), but rather because they bear manifest similarities to phenomena that have legal status today.

Analytical jurisprudents who criticize my conventionalist approach to the identification of law fail to realize that they use the same starting point. They too begin with what people conventionally label "law" within a community. When Hart posited municipal law as the central case of what an "educated man" views as law, he jumped directly to assertions about the folk concept of law and to analysis – stages two and four. He identified this as his starting point precisely because people in contemporary England (and many other countries) conventionally consider state law "law" – stage one. The conventionalist approach merely makes explicit the first stage of identification that Hart, Raz, and others took for granted and skipped over without thinking about it.

Raz's essay "Why the State?" exposes that analytical jurisprudents rely on the conventionalist identification of law. As mentioned, he now urges analytical jurisprudents to examine "other kinds of law," including *"international law, or the law of organizations like the European Union, but also Canon Law, Sharia Law, Scottish Law, the law of native nations, . . . "*[108] Now ask, how did Raz come up with his list of other kinds of law? Notice the label "law" is in their names and they are collectively perceived as law – that is what I mean by "conventionalist identification of law." When articulating my conventionalist proposal, I offered the same sorts of examples Raz does: "international law," "Islamic Law, Hebrew Law, and the canon law," "Yapese customary law,"[109] etc. We came up with the same kinds of examples because they are seen as "law" by people within communities. Whatever one posits as the pre-theoretical data set for law ultimately is rooted in the conventional (folk) identification of law.

The main difference is not in how we initially identify what counts as law, but that I do not assume people identify only *one* concept of law or that there is only *one* central case of law. Raz now quizzically wonders why legal philosophers have heretofore ignored other forms of law.[110] Part of the explanation, I suggest, in addition to their limited familiarity with other forms of law, is the classic question "What *is* law?" has misled theorists. Thus posed in singular terms, theorists have striven to find a set of elements for a single correct notion of law, their minds closed to the possibility that there might be multiple forms of law. It is not just that law is a cluster concept, as Schauer contends. There are multiple manifestations of law, each with a collection of characteristics, none essential or necessary, and much

---

[108]   Raz, "Why the State?" supra 3 (emphasis added).
[109]   Tamanaha, *A General Jurisprudence of Law and Society*, supra 226–29, 193–99.
[110]   See Id. 138–48, 151.

variation amongst them. One must be open to a multiplicity of conventionally recognized forms of law to see this.

A final objection has been raised against the conventionalist approach. "If 'Law' simply is whatever people identify and treat through their social practices as law," a critic laments, "there is a danger of a resigned nominalism taking over, rendering law ephemeral and contingent in nature."[111] Theorists might be uneasy at the thought of it, but law *is* contingent, like any social construction that varies and changes over time.

The contingency of law, however, does not render it ephemeral. The multiple conventionally recognized forms of law are solid, deeply rooted, evolving, long-standing social growths, as demonstrated in the next chapter. Their enduring resilience is reflected in the fact that the three angles on law identified more than two millennia ago in *Minos* – customary law, state law, and natural law – still form streams of thought about law today. Though they wax and wane and change in form and function over time, conventionally recognized legal forms are anything but ephemeral.

The belief that the conventionalist approach deprives law of substance is based on a misunderstanding. The fact that law is whatever people conventionally identify as law does not mean people are able to call whatever they want to "law." One can try to secure this label for a given social form, but general social acceptance must be achieved to become *conventional*. Because law carries connotations of fundamental social significance, coercive authority by a polity, and right – the three streams in *Minos* – communities do not lightly attach the label "law" in a non-metaphorical sense to social phenomena. The list of kinds of social forms recognized as law is short because the term is laden with weighty meaning.

SHIELDING THEORIES FROM EMPIRICAL REFUTATION

Theories of law must in some way answer to the empirical reality of law. In the passage quoted earlier, Leslie Green asserts, "We begin with the most reliable knowledge we have of actual legal systems, then we test conjectures about which of their universal features are necessary features by seeing whether they can resist contrived but intelligible counter-examples." This appears to envision an empirical check on the validity of a concept. Subjecting a given theory to testing, however, is far from straightforward. Questions about this are heightened when John Gardner dismisses the critical weight of counterexamples:

[111] Sionaidh Douglas-Scott, "Brave New World? The Challenges of Transnational Law and Legal Pluralism to Contemporary Legal Theory," in *Law, Society, and Community: Socio-legal Essays in Honour of Roger Cotterrell*, edited by Richard Nobles and David Schiff (Surrey: Ashgate 2014) 82. Douglas-Scott does not explicitly attribute this conception to me, but the wording she uses is identical to my formulation.

One single counter-example suffices to show that a proposed explanation of the nature of something is mistaken at the limits. But no number of supposed counter-examples can show that a proposed paradigm is not a paradigm. That is because a paradigm or central case is simply the case that shows how the other cases – including those supposed counter-examples – ought to be. It is part of the very idea of a central case that there might be cases (even statistically preponderant cases) that do not exhibit all the features that make the central case a central case.[112]

Notice that Gardner's stance presupposes that the theorist pre-theoretically identified the correct central case of law, which, as indicated previously, is typically assumed without justification. He suggests in this passage that a theoretical account of the necessary features of law cannot be shown incorrect even if many contemporary and historical manifestations of law lack those features. But if even a statistically preponderant number of counterexamples is not enough, then how does one show that the proffered theory of law is incorrect? Absent standards for testing its validity against existing and historical legal systems (never mind all possible ones), a theory of law is not falsifiable.

The issue is not only their failure to specify criteria by which to determine when a proffered theory of law is incorrect. Analytical jurisprudents have two avenues to insulate their theories of law from empirical refutation. The first is to declare that an existing or historical legal system that does not meet the features of their theory of law, ipso facto, is *not* a legal system – leaving the theory unscathed. This conclusion, as explained earlier, directly follows from the fact that the theorist pre-theoretically excluded those versions of law from the data set used to determine the features of law. Had those versions initially been included as exemplars of law, the resultant theory of law would match their features.[113] Danny Priel explains how this operates to shield a given theory of law:

> [T]he theorist has no way of distinguishing between true examples of law (which as such could serve as counter-examples to an account of the nature of law) and false examples of law (that do not affect the theorist's account for they are not members of the same kind of thing the theorist is trying to explain). Since, unlike in natural science, the legal philosopher can always treat supposedly counterfactual cases as members of the second group, the account becomes immune to refutation by begging the most important question, namely, which cases belong to the set of things that are laws.[114]

Thus, if one shows manifold respects in which a particular theory of law is inconsistent with law in the medieval period, with colonial legal regimes, and with law in rural areas of the Global South today, as I show in the next chapter, analytical

---

[112]   Gardner, *Law as a Leap of Faith*, supra 152.
[113]   See Webber, "Asking Why in the Study of Human Affairs," supra 12–13.
[114]   Priel, "Jurisprudence and Necessity," supra 187.

jurisprudents may respond that the counterexamples are *not law* (since they lack law's essential features) and therefore do not refute the theory. Keep in mind, this result follows from the fact that they presupposed at the outset "our" concept of state law in the here and now when constructing their theory.

A second avenue to shield theories of law from empirical refutation is to declare that legal systems inconsistent with a given theory of law are corrupt, defective, exceptional, or marginal (per Gardner). Denis Galligan articulates this out:

> To find in an actual legal order some feature inconsistent with, a corruption of, or an exception to, the concept of law does not render the concept invalid or wrong. It does not because, as should now be clear, a concept is not a generalization from empirical evidence. An inconsistent feature at the empirical level is at best reason for reconsidering, potentially revising, the concept; odd or unusual cases in the realm of experience ought to be taken into account in the domain of concepts, just because such cases are cause to pause, to consider whether the conceptual analysis needs revising. Theorists ought to direct their minds to corrupt, defective, exceptional, or marginal legal systems, but having done so, are likely to conclude, as Hart concluded, that they make no difference to the concept. That there exist such variations in practice does not affect the concept of which they are variations.[115]

Once again, this position presupposes that analytical jurisprudents have picked the singularly correct central case of law – which is the issue multiple counterexamples put in dispute. Without indicating how many counterexamples one must show, or how extensively deviations must be to refute a given theory, a legal philosopher is able to dismiss inconsistent manifestations as corruptions, exceptions, marginal, or defective – leaving the theory of law unscathed.

Proceeding on the assumption that state law is the paradigm of law, various analytical jurisprudents assert law is unified and systematic (Hart), claims supreme legitimate authority (Raz), and solves complex moral problems (Shapiro).[116] They do not contemplate that state law as they portray it is exceptional. Many legal systems past and present are contrary to the essential features identified by these theories of law. Not only are their accounts based on contemporary state law, but their intuitions and assumptions are idealizations.[117] If one looks at what legal systems do and how they actually operate, the picture is altogether messier, with legal systems splayed across a spectrum of variation on multiple dimensions.

---

[115] Denis J. Galligan, "Concepts in the Currency of Social Understanding of Law: A Review Essay on the Later Work of William Twining," 35 *Oxford Journal of Legal Studies* 373, 392 (2015).

[116] Lately a few analytical jurisprudents have moved beyond the state law model. A fine example is K. Culver and M. Giudice, *Legality's Borders* (Oxford: Oxford University Press 2010).

[117] Jeremy Waldron criticizes Hart for idealizing the systematicity of state law when he dismissed international law as law. Waldron, "International Law: 'A Relatively Small and Unimportant' Part of Jurisprudence?" *supra*.

These two shields – declaring counterexamples to be *not* law or a corruption of law – rest on contestable assumptions, lack clear criteria, and are devoid of analytical rigor and accountability. The counterexamples provided in the next chapter inconsistent with various aspects of analytical jurisprudents' theories of law are so plentiful that the declaration their theories hold true for all places and times is strained beyond credibility. The idealized state law model analytical jurisprudents work from, as we shall see, is a relatively recent historical development and dominates today mainly in parts of the world immediately familiar to analytical jurisprudents.

DOES LAW HAVE A NATURE?

After unpeeling the arguments of analytical jurisprudents, it appears the main basis for their claims of necessary, universal truths about law is simply their repeated insistence on it. Julie Dickson asserts a successful theory of law "consists of propositions about the law which (1) are necessarily true, and (2) adequately explain the nature of law."[118] "The nature of law" refers to "those essential properties which a given set of phenomena must exhibit in order to be law."[119] Presented in these terms, "nature" has no independent content beyond essential and necessary properties of law. If one concludes law lacks essential and necessary features, talk about "the nature of law" can then be dispensed with, superfluous wrapping tossed aside because it no longer has a point.

Perhaps there is a different way to understand the "nature of law," though, one still meaningful in the absence of essential and necessary properties. In his Introduction to the third edition of Hart's *Concept of Law*, Green characterized Hart's view thus: "Laws and legal systems are not matters of nature but artifice." "We might say they are social constructions."[120] "Anything in the law is there because some person or group put it there, either intentionally or accidentally. It all has a history; it can all be changed; it is all either known or knowable."[121]

Green's depiction reaches core aspects of the nature of law: it is a social construction that exists owing to the meaningful actions of people and groups, it has a history, it could all have been constructed differently and can all be changed. People and groups have conventionally identified and constructed multiple forms of law (*ius, droit, recht, diritto, derecho, prawo*, etc.) in the course of history and today, including customary law, natural law, religious law, state law, international law, transnational law of various types, and human rights, and each of these forms of law comes in a range of variations. These forms of law arise and change over time in connection with social, cultural, economic, political, ecological, and technological factors. That is the nature of law.

---

[118] Dickson, *Evaluation and Legal Theory*, supra 17.   [119]   Id.
[120] Leslie Green, "Introduction," *The Concept of Law*, 3rd ed. (Oxford: Oxford university Press 2012) xvii.
[121] Id. xviii.

The pragmatic method is "the attitude of looking away from first things, princi-ples, 'categories,' supposed necessities; and of looking towards last things, fruits, consequences, facts."[122] My realistic theory is built on attention to how manifesta-tions of law have been constructed and operate in the course of human history, what people think of them, what they are used for, what they do, and what their consequences are. A genealogical view helps expose these aspects of law across a broad range of contexts.

[122] William James, *Pragmatism and the Meaning of Truth* (Cambridge, MA: Harvard University Press [1907] 1975) 32.

4

A Genealogical View of Law

When declaring what law is, as we have seen, analytical jurisprudents abstract from their intuitions about state law and use this as the measure of law for all places and times. This approach begs large questions: Why should contemporary state law serve as *the* universal standard for law? Does law have only one form and set of fixed features? Can law vary and change over time? In this chapter, I apply a different approach. I trace law backward – thence forward – looking for earlier manifestations, continuities, variations, and growths, observing how law is structured, what it does, and how it is manifested in different social contexts. This is a genealogical perspective, situating law at various levels of social complexity, developing in relation to social, political, economic, ecological, technological, and cultural circumstances and changes over time.

My argument proceeds on two tracks, one discussing increasingly complex social arrangements, and the second making theoretical points about law. The first track draws mainly from anthropologists, archeologists, sociologists, political scientists, and historians, and the second refers to arguments by analytical jurisprudents, legal positivists in particular. We see law among hunter-gatherers, in chiefdoms, and in early states; law in empires; the consolidation of state law; the establishment of professional legal cultures; and the modern thickening of state law. Although set forth in roughly chronological order, this is not a history of law. It is a sampling of law in different times and places used to show what law is like and to cast doubt on theories of law propounded by analytical jurisprudents while laying the groundwork for my realistic alternative.

BASICS OF SOCIAL LIFE

We are energy-consuming beings who reproduce and live within communities. We seek to satisfy our basic needs (food, shelter, safety, reproduction, meaningful existence), desires, and tendencies (cooperation, affection, material comforts, competition, status, power, wealth, etc.). We perceive and communicate through the symbolic mediation of language and concepts. We act informed by culturally generated and conveyed ideas and beliefs. We create webs of relationships, pursue projects, and coordinate and compete with others. Ecological, technological, and economic resources and constraints are materialist aspects of our existence.[1] Equally fundamental are idealist aspects: knowledge, beliefs, values, concepts, and habits inform and shape our behavior. "This heritage of culturally generated past experience supplies most of the knowledge that each individual has at her or his disposal for coping with social and ecological realities."[2] Social development involves the interaction of materialist and idealist elements woven through and overlaid with social institutions and practices.[3]

Group size is a crucial factor in the development of social institutions.[4] A hierarchy of decision making and organized implementation is required to coordinate activities across many people.[5] "The larger the group of people who interact, the more ramified their organizational structure needs to be. There is a limit to the number of people whom a leader can effectively control without intermediaries; the less the activity in question follows a fixed and preunderstood pattern and the more group decisions need to be made, the smaller the number of people one leader can directly control"[6] (though modern mass communication technology enhances the capacity to organize large numbers of people). Groups of more than 500 require leaders, "and if they contain over a thousand, some kind of specialized organization or corps of officials to perform police functions."[7] Hence "social complexity increases with group size."[8]

All large communities handle basic tasks: supply water, food, and housing, produce and distribute goods and services, provide transportation, facilitate trade, manage waste disposal, provide effective communication, protect health and safety (injuries, disease, fire, and natural hazards), coordinate behavior on collective projects, and maintain internal order and defense against outsiders. Complex societies consist of institutions organized in terms of these and other functions.[9] Over time, societies have become increasingly layered with hierarchical organization and heterarchy,[10] using

---

[1]   See Bruce G. Trigger, "Distinguished Lecture in Archeology: Constraint and Freedom – A New Synthesis for Archeological Explanation," 93 *American Anthropologist* 551 (1991).

[2]   Id. 560.

[3]   Bruce G. Trigger, *Understanding Early Civilizations* (Cambridge: Cambridge University Press 2003) 13.

[4]   See Gregory J. Johnson, "Information Sources and the Development of Decision-Making Organizations," in *Social Archeology: Beyond Subsistence and Dating*, edited by Charles L. Redman, Mary Jane Berman, Edward V. Curtain, William T. Langhorne, Nina M. Versaggi, and Jeffrey C. Wansner (New York: Academic Press 1978) 87–112.

[5]   See Johnson, "Information Sources and the Development of Decision-Making Organizations," supra 100–04.

[6]   Raoul Naroll, "A Preliminary Index of Social Development," 58 *American Anthropologist* 687, 690 (1956).

[7]   Id.

[8]   Joseph A. Tainter, *The Collapse of Complex Societies* (Cambridge: Cambridge University Press 1988) 23.

[9]   See C. R. Hallpike, *The Principles of Social Evolution* (Oxford: Clarendon Press 1986) 142.

[10] See Henri J. M. Claessen, "Was the State Inevitable?" 1 *Social Evolution & History* 101, 101 (2002). Heterarchy is a network or organization that is not structured in hierarchical terms and can have various nodes of authority.

differentiated organizations to coordinate and carry out these tasks.[11] The larger the group, the more ramified the organizational structure must be, combining horizontal specialization (distributed power among functional units at the same level) and vertical specialization (managing hierarchy). Interaction across organizations takes place through networks of formal and informal links between people located in different organizations sustained through reciprocal relations and shared interests.[12]

In a long-delayed and halting fashion, human history has witnessed a massive increase in the size, density, and complexity of social groups and the development of thick networks of interaction across social groups.[13] Law, as we shall see, takes on different forms and functions in connection with different degrees of social complexity, manifesting one way in simple societies, becoming something else in complex societies, and changing yet again in modern societies.

EXAMPLES OF LAW IN BANDS, TRIBES, AND CHIEFDOMS

"Those who live in bands don't have law," analytical jurisprudent Scott Shapiro declares.[14] "Anthropologists now believe that humans mostly *lived without law* for the vast majority of their time on earth,"[15] he asserts. But this is too sweeping if attributed to anthropologists. "No society is without law,"[16] in the view of prominent legal anthropologist Sally Falk Moore. Julius Lips wrote, "there is no people without fire, without language, without religion, or without law. Our social, religious, and legal concepts do not coincide with those of the primitives; what we must do is to find the correct equivalent for our modern institutions in primitive societies."[17]

Several features are characteristic of hunter-gatherers.[18] They lived in family-based groupings of twenty-five or so people, among a larger network of neighboring bands that gathered together and moved apart throughout the year, comprising

---

[11]   The seminal article on complexity is Herbert A. Simon, "The Architecture of Complexity," 106 *Proceedings of the American Philosophical Society* 467 (1962). Using increasing complexity as a measure of evolution is in tension with Darwinian theory because the former is directional while the latter does not have any built-in progressive arrow.

[12]   See France S. Berry, Ralph S. Brower, Sang Ok Choi, Wendy Xinfang Goa, HeeSoun Jang, Myungjung Kwon, and Jessica Ward, "Three Traditions of Network Research: What the Public Management Research Agenda Can Learn from Other Research Communities," 64 *Public Administration Review* 539 (2004).

[13]   See generally Kent V. Flannery, "The Cultural Evolution of Civilizations," 3 *Annual Rev. of Ecology and Systematics* 399 (1972); Julian H. Steward, "Cultural Causality and Law: A Trial Formulation of the Development of Early Civilizations," 51 *American Anthropologist* 1 (1949).

[14]   Scott Shapiro, *Legality* (Cambridge, MA: Harvard University Press) 35.

[15]   Id. 35 (emphasis added).

[16]   Sally Falk Moore, *Law as Process: An Anthropological Approach* (London: Routledge & Kegan Paul 1978) 215.

[17]   Quoted in Morton H. Fried, *The Evolution of Political Society: An Essay in Political Anthropology* (New York: Random House 1967) 16–17.

[18]   See Eleanor Leacock and Richard Lee, "Introduction," in *Politics and History in Band Society* (Cambridge: Cambridge University Press 1982) 1–20, 8–9.

tribes of several hundred members.[19] With the major exception of gender relations,[20] they were egalitarian and group leadership was determined by personal qualities (prowess as a hunter or warrior, persuasive ability or demonstrated judgment, or elder status).[21] A basic division of labor existed between males and females on food production and other tasks.[22] Sharing and reciprocity within the camp was common.

Anthropologists define property rights in terms of the right to possess, to use, and to exclude. There is a "wide measure of agreement" in the field that hunter-gatherers had property rights, some collectively and some individually held.[23] "Movables – tools, weapons, cooking utensils, procured food, occasionally trees, and so on"[24] – were owned individually, reflecting the time, effort, and access to materials required to make them. "Hence individual ownership forms the basis for individual gift-giving and for inter-band exchange systems that make possible farflung networks of reciprocity."[25] Five basic categories of property rights have been found in hunter-gatherer societies: rights over land and water sources; rights over movables (tools, weapons, cooking pots, etc.); rights over killed game, harvested food, and procured raw materials; rights over people (their labor, their sexual and reproductive capacity); and rights over sacred knowledge.[26]

Land rights of hunter-gatherers varied in connection with cultural views and ecological surroundings, though collective ownership by the band was common.[27] Members of the band could collect and consume fruits of the land, with certain restrictions; access to sacred sites was forbidden to women, children, and uninitiated men.[28] Property rights vested in individuals or families were tied to concentrated resources like watering holes and fruit or nut groves.[29] Many studies have found that

[19] See David Riches, "Hunter-Gatherer Structural Transformations," 1 *Journal of the Royal Anthropological Institute* 679 (1995).

[20] See James G. Flanagan, "Hierarchy in Simple 'Egalitarian' Societies," 18 *Annual Review of Anthropology* 245 (1989).

[21] See James Woodburn, "Egalitarian Societies," 17 *Man* 431 (1982).

[22] Allen W. Johnson and Timothy Earle, *The Evolution of Human Societies: From Foraging Group to Agrarian State*, 2nd ed. (Palo Alto, CA: Stanford University Press 2000) 44–45.

[23] Alan Barnard and James Woodburn, "Property, Power and Ideology in Hunter-Gathering Societies: An Introduction," in *Hunters and Gatherers 2: Property, Power and Ideology*, edited by Tim Ingold, David Riches, and James Woodburn (Oxford: Berg 1988) 4–31, 10.

[24] Richard B. Lee, "Reflections on Primitive Communism," in *Hunters and Gatherers 1: History, Evolution and Social Change*, edited by Tim Ingold, David Riches, and James Woodburn (Oxford: Berg 1988) 252–68, 257.

[25] Leacock and Lee, "Introduction," supra 9.

[26] Barnard and Woodburn, "Property, Power and Ideology in Hunter-Gathering Societies," supra 14.

[27] Leacock and Lee, "Introduction," supra 8. One theory of land rights is "territorial exclusion is expected whenever resource density and predictability is sufficient to make the benefits of exclusive use outweigh the cost of defense." Eric Alden Smith, "Risk and Uncertainty in the 'Original Affluent Society': Evolutionary Ecology of Resource-Sharing and Land Tenure," in Ingold, Riches, and Woodburn, *Hunters and Gatherers 1*, supra 222–51, p. 244.

[28] Annette Hamilton, "Descended from Father, Belonging to Country: Rights to Land in the Australian Western Desert," in Leacock and Lee, *Politics and History in Band Society*, supra 85–108, p. 90.

[29] Timothy Earle, "Property Rights in the Evolution of Chiefdoms," in Timothy Earle, *Chiefdoms: Power, Economy, and Ideology* (Cambridge: Cambridge University Press 1991) 72.

bands would allow other bands reciprocal access to land (after permission was sought), and "that tribal areas are defined and subject to laws of trespass"[30] – with punishment for violations up to death.[31]

Anthropologists draw a distinction between "immediate return" and "delayed return" hunter-gatherers. Those in immediate return systems consume the food they procure immediately. "They use relatively simple, portable, utilitarian, easily acquired, replaceable tools and weapons made with real skill but not involving a great deal of labor."[32] Delayed return systems among hunter-gatherers exhibit a cluster of four characteristics. They have "valuable technical facilities used in production: boats, nets, artificial weirs, stockades, pit-traps, beehives and other such artifacts which are a product of considerable labor and from which food yield is obtained gradually over a period of months or years."[33] They process and store food. They cull wild herds and tend wild food patches. And men have rights to bestow their female kin in marriage. "Delayed return systems depend for their operation on sets of ordered, differentiated, jurally-defined relationships through which crucial goods and services are transmitted."[34]

Immediate return societies are more flexible and family units are less dependent on long-term commitments from others, with groups free to strike out on their own. In contrast, "for people to build up, secure, protect, manage and transmit the delayed yields on labour, or the other assets which are held in delayed-return systems, load-bearing relationships are necessary."[35] This difference is reflected in more extensive property rights in delayed return societies. "The *particular* form the organization will take cannot be predicted, nor can one say that the organization exists in order to control and apportion these assets because, once in existence, the organization will be used in a variety of ways, which will include the control and apportionment of assets but which are not otherwise determined."[36]

Chiefdoms are larger, settled groups,[37] which emerged "around the world between about 1,000 and 7,000 years ago,"[38] ranging in size from hundreds to tens of thousands of people, marked by hereditary social stratification and inequality.[39]

---

[30] Hamilton, "Descended from Father, Belonging to Country," supra 90; on land rights, see also Nicolas Peterson, "Hunter-Gatherer Territoriality: The Perspective from Australia," 77 *American Anthropologist* 53 (1975).

[31] See Robert Layton, "Political and Territorial Structures among Hunter-Gatherers," 21 *Man* 18, 21–23 (1986).

[32] James Woodburn, "Egalitarian Societies," 17 *Man* 431, 432 (1982).   [33] Id. 432–33.

[34] James Woodburn, "African Hunter-Gatherer Social Organization: Is It Best Understood as a Product of Encapsulation?" in Ingold, Riches, and Woodburn, *Hunters and Gatherers* 1, supra 31–64, p. 33.

[35] Id.   [36] Id. 33–34.

[37] See Gil J. Stein, "Heterogeneity, Power, and Political Economy: Some Current Research Issues in the Archaeology of Old World Complex Societies," 6 *Journal of Archaeological Research* 1 (1998).

[38] Robert D. Drennan and Christian E. Peterson, "Patterned Variation in Prehistoric Chiefdoms," 103 *Proc. National Academy of Sciences* 3960, 3960 (2006).

[39] An excellent overview is Robert L. Carneiro, "The Chiefdom: Precursor of the State," in *The Transition to Statehood in the New World*, edited by Grant D. Jones and Robert R. Kautz (Cambridge: Cambridge University Press 1981) 37–75. See also Colin Renfrew, "Beyond Subsistence

Complex chiefdoms were "strongly theocratic," led by priest-chiefs, "there usually being a royal class ruling over other nobility, warriors, craftsmen, and a large population of commoners."[40] They interacted with neighboring chiefdoms in extensive networks of trade, mutual defense, and warfare.

How chiefdoms came to be hierarchical and inegalitarian are open questions.[41] *Functionalist* explanations point to the necessity for political leadership and coordination in economic activities when populations reach a certain size. Politically, this involves exerting force to keep internal order and lead battles against outsiders;[42] economic activities involve the intensification of subsistence production through major projects like irrigation works or terracing. *Conflict* explanations invoke competition over status, wealth, and power in larger, settled communities, leading to consolidation of rule by winners, supported by ideological justifications, perpetuated by property rights that pass through kin groups.[43] Wealth is obtained from the acquisition of surplus production from commoners (redistributed to priests, nobility, and warriors), as well as the accumulation of prestige goods (ritual objects, shells, obsidian, etc.) via long-distance exchange, which cements social and religious standing.[44] Power is a function of wealth and social status, and is tied to the strength/size of the kin group.[45]

Leadership roles, bolstered by religious authority, harden into kin-based organization and social stratification that establish unequal access to resources.[46] Only members of noble families were eligible to be a chief. A common arrangement saw layers of chiefs, with paramount chiefs at the top, major chiefs below, and subchiefs in each village. Chiefs held authority through religious ideology, by the possession of status goods, and by wealth and economic redistribution secured to them by property rights and exchanges with neighboring chiefdoms.[47]

Property rights were central to the power of chiefs and social stratification in chiefdoms. In the Hawaiian Islands, for example, "Since all lands were owned by the paramount chiefs, the allocation of community lands to his supporters and the further allocation of small subsistence plots to commoners formed the basis for

---

Economy: The Evolution of Social Organization in Prehistoric Europe," in 20 *Bulletin on the American Schools of Oriental Research* 69, 79 (1974).

[40] William C. Noble, "Tsouharissen's Chiefdom: An Early Historic 17th Century Neutral Iroquoian Ranked Society," 9 *Canadian Journal of Archaeology* 131, 132 (1985).

[41] See Jerome Rousseau, "Hereditary Stratification in Middle-Range Societies," 7 *J. Royal Anthropological Institute* 117 (2001).

[42] See Robert L. Carneiro, "A Theory of the Origin of the State," 169 *Science* 733 (1970).

[43] See Earle, "Property Rights in the Evolution of Chiefdoms," supra 71–99.

[44] See Gary M. Feinman, "Demography, Surplus, and Inequality: Early Political Formation in Highland Mesoamerica," in Earle, *Chiefdoms: Power, Economy, and Ideology*, supra 229–62.

[45] Stein, "Heterogeneity, Power, and Political Economy," supra 6.

[46] See Johnson and Earle, *The Evolution of Human Societies: From Foraging Group to Agrarian State*, supra 265–67.

[47] See Timothy Earle, "The Evolution of Chiefdoms," in Earle, *Chiefdoms: Power, Economy and Ideology*, supra 1–15.

requiring payments in labor and goods."[48] Chiefs kept the most fertile lands from which they obtained the greatest surplus for themselves. On their part, chiefs coordinated major projects that provided sufficient food supplies, led wars for plunder, defended the community from external threats, and resolved internal disputes.[49]

Thus far, I have emphasized property rights in hunter-gatherer bands and chiefdoms, but other familiar legal provisions were present as well. In *The Law of Primitive Man*,[50] Adamson Hoebel collected restrictions against theft, adultery, incest, assaults, and other delicts from hunter-gatherer bands and tribal groups around the world, focusing especially on responses to murder. Distinctions were made between accidental deaths, deaths from anger, and homicidal recidivists, the latter posing the gravest danger to the community. "The single murder is a private wrong redressed by the kinsman of the victim. Repeated murder becomes a public crime punishable by death at the hands of an agent of the community."[51] Often the decision to carry out the appropriate punishment was made by chiefs or a council of elders, or by consensus of the community, and carried out by the victim's kin. What distinguishes these actions from pure personal retaliation is that punishment receives authorization.[52] Prior approval lessens the potential for a tit-for-tat cycle of violence between families (feuds were circumscribed by rules[53]). Decision makers aimed to restore ruptured relations within the social group. Punishments ranged from fines, to labor obligations, to banishment, to death.

In *The Cheyenne Way*, Hoebel and Karl Llewellyn described a series of murder and suicide cases among nineteenth-century Cheyenne (told by informants), who were nomadic, semi-pastoral tribal hunters. Here is a portion of their reconstructed legal provisions: "Killing within the tribe is a crime, and a sin, but it is no longer even a fully recognized tort."[54] "The chiefs present in a body of Cheyenne at the time of a homicide shall have exclusive jurisdiction over the offense of killing, if they exercise jurisdiction; but, in the absence [pending?] of a ruling by the chiefs, a military society may take such [minor?] measures as they may deem required, including temporary banishment during a hunt [or even a general banishment?]."[55] "The chiefs shall decree the banishment of the killer. Unless otherwise expressly provided in the decree, the banishment shall be for a period of five [ten?] years."[56] (After two years, if persuaded of penitence and no further risk, chiefs had the

---

[48] Johnson and Earle, *Evolution of Human Societies*, supra 291.   [49] Id. 92.

[50] See Adamson Hoebel, *The Law of Primitive Man* (Cambridge, MA: Harvard University Press 1954) 88–91, 276–77, 298–307.

[51] Id. 88.

[52] See also Richard G. Dillon, "Capital Punishment in Egalitarian Society: The Meta Case," 36 *Journal of Anthropological Research* 437 (1980).

[53] William Ian Miler, *Bloodtaking and Peacemaking* (Chicago, IL: University of Chicago Press 1990).

[54] Karl Llewellyn and Adamson Hoebel, *The Cheyenne Way* (Norman: University of Oklahoma Press 1941) 166.

[55] Id.   [56] Id. 167.

discretion to remit the banishment.) And various "exceptions and mitigations" were specified for killings in self-defense, accidental killings, provoked killings, and so forth.[57] This was carried out without an organized legal system.

Anthropologist Max Gluckman observed that there have been many societies with "no governmental institutions," no officers to judge disputes or enforce decisions, yet they have "well known codes of morals and laws," laws that address personal injury, property, inheritance, and marriage restrictions.[58]

WHY THIS COUNTS AS LAW

Anthropologists differ on whether bands and chiefdoms had law. The answer depends on how one defines law. A scholar who adopts a definition of law as a command of the sovereign backed by publicly administered sanctions and enforced by courts – the state law model – as Morton Fried did, would conclude that any social group below complex chiefdoms did not have law.[59] Stanley Diamond concurred: "law is the instrument of civilization, of political society sanctioned by organized force, presumably above society at large, and buttressing a new set of social interests."[60] Many chiefdoms lacked "true government to back up legal decisions by legalized force,"[61] and chiefs often did not have a monopoly on force.[62] Hence they did not have law.

A conception of law that does not require an institutionalized system, in contrast, can locate law in hunter-gatherer bands and in rudimentary chiefdoms. Hoebel's formulation does that: "A social norm is legal if its neglect or infraction is regularly met, in threat or in fact, by the application of physical force by an individual or group possessing the socially recognized privilege of so acting."[63] Even when the victim's kin carries out the punishment, as was frequently the case, this would constitute law if some form of community approval was required (via elders or accepted decision makers).

Analytical jurisprudents insist this is insufficient. Only a well-organized legal system counts as law in their view. Hart insists that primitive societies were prelegal because they lacked unified secondary rules. "Indeed," Shapiro asserts, "it is plausible to suppose that law is a comparatively recent invention, postdating the wheel, language, agriculture, art, and religion."[64] Yet we see recognizable forms of law

[57] Id. 168. [58] Max Gluckman, "The Peace in the Feud," 8 *Past and Present* 1, 1 (1955).

[59] See Morton H. Fried, *The Evolution of Political Society: An Essay in Political Anthropology* (New York: Random House 1967) 3–26. Elman Service takes an intermediate stance, recognizing that chiefdoms have basic elements of law, while lacking formal legal institutions. Elman R. Service, *The Origins of the State and Civilization: The Process of Cultural Evolution* (New York: Norton 1975) 83–90.

[60] Stanley Diamond, "The Rule of Law Versus the Order of Custom," 38 *Social Research* 42, 47 (1971).

[61] Renfrew, "Beyond a Subsistence Economy," supra 73.

[62] See Phyllis Kaberry, "Primitive States," 8 *British Journal of Sociology* 224 (1957).

[63] Hoebel, *Law of Primitive Man*, supra 28. [64] Shapiro, *Legality*, supra 36.

relating to persons and property among hunter-gatherers and chiefdoms. What supports their assertion that this is *not* law?

Hart constructed his account of law by identifying three "defects" suffered by regimes of primary rules of obligation alone. First, the rules are *uncertain*, because "if doubts arise as to what the rules are or as to the precise scope of some given rule, there will be no procedure for settling this doubt, either by reference to an authoritative text or to an official whose declarations on this point are authoritative."[65] The second defect is rules are *static*: "There will be no means, in such a society, of deliberately adapting the rules to changing circumstances, either by eliminating old rules or introducing new ones."[66] "The third defect of this simple form of social life is the *inefficiency* of the diffuse social pressure by which the rules are maintained."[67] Without legal officials enforcing rules, "the waste of time involved in the group's unorganized efforts to catch and punish offenders, and the smoldering vendettas which may result from self help in the absence of an official 'monopoly' of sanctions, may be serious."[68] Secondary rules remedy these defects. A "rule of recognition" specifies the criteria for valid legal rules, solving uncertainty; "rules of change" empower a body or person to enact new rules and abolish old ones; "rules of adjudication" empower individuals to identify when rules have been broken and specify the procedure to be followed in response.[69] Secondary rules are "the heart of a legal system,"[70] he concluded, because they facilitate the efficient operation of law.

Notice, however, that the absence of secondary rules is a defect only if there is substantial uncertainty about the rules, if society is rapidly changing, and if existing enforcement mechanisms are not functioning. None of these conditions was typical of bands and chiefdoms. They were homogeneous societies with shared understandings of their laws and what ought to be done in situations of disruption, with the response usually oriented to restoring relations within the community. Many of these groups, as an anthropologist described in connection with an Indian community, "had a strong feeling for the definition of rights and obligations, and recognized certain appropriate damages for any private delicts. Nevertheless this code was maintained not only without any court, but without any formal procedure at law."[71] Hart's concept of law privileges forms of law necessary to fast-changing heterogeneous societies, discounting non-systematized legal forms suited to slow-changing, close-knit communities.

A genealogical approach holds that primitive legal provisions that resemble our own law in function and subject matter – like property rights, debt obligations, marriage rights, and responses to personal injuries – are "law" regardless of the absence of an organized system. Systems of primary and secondary rules did not suddenly emerge fully formed, but rather evolved when additional institutionalization (secondary rules) became necessary as groups grew much larger, requiring

---

[65] Hart, *Concept of Law*, supra 90.   [66] Id.   [67] Id. 91.   [68] Id.   [69] Id. 92–95.   [70] Id. 95.
[71] Robert Redfield, "Primitive Law," 33 *University of Cincinnati Law Review* 1, 9 (1964).

coordination across many people and different types of activities. The emergent legal system was a component of advancing social complexity.

Jurgen Habermas understood this. "As we learn from anthropology, law as such precedes the rise of the state and of political power in the strict sense, whereas politically sanctioned law and legally organized political power arise simultaneously."[72] "Archaic law" paved the way for and "first made possible the emergence of a political rule in which political power and compulsory law mutually constituted one another."[73] Full systems of procedures and standing institutions were not possible nor necessary given the limited social complexity of bands, though laws on core aspects of social intercourse still existed.

Immanuel Kant presented the argument on logical grounds. "If it were held that no acquisition, not even provisional acquisition, is juridically valid before the establishment of a civil society," Kant wrote, "then the civil society itself would be impossible. This follows from the fact that, as regards their form, the laws concerning Mine and Yours in a state of nature contain the same things that are prescribed by the law in civil society insofar as they are considered merely as pure concepts of reason."[74] What the state adds is a layer of public law that enforces preexisting private law of property rights and personal injuries. "The original community of the land and, along with the land, of the things on it (*communio fundi originaria*) is an Idea that has objective (juridical-practical) reality."[75] Based on this view, Kant condemned as "reprehensible" the colonial taking of land from indigenous people[76] – a practice justified at the time on grounds that natives lacked law and had no property rights.

The thread of familiar legal proscriptions on core matters of social intercourse from hunter-gatherer bands, to chiefdoms, to early states, to modern society connects law across these very different social arrangements. Anthropologists naturally invoke legal terms like "juridical" and "rights" to characterize rules, sanctions, and procedures in simple societies notwithstanding the absence of an institutionalized system.

Analytical jurisprudents go wrong when they unthinkingly conflate "law" and "legal system." "Such is the standard case of what is meant by 'law' and 'legal system,'"[77] Hart said, merging the two. "Yet if they lack the essential features of the law," Raz wrote, "they are not legal systems."[78] Shapiro pronounces it self-evident

---

[72] Jurgen Habermas, *Law and Morality*, Tanner Lectures (1986) 263, available at http://tannerlectures .utah.edu/_documents/a-to-z/h/habermas88.pdf.

[73] Id. 264. These were not just empirical claims by Habermas, who was "primarily concerned with the clarification of conceptual relations," 266.

[74] Immanuel Kant, *Metaphysical Elements of Justice*, 2nd ed. Translated by John Ladd (Indianapolis, IN: Hackett [1979] 1999) 116–17. Kant uses the term "provisionally" to represent the right to possess given property in a state of nature; he contrasts this with "peremptorily," which is property rights in civil society backed by institutionalized enforcement.

[75] Id. 183. [76] Id. 65–66. [77] Hart, *Concept of Law*, supra 5.

[78] Joseph Raz, "Can There Be Theory of Law?" in *The Blackwell Guide to the Philosophy of Law and Legal Theory*, edited by Martin P. Golding and William A. Edmundson (Oxford: Blackwell 2005) 328.

that "Laws are always members of legal systems."[79] Raz and Shapiro categorically insist that an organized system is essential to the nature of law, so whatever lacks this form does not count as law. Hart was more flexible, acknowledging: "There are no settled principles forbidding the use of the word 'law' of systems where there are no centrally organized sanctions"[80] (though he did not embrace this usage).

The presupposition that law is a system – based on their starting assumption that state law is the epitome of law – obscures fundamental continuities tracing back to before law took systematic form. In small social groups, law effectively preserves property and persons and resolves disruptions without an organized system. Put in Searle's terms, community members collectively recognized certain objects and arrangements as property, marriage, etc., with attendant rights, duties, obligations, and remedies. This is what law has been for most of human existence and still is in remote areas around the world.

Dropping the system requirement raises an old jurisprudential puzzle. Analytical jurisprudents have long thought it necessary to find a way to distinguish law from other normative orders. Andrei Marmor writes, "Law is not the only normative domain in our culture; morality, religion, social conventions, etiquette, and so on, also guide human conduct in many ways which are similar to law. Therefore, part of what is involved in the understanding of the nature of law consists in an explanation of how law differs from these similar normative domains, how it interacts with them, and whether its intelligibility depends on such other normative orders, like morality or social conventions."[81] Because the presence of an organized system helps distinguish law from these other normative orderings, discarding this as a defining feature of law appears to make it impossible to draw the distinction.

This is an artificial puzzle created by a poorly posed question that presupposes current circumstances. We have little trouble making these distinctions in our own societies using commonsense conventional criteria. Sharp distinctions cannot be drawn between law, custom, morality, etiquette, and religion in early social groups because low levels of social differentiation did not have the normative variations present at higher levels of social complexity. It was a primordial normative soup. If one points at the lack of differentiation to conclude that law did not exist, then it would also follow that customs and morality did not exist because they too cannot be clearly distinguished – which reinforces the point that these distinctions are inapposite. A genealogical approach need not make these distinctions, for it can identify law in early social groups by locating recognizably familiar legal proscriptions.

An essential clarification must be made to avoid confusion. When I assert "law" existed in bands and chiefdoms, I am not saying this is law in an objectively true universal sense or that they conventionally labeled this "law." Law is our concept, not theirs. My claim is that what we think of as law was present despite the absence of

---

[79]   Shapiro, *Legality*, supra 15.   [80]   Hart, *Concept of Law*, supra 195.
[81]   Andrei Marmor, "The Nature of Law," *Stanford Encyclopedia of Philosophy*, at http://plato.stanford
       .edu/entries/lawphil-nature/.

a system, even if they had no conception of law or of property or murder in our terms. We cannot help but use our own concepts in these inquiries, and must proceed mindful of not mistaking our categories for theirs.[82]

LAW AND INEQUALITY

Pristine or primary states arose independently in several parts of the world – Mesopotamia, Egypt, Indus Valley, China, Peru, Mesoamerica – 3,000 to 5,000 years ago.[83] States had populations of 100,000 or more, established legal systems, and a stratified society, including administrators, nobility, priests, warriors, manual workers, artisans, traders, slaves, etc.[84] A centralized government with control over the surrounding area was typically headed by a kingship enjoying religious support, bolstered by cultural, religious, and political ideologies that justified the social-political arrangement. Officials carried out specialized functions, funded by taxation, tribute, and plunder. Leaders managed large projects (irrigation works, public buildings and temples, monuments, transportation byways). They controlled external trade, whether by the state itself or in private hands subject to approval and fees. They had the capacity to exert force within society and hold court, and they waged offensive and defensive wars.[85]

As with chiefdoms, scholars put forth functionalist and conflict theories of state formation.[86] Functionalist theories focus on the needs of society in organic or holistic terms. They emphasize the benefits of the state in providing coordination, order, protection, defense, food provision to offset bad harvests, markets, information and communication, public works, and other projects for community benefit. These theories "argue that complexity and stratification arose because of stresses impinging upon human populations, and were positive responses to those stresses."[87] Conflict theories, in contrast, see the state as managing individual and group conflict within society in the interest of power holders. "More specifically, the governing institutions

---

[82] This hearkens to the famous Gluckman–Bohannan debate of the 1950s over the potential misuse of Western legal categories to study other societies. The lesson of this exchange was that folk terms cannot be compared, but analytic categories abstracted from folk ideas and practices can be compared. See Sally Engle Merry, "Transnational Human Rights and Local Activism: Mapping the Middle," 108 *American Anthropologist* 38, 41 (2006).

[83] See Elman R. Service, *Origins of the State and Civilization: The Process of Cultural Evolution* (New York: Norton 1978). See Robert J. Wenke, *Patterns in Prehistory: Humankind's First Three Million Years*, 4th ed. (New York: Oxford University Press 1999) 331–36.

[84] Elman Service uses the presence of formal legal institutions to distinguish states from chiefdoms. Service, *The Origins of the State and Civilization*, supra 14–16. For the features of early states, see Henry T. Wright, "Recent Research on the Origin of the State," 6 *Annual Review of Anthropology* 379 (1977); Henri M. Claessen, "The Internal Dynamics of the Early State," 25 *Current Anthropology* 365 (1984); Robert L. Carneiro, "Cross-Currents in the Theory of State Formation," 14 *American Ethnologist* 756–70 (1987); Rita Smith Kipp and Edward M. Schortman, "The Political Impact of Trade in Chiefdoms," 91 *American Anthropologist* 370 (1989).

[85] Henri J. M. Claessen, "Was the State Inevitable?" supra 107–12.

[86] See Tainter, *Collapse of Complex Societies*, supra 33.   [87] Id. 34.

of the state were developed as coercive mechanisms to resolve intra-societal conflicts arising out of economic stratification. The state serves, thus, to maintain the privileged position of a ruling class that is largely based on the exploitation and economic degradation of the masses."[88] A leading scholar of state development, Henri Claessen, remarked, "there is always found great inequality in (early) states. Some people, the happy few, are rich and powerful and all others, the great majority, are poor and powerless."[89] Law maintained this arrangement.

Law in early states was intertwined with religious and supernatural beliefs. Archeologist Bruce Trigger provides a few examples (citations omitted):

> Laws were often claimed to originate with the gods, who transmitted them to humans through the proclamations of rulers. The Aztec term for "laws," *nahuatilli*, meant "a set of commands." Laws were a means by which human society was not only regulated but also aligned with a cosmic order that was profoundly hierarchical. The Babylonian word *mesaru* and the Egyptian *m3't* referred both to the cosmic order and to legal justice. The Inka state claimed that subjects' commission of crimes such as murder, witchcraft, theft, and neglect of religious cults threatened the health of the king and considered them sacrilege. Later evidence from China indicates that law (*fa*) was believed to have been created by superhuman beings in accordance with divine models and interests. To promote order on earth, rulers sought to suppress blood feuds and punish murder, treason, theft, incest, and many other forms of misconduct.
>
> Supernatural powers were believed to support the legal process by revealing guilt or innocence through oracles and ordeals and by punishing oath-breakers. The gods punished individuals whose crimes went undetected or unpunished by humans. The Babylonian king Hammurabi claimed to have assembled his law code at the command of the god Utu, or Shamas, who, because as the sun god he saw everything that humans did, was also the patron deity of justice. Promulgating this law code gave Hammurabi an earthly role analogous to that of Enlil, the chief executive deity of the Sumerian pantheon. The laws proclaimed by Aztec ruler Mochtezuma I were described as "flashes that the great king [had] sown in his breast, from the divine fire, for the total health of his kingdom." This claim referred to the divine powers that were implanted in the Aztec monarch at the time of his enthronement. The early Chinese believed that improper conduct was supernaturally punished.[90]

Another common characteristic of law in early states was the enforcement of social hierarchy and status differences. Hammurabi's Code is replete with status distinctions. "If any one strikes the body of a man higher in rank than he, he shall receive sixty blows with an ox-whip in public."[91] Anyone who steals property from the court or temple is put to death, whereas thieves who steal from others suffer lesser

[88] Id. 33.   [89] Claessen, "Was the State Inevitable?" supra 104.
[90] Trigger, *Understanding Early Civilizations*, supra 221–22.
[91] Hammurabi's Code of Law, translated by L. W. King, available at http://eawc.evansville.edu /anthology/hammurabi.htm #202.

punishments.[92] A husband can sell his wife and children into forced labor to pay off debt, though they must be set free in the fourth year.[93] Runaway slaves must be returned to their master, and anyone who harbors them shall be put to death.[94] The overall governing norm was rough equivalence (factoring in hierarchy), matching their sense of justice: an eye for an eye, a broken bone for a broken bone, a tooth for a tooth (except that a tooth knocked out of a lower-status person results in a fine).[95] "If a builder build a house for some one, and does not construct it properly, and the house which he built fall in and kill its owner, then that builder shall be put to death."[96] If the son of the owner is killed by the falling building, the builder's son is put to death;[97] if the owner's slave is killed, the builder "shall pay slave for slave to the owner."[98]

Roman law also enforced status distinctions: "The 'standard unit' of the Roman law was the freeborn Roman citizen, male, of age and sound mind and head of his family. Everyone else was legally inferior and by comparison subject to some sort of restriction, ranging from minor to total, upon his legal powers, rights or personality. There thus developed a stratified society in which every man had his legally appointed and legally defined place."[99]

Modern states have status-based laws as well, notoriously exemplified by slave laws in the United States. Slave status was inherited through the mother (including mulatto offspring of the slave owner), making slavery a legal condition passed through generations.[100] Whipping was the penalty for a slave striking or attempting to strike a white; second or third offenses were punishable by death.[101] Attempts to escape or advocating escape were punishable by whipping, branding, cutting off an ear, or death; when slaves were executed by the state, owners could seek compensation for lost property.[102] Slaves were prohibited from owning cattle, horses, sheep, pigs, and boats, and from engaging in commercial activities, so as not to compete with whites.[103] There were sumptuary laws that restricted slaves to low-status clothing.[104] After slave laws were abolished, legally enforced status distinctions were perpetuated in Jim Crow laws on the books through the 1950s, along with legally enforced ideological and political controls to maintain white dominance over blacks.[105] Although explicit status-based laws directed at African Americans

---

[92] Id. #6–8.   [93] Id. #117.   [94] Id. #17–19.   [95] Id. #196–97; #200–01.   [96] Id. #229.

[97] Id. #230.   [98] Id. #231.

[99] Colin F. Kolbert, *Justinian: The Digest of Roman Law, Theft, Rapine, Damage, and Insult* (Middlesex: Penguin Books 1979) 49.

[100] See William M. Wiecek, "The Statutory Law of Slavery and Race in the Thirteen Mainland Colonies of British America," 34 *William and Mary Quarterly* 258, 262–63 (1977).

[101] Id. 273.   [102] Id. 270.   [103] Id. 276.   [104] Id. 268.

[105] A Mississippi statute still on the books in the 1950s read: "Any person . . . who shall be guilty of printing, publishing or circulating printed, typewritten or written matter urging or presenting for public acceptance or general information, arguments or suggestions in favor of social equality or of inter-marriage between whites and negroes, shall be guilty of a misdemeanor and subject to fine of not exceeding five hundred (500.00) dollars or imprisonment not exceeding six (6) months or both." See Examples of Jim Crow Laws, *The Jackson Sun*, at. www.ferris.edu/jimcrow/links/misclink/examples/.

have since been removed, social factors and cultural attitudes continue to result in systematically disproportionate harsh treatment of blacks in the U.S. criminal justice system.[106]

Legal theorists have presented law as the hallmark of civilization. "Civilization is possible only with a very high degree of social cooperation and interdependence," Shapiro writes, "which, in turn, is possible only when a community has the ability to regulate social relations efficiently and effectively. Law was a revolutionary invention precisely because it permitted this regulation."[107] Law, he concludes, "is a self-certifying compulsory planning organization whose aim is to solve those moral problems that cannot be solved, or solved as well, through alternative forms of social ordering."[108]

This idealization emphasizes the functional benefits law provides while shunting to the margins its oppressive aspects backed by force, painting the former as central and the latter as contingent, although they are constant companions in the history of law. This way of thinking about law is one-sided. To determine the character of an institution, Jeremy Bentham insisted, all its effects must be considered. "The abuse of a thing is as much the effect of it as the use is. When a thing has various effects, some good and some bad, it is not by calling the bad by the name of abuses that will make them the less its effects than they were before. An abuse is a bad effect: now a bad effect of a thing is as much its effect as a good one: the one has as much claim to consideration as the other."[109] As John Dewey put it: "a thing is – is defined as – what it does, 'what-it-does' being stated in terms of specific effects extrinsically wrought in other things."[110]

History suggests that oppression in varying ways and degrees is a common aspect of state legal systems. This is a pervasive *feature* of state law, not an aberration. David Hume did not sugarcoat the reality that "Almost all of the governments which exist at present, or of which there remains any record in history, have been founded originally either on usurpation or conquest or both, without any pretense of a fair consent or voluntary subjection of the people."[111] Adam Smith provided an evolutionary account of social-legal development that highlights the connection between law and inequality.[112] "When some have great wealth and others nothing, it is necessary that the arm of authority should be continually stretched forth, and permanent laws or

---

[106]   See Michelle Alexander, *The New Jim Crow: Mass Incarceration in the Age of Colorblindness* (New York: The New Press 2010). See *Investigation of the Ferguson Police Department*, U.S. Department of Justice Civil Rights Division, March 4, 2015, http://apps.washingtonpost.com/g/documents/national/department-of-justice-report-on-the-ferguson-mo-police-department/1435/.

[107]   Shapiro, *Legality*, supra 36.   [108]   Id. 225.

[109]   Quote from Bentham's journal, "Abuse and Use – Both Equally Effects," in John Bowring, "Memoirs of Jeremy Bentham," 37 *Westminster Review* 265, 270 (1842).

[110]   John Dewey, "The Historic Background of Corporate Legal Personality," 35 *Yale Law Journal* 655, 660 (1926).

[111]   David Hume, *Political Essays*, Charles W. Hendel, ed. (New York: Liberal Arts Press 1953) 47.

[112]   See Andrew Skinner, "Adam Smith: Society and Government," in *Perspectives in Jurisprudence*, edited by Elspeth Attwooll (Glasgow: University of Glasgow Press 1977) 195–220.

regulations made which may ascertain the property of the rich from the inroads of the poor, who would otherwise continually make incroachments upon it, and settle in what the infringement of this property consists and in what cases they will be liable to punishment."[113] Rudolph von Jhering observed, "Whoever will trace the legal fabric of a people to its ultimate origins will reach innumerable cases where the force of the stronger has laid down the law for the weaker."[114]

Law in states is an organized system of coercive power that individuals, social groups, and officeholders seek to utilize to serve their ends. A prominent aspect of law throughout history is the service of political and economic power, social stratification, various forms of inequality (including husbands over wives), and the power of the polity itself.

It is widely thought that the shift from status-based societies to modern liberal legal systems with property rights and freedom of contract creates a society free of coercion, but what has changed are the underlying bases for coercion. Whether this represents an actual reduction of coercion, Max Weber observed, "depends entirely upon the concrete economic order and especially on the property distribution."[115] In market systems, owners of the means of production and those with capital utilize legal empowerment to their advantage, dictating the terms of employment relationships for people lacking property. "A legal order which contains ever so few mandatory and prohibitory norms [lacking restrictions on what conditions employers can impose] and ever so many 'freedoms' and 'empowerments' can nonetheless in its practical effects facilitate a quantitative and qualitative increase not only of coercion in general but quite specifically of authoritarian coercion."[116] Legal philosopher Morris Cohen noted, "The greater economic power of the employer exercises a compulsion as real in fact as any now recognized by law as duress."[117]

In capitalist societies, moreover, wealthy interests pervasively influence law to their benefit. This was plain at the turn of the twentieth century when criminal conspiracy laws and antimonopoly statutes were applied to squelch labor actions, courts issued labor injunctions against strikes and boycotts, and public and private police forces killed and imprisoned strikers.[118] Today, billions of dollars in lobbying and campaign contributions flow through the political system sent by corporations and rich individuals seeking favorable legislation and regulations, and representatives of industry

---

113 Adam Smith, *Lectures on Jurisprudence*, edited by R. L. Meek, D. D. Raphael, and P. G. Stein (Indianapolis, IN: Liberty Fund 1982) 208 (emphasis added).

114 Rudolph von Jhering, *Law as a Means to an End*, translated by Issack Husik (1914) 185.

115 Max Weber, *Economy and Society*, vol. 2, edited by Guenther Roth and Clause Wittich (Berkeley: University of California Press 1978) 730.

116 Id. 731. See Robert L. Hale, "Coercion and Distribution in a Supposedly Non-coercive State," 36 *Political Science Quarterly* 470 (1923).

117 Morris Cohen, "The Basis of Contract," 46 *Harvard L. Rev.* 553, 569 (1933).

118 See generally Michael Mann, *The Sources of Social Power: Volume 2: The Rise of Classes and Nation-States*, 1760–1914, 2nd ed. (Cambridge: Cambridge University Press 2012) chapters 17 and 18.

cycle through high-level positions in administrative agencies to implement desired legal initiatives.[119]

Attention to the actual workings of law across time and place reveals that legal systems and inequality are linked, the former maintaining the latter. Analytical jurisprudents and legal theorists generally who write about the nature of law tend to emphasize that law has social and moral functions (as I detail shortly). Critical theorists emphasize that law entrenches, normalizes, and enforces hierarchy and inequality, reinforced by ideological support from cultural, religious, and political beliefs. Each emphasizes one side of law, downplaying the other. A realistic understanding incorporates both. Adam Smith's perspective, conveyed in the Introduction, conveys the social utility of law while also indicating how natural human motivations result in uses of legal coercion by individuals and groups (and the polity itself) to maintain domination over others and instrumentally advance objectives.

LEGAL COVERAGE OF EARLY STATES

Legal proscriptions commonly found in early states can be broken down into eight broad (overlapping) categories: laws in the interest of the state itself; laws enforcing social hierarchy; religious-supernatural laws; laws involving the family and regulating sex; laws involving personal injuries; laws protecting property; laws controlling labor; laws involving trade.[120] These categories are informative groupings, not fixed and mutually exclusive classifications. For instance, I discuss slavery as regulation of labor, though it can be seen as property. Here are a few illustrations of each:

1) Maintaining the state apparatus (including royalty and officials) are laws securing revenues (rents, taxes, customs duties); laws punishing treason, disloyalty, disobedience, and threats to officials; and laws requiring corvee (obligatory unpaid labor).

2) Enforcing social and economic hierarchy are laws on proper conduct toward superiors; sumptuary laws restricting food consumption, clothing, and possession of luxury items by social rank; status-based legal distinctions on treatment of nobles, warriors, commoners, women, children, and slaves.

3) Religious-supernatural laws deal with witchcraft, sacrilege, heresy, violation of religious prohibitions, failure to meet religious obligations, and supplying human sacrifices, as well as mystical-legal ordeals, oracles, and punishments.

4) Family laws and sexual regulation include legal prohibitions against incest, adultery, rape, seduction, sex outside of marriage, and laws about marriage and divorce (including age restrictions, who has the right of permission, dowry,

---

[119]   See Brian Z. Tamanaha, *Law as a Means to an End: Threat to the Rule of Law* (New York: Cambridge University Press 2006) chapter 11.

[120]   For examples, see "Law," in Trigger's *Understanding Early Civilizations*, supra 221–39, along with the other sources cited earlier. The categories and summaries are my own.

which family the new spouse lives with, grounds for divorce, who the children belong to).

5) Personal injury laws deal with killings (intentional and accidental), assaults or wounding in attacks, accidental injuries, kidnapping, and feuds.

6) The preservation of property includes laws against robbery and theft, trespass, damage to property, disputes over ownership of personal property and land (including use rights), and inheritance law.

7) Laws regulating labor cover slave ownership and rules about the disposition, treatment, and return of slaves, restrictions on who can do what types of work, indentured or debt servitude, labor obligations, and rights in the labor of others (wives and children, serfs, servants).

8) Laws relating to economic exchanges address breaches of agreements between merchants, dishonest traders defrauding buyers, the selling of faulty goods or non-delivery, payment of debts, and restrictions that protect guilds.

These categories of legal regulation extend as far back as early states several thousand years ago. That today we regulate most of same categories suggests there are certain constants of social life in large polities. This includes enforcing social, economic, and political hierarchy, control over family unions, sexuality and off-spring, rules for economic exchange and debt, protection of property, regulation of labor, protection from physical injury, and ideological maintenance (i.e., religion, political legitimation). These legal constants flow from the needs of social-sexual beings living in large groups, who pursue material comforts and require food, safety, and shelter, who reproduce, who require cooperation and coordination with others, who compete with others and seek status and wealth, who are threatened by others, and who strive to make sense of the world and find meaning in their lives. Another constant is that the state apparatus uses law to protect and consolidate its own power; once states and legal systems exist, they preserve their own (and officeholders' personal) interests in addition to the social interests they advance.

H. L. A. Hart suggested there is a "minimum content of natural law" that exists in all societies. The human condition (vulnerability, approximate equality of capacities, limited altruism, limited resources, limited understanding and will) requires basic legal rules for the ordered maintenance of social life, he argued, including the protection of persons, property, and promises.[121] The legal coverage of early states is consistent with Hart's observation, although four additional legal constants he failed to mention might be added (at least in larger social groups): legal regulation of family unions, sexual relations and offspring, legal regulation of labor, legal enforcement of social, economic, and political hierarchy (including patriarchy), and maintenance of the power of the legal system itself and the polity to which it is attached. Hart's legal minimums focus on functional benefits, whereas the list of legal constants also includes family unions and oppressive aspects of law.

---

[121]   Hart, *The Concept of Law*, supra 189–95.

Leslie Green builds on Hart's minimum to assert that law's connection to morality is not contingent. The minimum content Hart identified (protection of property, persons, and promises) are universally valuable social needs that law is especially suited to provide:

> The minimum content thesis does not depend on the idea that supporting morality is what law *is for* in the sense of "constitutively for." And law's structural features of institutionalization, systematicity, comprehensive authority, etc. are not design features that exist *in order* to enable law to support morality. The connection runs the other way round. It is law's having such features that explains why law is so apt for supporting morality (among other things).[122]

Like Hart, Green stops short. The same argument applies to state law's association with domination and the enforcement of social, economic, and political hierarchy. Indeed, an argument can be made that the link between domination and state law as organized force is stronger than the connection between law and morality because it rarely lacks domination but regularly deviates from morality.

A few changes with respect to the list of law in early states have taken place over time. Magic and religion were integrated with law up through the medieval period: priestly figures declared norms in prophesies or oracles, agreements were sealed with sacred oaths, violations of rights were punished by supernatural sanctions (curses), guilt was determined by omens and ordeals, blasphemy, heresy, and witchcraft were punished.[123] With the Enlightenment rise of science and the advance of legal rationalization, these irrational elements of law diminished.[124] A range of theocratic arrangements intertwining religious law within the polity still exist around the world today. In most liberal societies, however, religious institutions are no longer state-enforced orthodoxy beyond a number of remaining religiously motivated legal restrictions, though they retain special privileges in civil and criminal law. Another major shift is that law in early states directly enforced hereditary social status, whereas in liberal societies, hierarchy is largely based on wealth and occupational status supported by property rights, along with special access to legal mechanisms for those who can afford them.

Additional differences between early states and most states today (liberal and non-liberal) involve a huge growth in the size and scopes of the first and last categories, dealing respectively with the government and the economy, which now dwarf the other categories. Entirely new realms of activities in society are undertaken by the

---

[122]   Hart's argument is developed in Leslie Green, "The Morality in Law," http://papers.ssrn.com/sol3/papers.cfm?abstract_id=2223760.

[123]   See Georges Gurvitch, "Magic and Law," 9 *Social Research* 104 (1942); Weber, *Economy and Society*, vol. 2, supra 647, 761–62, 765, 768–70, 809–31.

[124]   As late as 1697, the Scottish legal system executed for blasphemy a twenty-year-old man who jokingly said to friends on a cold day, "I wish right now I were in a place Ezra called hell, to warm myself there." Arthur Herman, *How the Scots Invented the Modern World* (New York: Broadway Books 2001) 2.

modern administrative state, much of it carried out through law, including constructing the government itself and advancing its purposive pursuits. Laws dealing with economic activities have likewise ballooned, including laws relating to corporations, finance and banking, and regulation and support of the market. The aggregate effect of these two changes is the creation of a legal fabric within society, taken up in the next chapter.

EMPIRES AND LAW

Empires are incorporative states that exercise control over other societies through military force: the Roman, Byzantine, Persian, Mongol, Mughal, Ottoman, and British Empires, to name a few of the best known.[125] They are economically motivated, seizing labor (slaves, warriors), material resources (copper, gold, silver, etc.), and taxes and tributes.[126] Owing to the difficulty of controlling large expanses of people with diverse languages and cultures, empires typically allowed a substantial degree of local autonomy after forcibly and often brutally pacifying the subject populace. A relatively small contingent of administrators and an armed force maintained imperial rule, relying on local elites to keep order and collect taxes, allowing local laws to continue undisturbed except when they clashed with imperial interests. Empires bare the extractive side of states, as extortion rackets that offer protection from plundering by the state itself and others in exchange for material wealth.[127]

The East India Company (EIC), a private corporation that ruled large areas of India from the mid-eighteen to the mid-nineteenth century, was a particularly naked example of the connections between empire, law, and economic interests.[128] It was "the sole British administrative, judicial, and commercial representative in India during this period. The monopolistic company acted as the upholder of British interests and served as the vehicle for territorial expansion on the subcontinent."[129] EIC supplemented revenues from its commercial activities (a legal monopoly) with substantial territorial revenues it took over from the Mughal emperor. EIC set up a dual court system, one for employees applying English law, a second for natives

---

[125] For a history of the world told through empires and the commerce they generated, see J. R. McNeill and William H. McNeill, *The Human Web* (New York: Norton 2003).

[126] See generally Carla M. Sinopoli, "The Archeology of Empires," 23 *Annual Review of Anthropology* 159 (1994).

[127] See Charles Tilly, "War Making and State Making as Organized Crime," in *Bringing the State Back In*, edited by Peter Evans, Dietrich Rueschemeyer, and Theda Skocpol (Cambridge: Cambridge University Press 1985).

[128] See L. S. Sutherland, "The East India Company in Eighteenth Century Politics," 17 *Economic History Review* 15 (1947); Amar Farooqui, "Governance, Corporate Interest and Colonialism: The Case of the East India Company," 35 *Social Scientist* 44 (2007).

[129] Huw V. Bowen, "The 'Little Parliament': The General Court of the East India Company, 1750–1784," 34 *Historical Journal* 857, 858 (1991).

applying Hindu and Muslim personal laws, and Islamic criminal law.[130] Native courts were prohibited from trying British citizens; the expense of traveling to Calcutta, where the English court was located, meant that Indians in the interior were "extremely vulnerable to European violence and exploitation in both civil and criminal matters."[131]

British colonial practices are telling because the English saw themselves as a rule-of-law society spreading civilization to backward lands. Yet law was above all an enforcer of imperial interests. "Colonial rule created new 'crimes,' many of which were offences against the imposed structure of colonial management."[132] To facilitate acquisition by expatriate settlers of land for plantations and mining, preexisting collective property rights of the community were abolished and replaced with individually held titles that could be sold or leased, benefiting settlers and savvy traditional elites while dispossessing the collective.[133] Historian C. A. Bayly writes, "In areas of European settlement, these new definitions of property rights could become blunt instruments to bludgeon the weak. They made it possible for white settlers, and sometimes for indigenous elites, to expropriate the common lands and labor of the original inhabitants."[134] Lawyers, most of them expatriates, also benefited. "These lawyers enriched themselves by battening on land litigation, and especially on buoyant sales of land rights, which were being expropriated from indigenous people."[135]

A common colonial legal initiative was to impose Hut taxes or head taxes on natives to secure revenues to run the colony. To pay taxes owed, natives were forced to seek employment in the money economy, supplying labor for settler farms growing export crops.[136] A colonial administrator in Rhodesia lamented in 1935 that the district officer came into contact with the African population "almost only in the guise of public authority and power – that is as the avenging magistrate and the tax collector."[137] Labor laws were also exploitative. In Papua New Guinea, for example, taxes forcing native people to seek paid work were backed by a indentured servitude system that locked plantation workers into multiyear terms of employment enforced by criminal sanctions against "desertion."[138]

---

[130] Elizabeth Kolsky, "Codification and the Rule of Colonial Difference: Criminal Procedure in British India," 23 *Law and History Review* 631, 641 (2005).

[131] Id.

[132] David Killingray, "The Maintenance of Law and Order in British Colonial Africa," 85 *African Affairs* 411, 413 (1986). This article provides an excellent look at the impact of colonial policies.

[133] See Martin Chanock, "The Law Market: The Legal Encounter in British East and Central Asia," in *European Expansion and Law*, edited by W. J. Mommsen and J. A. de Moor (Oxford: Berg Publishers 1992).

[134] C. A. Bayly, *The Birth of the Modern World, 1780–1914* (Oxford: Blackwell 2004) 112, 132.

[135] Id. 145.

[136] See John Lonsdale and Bruce Berman, "Coping with the Contradictions: The Development of the Colonial State in Kenya, 1895–1914," 20 *Journal of African History* 487 (1979).

[137] Quoted in Killingray, "The Maintenance of Law and Order in British Colonial Africa," supra 411 n. 1.

[138] See Peter Fitzpatrick, "Law and Labor in Colonial Papua New Guinea," in *The Political Economy of Law: A Third World Reader*, edited by Yash Ghai, Robin Luckham, and Francis Snyder (Delhi: Oxford University Press 1987) 130–43.

Colonial law is an unadorned instrument of oppressive rule, preserving the colonial state and advancing imperial economic enterprises, while providing scant services to indigenous people. The state legal system in many colonial settings initially made little effort to maintain social order outside colonial towns and enterprises, leaving those tasks to local leaders and institutions. This did not contravene rule-of-law ideology, at least on the surface. Indentured servitude contracts imposed legal obligations on both parties, plantation owners and laborers alike, although natives "had, in practical terms, almost no access to courts to enforce his side."[139] And while they suffered significant legal disadvantages, indigenous people were in limited ways occasionally able to invoke law against colonial government, settlers, missionaries, and local elites.[140]

Western common law and civil law systems spread around the globe through imposition by colonial powers and voluntary copying. (International law was also a companion of imperialism, discussed in Chapter 6.) An unintended consequence of empires was a mishmash of legal pluralism and hybridity through the juxtaposition of law derived from one society onto others with different cultural-political-economic arrangements, transforming both law and society in various ways.[141]

Legal theorists construct theories of law assuming law is a mirror of society that maintains social order. In colonial contexts, however, law was exploitative, clashed with prevailing social norms, and was avoided by the populace. Basic aspects of the everyday lives of indigenous peoples were governed by customary and religious law and institutions, not by colonial legal regimes, including property rights outside areas taken over by settlers. Raz's claim that law "provides the general framework within which social life takes place" was belied by colonial law. The legacy of colonization and legal transplantation continues to this day with multiple coexisting legal regimes (state law, customary law, religious law, and various mixtures) operating in the same social space throughout the Global South, giving rise to manifold conflicts and uncertainties. Attention to the imposition and spread of law by empires also corrects the erroneous image projected by historical and sociological jurisprudence, conveyed in Chapter 1, that law develops exclusively through forces and conditions *within* a society; historical and contemporary interaction with external societies and legal traditions has significant consequences for law in every society (exemplified by the spread of Roman law, discussed shortly).

Legal systems, as colonial law shows, are complexes of coercive power that do things in the name of law with no necessary or inherent connections to the society

---

[139] Id. 131.
[140] See Lauren Benton, *Law and Colonial Cultures: Legal Regimes in World History, 1400–1900* (New York: Cambridge University Press 2002).
[141] See generally Brian Z. Tamanaha, *A General Jurisprudence of Law and Society* (Oxford: Oxford University Press 2001) 112–20; Sally Engle Merry, "Law and Colonialism," 25 *Law & Society Review* 889 (1991).

they purport to rule and no inherent moral purpose. Legal systems can operate contrary to prevailing social norms and interests and morality when legal officials enforce an agenda and set of values different from that of the surrounding social group. The tendency of analytical jurisprudents to deny that legal systems can be fundamentally about coercive oppression makes it hard to account for colonial law. "Law surely is not the gunman situation writ large, and legal order is surely not to be thus simply identified with compulsion," Hart writes.[142] Yet "Gunman writ large" is an apt description of many legal regimes in human history. Legal positivists are well aware that legal systems can have immoral laws or be evil (Hart emphasized the separation thesis to highlight this[143]), but nonetheless they insist law by nature is distinct from raw coercion. "Every legal system contains obligation-imposing norms and claims legitimate authority to impose them,"[144] Green says, incorporating a moral element in law.

"If we want to explain what makes the law *the law*, we must see it as necessarily having a moral aim,"[145] Shapiro states.[146] Green asserts, "Necessarily, law deals with moral matters." "Necessarily, law makes moral claims on its subjects."[147] Law "would inevitably deal with morality's subject matter," he adds, and "a regime of "stark imperatives" would not be a system of law, for it could not "even lay claim to obligate its subjects."[148] Contrary to these confident assertions, the plain objective of colonial law was exploitation, and its claim to obligate subjects was grounded on coercive legal force, perceived as a regime of stark imperatives by indigenous people. The British Empire enacted colonial legal regimes in the name of spreading civilization to backward lands, but self-justifications uttered sincerely (or not) by colonial officials to subjugated populations that had no choice lays no claim of legitimate authority upon them.

To defend their theories of law against this critique, analytical jurisprudents might respond that colonial legal regimes had moral aims aside from their exploitative orientation (stretching morality beyond recognition), or that colonial law was a corruption or not law at all – never mind that it occurred in numerous locations around the world and consisted of statutes, magistrates, judicial decisions filled with legal analysis, and other standard legal trappings. Analytical jurisprudents who proffer this response would put themselves on the receiving end of John Austin's

---

[142] H. L. A. Hart, "Positivism and the Separation of Law and Morals," 71 *Harvard L. Rev.* 593, 603 (1958).
[143] Id. 596–99, 606, 616–17; Hart, *Concept of Law*, supra 204–07.
[144] Leslie Green, "Positivism and the Inseparability of Law and Morals," 83 *New York University Law Review* 1035, 1048 (2008).
[145] Shapiro, *Legality*, supra 215.
[146] Shapiro's view of the moral function of law appears to commit him to a weak anti-positivist position (or weak natural law position), although he lacks a moral theory to provide criteria to determine what counts as moral. See William A. Edmundson, "Why Legal Theory Is Political Philosophy," 19 *Legal Theory* 331 (2014).
[147] Leslie Green, "Legal Positivism," *Stanford Encyclopedia of Philosophy* (Fall 2009 edition), Edward N. Zalta (ed.), http://plato.stanford.edu/entries/legal-positivism/.
[148] Id.

objection to natural lawyers that a hangman would not hear pleas by a condemned man that an evil system of law is not law at all. A realistic clear-eyed view tells us that law can be constructed to advance all sorts of aims, from moral, to immoral, to having nothing to do with morality.

THE CONSOLIDATION OF LAW-STATE

Hart asserted that legal systems contain an "ultimate rule of recognition," necessary for coherence and unity of the system.[149] In addition to a claim of legitimate authority, Raz identified three essential features of legal systems: 1) "they claim to regulate any type of behavior"; 2) they claim supremacy over all other normative systems in society; and 3) they "maintain and support other forms of social group-ing." Law is "the most important institutionalized system in society" and "provides the general framework within which social life takes place."[150] "By making these claims, the law claims to provide the general framework for the conduct of all aspects of social life and sets itself up as the supreme guardian of society."[151] John Gardner likewise emphasizes "the importance . . . of every legal system's claim to be supreme among all institutionalized normative systems (including but not limited to other legal systems)."[152]

The vision of unified, supreme state law, however, is a late entry on the historical stage – and might already be passing. In many early societies, God's law was thought to be supreme law, enforced by supernatural sanction in this life or the next. Until well into the nineteenth century, state law in many locations did not have the capacity to make this claim credible. Far from inherent to the nature of law, assertions of unity and supremacy on behalf of state law is a long-term political-legal project.

Law in medieval Europe was a jumble of different laws and institutions occupying the same space, lacking any overarching hierarchy or organization.[153] Law was the product of social groups and associations, Max Weber tells us, each forming a special legal order "either constituted in its membership by such objective characteristics of birth, political, ethnic, or religious denomination, mode of life or occupation, or arose through the process of explicit fraternization."[154] These forms of law included unwritten local customary law; residual Roman law; Germanic customary law;

---

[149] Hart, *Concept of Law*, supra 102–03, 98. Alf Ross was critical of Hart's assertion, pointing out that it is "more of a fiction or a postulate than a reality." Alf Ross, "Reviews: The Concept of Law," 71 *Yale Law Journal* 1185, 1186 n. 8. (1962).

[150] Joseph Raz, *The Authority of Law* (Oxford: Oxford University Press 1979) 116–21.   [151] Id. 121.

[152] John Gardner, *Law as a Leap of Faith* (Oxford: Oxford University Press 2010) 278.

[153] See generally Olivia Robinson, Thomas Fergus, and William Gordon, *European Legal History* (London: Butterworths 1995); Harold Berman, *Law and Revolution: The Formation of the Western Legal Tradition* (Cambridge, MA: Harvard University Press 1983).

[154] Weber, *Economy and Society*, vol. 2, supra 695.

feudal law; municipal law; merchant law (*lex mercatoria*); law of specific guilds; canon law of the Roman Catholic Church; royal legislation; and revived Roman law developed in universities. Various types of courts coexisted: manorial courts staffed by barons or lords of the manor; municipal courts staffed by burghers (leading citizens); merchant courts staffed by merchants; guild courts staffed by members of the guild; church courts staffed by bishops and archdeacons; and royal courts staffed by the king or his designees. "The demarcation disputes between these laws and courts were numerous."[155] Not only did separate systems and bodies of law coexist and compete, but also, under the "personality principle," a single court could apply different bodies of law.[156] Medievalist Walter Ullmann remarked, "This complex mosaic of legal systems presented many difficulties to the application of abstract legal rule to the given set of concrete circumstances."[157]

Concepts of law produced by contemporary analytical jurisprudents do not fit medieval law. Shapiro, for instance, declares a self-evident truism about law that "In every legal system, some person or institution has supreme authority to make certain laws."[158] This statement resonates with lawyers today, but would not have been self-evident in the medieval age when local customary law – no final authority, competing versions – was a primary form of law. "Every legal system has institutions for changing the law"[159] is another Shapiro truism. However, Weber noted, customary laws "were at first not conceived as the products, or even the possible subject matter, of human enactment. ... As 'traditional' they were, in theory at least, immutable. They had to be correctly known and interpreted in accordance with established usage, but they could not be created."[160]

Also ill-fitting to medieval times are Joseph Raz's essential features of law, particularly his (and Gardner's) assertion that "they claim supremacy over all other normative systems in society." This runs contrary to the long-standing medieval principle that "special laws were to prevail over the general law of the land."[161] Raz's assertion that law claims the "authority to prohibit, permit, or impose conditions on the institution and operation of all the normative organizations to which members of its subject-community belong"[162] is a projection of modern views of unified territorial law, which was absent in the Middle Ages. At the time, "Law was seen as central to a person's identity, a function of his or her ethnic heritage."[163]

---

[155]   Raoul van Caenegem, *Legal History: A European Perspective* (London: Hambledon Press 1991) 19.
[156]   See Van Caenegem, *Legal History*, supra 117–18; Patrick Geary, *The Myth of Nations: The Medieval Origins of Modern Europe* (Princeton, NJ: Princeton University Press 2003) 152–54.
[157]   Walter Ullmann, *The Medieval Idea of Law* (London: Methune 1969) 71.
[158]   Shapiro, *Legality*, supra 13.   [159]   Id.   [160]   Weber, *Economy and Society*, vol. 2., supra 760.
[161]   Id. 852.
[162]   Joseph Raz, *Practical Reason and Norms*, 2nd ed. (Oxford: Oxford University Press 1999) 151–54.
[163]   James A Brundage, *The Medieval Origins of the Legal Profession: Canonists, Civilians, and Courts* (Chicago. IL: University of Chicago Press 2008) 30.

Under this view, "every man was entitled everywhere to be judged by that tribal law by which he 'professed' to live."[164] No single legal regime claimed or held supremacy over all others (popes claimed supremacy for canon law on what it covered, though not entirely successfully[165]). "The result was the coexistence of numerous 'law communities,'" Weber wrote, "the autonomous jurisdictions of which overlapped, the compulsory, political association being only one such autonomous jurisdiction in so far as it existed at all."[166]

What analytical jurisprudents offer as truisms about law are contemporary assumptions based on an idealized image of state law. But even when applied to the present, their intuition-based assertions are contestable.[167] The assertion that every legal system has a supreme authority is problematic with respect to the European Union (EU).[168] The EU manifests constitutional pluralism, Neil Walker and other theorists have argued, with unsettled competing assertions of final authority on important legal matters.[169] "For the most part national courts have not accepted that EU law is the supreme law of the land. But nor have they simply assumed that national constitutional law is the supreme law of the land."[170] "This confers to EU law a kind of contested or negotiated normative authority."[171]

The consolidation of the state system across Europe took several centuries to achieve.[172] Monarchs had first to establish their separation from or dominance over rival sources of religious, political, and military power.[173] Internally, this meant pushing the church out of political affairs and pacifying major nobles by buying or co-opting their allegiance and denuding their military capability; externally, this meant absorbing neighboring territories through alliances (royal marriages) or

---

[164] Weber, *Economy and Society*, supra 696.   [165] Id. 830.   [166] Id. 697.

[167] Neil MacCormick pointed out two decades ago that theories of the sovereign state no longer applied to states within the European Union, raising serious questions about legal positivist theories of law. Neil MacCormick, "Beyond the Sovereign State," 56 *Modern Law Review* 1 (1993).

[168] An overview is provided in Julio Baquero Cruz, "The Legacy of the Maastricht-Urteil and the Pluralist Movement," 14 *European Law Journal* 389 (2008); see also Neil Walker, "The Idea of Constitutional Pluralism," 65 *Modern Law Review* 317 (2002). For a critical response, see Martin Loughlin, "Constitutional Pluralism: An Oxymoron?" 3 *Global Constitutionalism* 9 (2014).

[169] See Neil Walker, "Constitutional Pluralism Revisited," 22 *European Law Journal* 333 (2016).

[170] Mathias Kumm, "How Does European Union Law Fit into the World of Public Law?" in *Political Theory of the European Union*, edited by Jurgen Neyer and Antje Wiener (Oxford: Oxford University Press 2011) 127. This assertion applies not only to the substantive law, but also to which courts have final say.

[171] Miguel Poiares Maduro, "Courts and Pluralism: Essay on a Theory of Judicial Adjudication in the Context of Legal and Constitutional Pluralism," in *Ruling the World: Constitutionalism, International Law, and Global Governance*, edited by Jeffery L. Dunoff and Joel P. Trachtman (Cambridge: Cambridge University Press 2009) 357.

[172] See Martin van Creveld, *The Rise and Decline of the State* (Cambridge: Cambridge University Press 1999).

[173] For a detailed account of these developments, see Michael Mann, *The Sources of Social Power: Volume 1: A History of Power from the Beginning to AD 1760*, 2nd ed. (Cambridge: Cambridge University Press 2012); Michael Mann, *The Sources of Social Power: Volume 2: The Rise of Classes and Nation-States, 1760–1914*, 2nd ed. (Cambridge: Cambridge University Press 2012).

martial adventures and defending borders against incursion from other monarchs. The Reformation diminished the grip of the Church, allowing monarchs in Protestant countries to seize church assets and restrict ecclesiastical courts (though not finally deprived of jurisdiction in England until the 1850s[174]). The 1648 Treaty of Westphalia divided Europe into separate territories, reinforcing control by sovereigns over internal affairs.

State-building monarchial officials established administrative apparatuses that oversaw tax collection, law enforcement, and judging. Previously the main source of funding for monarchs had been revenues from their feudal holdings, special customs, and fees collected by royal courts; high officials were members of the king's household staff; many offices were privately owned, with occupants deriving rents from their official activities. A pivotal bureaucratic development was to create a separation between public and private positions, with public monies paying temporary holders of public offices.[175] Land was surveyed, free-hold tenure was created, and titles were recorded; people were counted and registered, border controls and passports were established, weights and measures were standardized, and administrative records were kept – much of this involving legal mechanisms.

Consolidation of law in the state involved establishing legal offices paying regular salaries from the state, creating and staffing courts not beholden to local magnates, and enacting territory-wide legal codes. In multiethnic and multi-religious societies where sub-communities recognized their own bodies of law, accommodations had to be made, and it took generations before comprehensive legal codes would be borne out in social life. The institutionalization of law in the state also involved building the legal profession, training people in specialized legal knowledge and legal practices. Professional police forces separate from the military were created in the nineteenth century at the national, regional, and municipal levels, and state-run prisons were built.[176] Only when a full comple-ment of bodies of law and effective legal institutions were created and consolidated in state offices, rationalized, and hierarchically organized did the unified vision of the law-state approximate reality.

The law-state with a monopoly over law reached its peak in the late twentieth century, when globalizing and privatizing forces began diminishing aspects of state monopoly, but even then the ideal was not reality in many lands. The hybrid and coexisting legal systems discussed in the previous section continued to persist

---

[174] R. B. Outhwaite, *The Rise and Fall of the English Ecclesiastical Courts, 1500–1860* (Cambridge: Cambridge University Press 2006).

[175] See Mann, *The Rise of Classes and Nation-States*, supra chapter 13; S. E. Finer, *The History of Government: Empires, Monarchies, and the Modern State* (Oxford: Oxford University Press 1999) 1266, 1298–99.

[176] See Mann, *The Rise of Classes and Nation-States*, supra 404; see Van Creveld, *The Rise and Decline of the State*, supra.

following decolonization. A recent report issued by the World Bank legal department finds:

> In many developing countries, customary systems operating outside of the state regime are often the dominant form of regulation and dispute resolution, covering up to 90% of the population in parts of Africa. In Sierra Leone, for example, approximately 85% of the population falls under the jurisdiction of customary law, defined under the Constitution as "the rules which, by custom, are applicable to particular communities in Sierra Leone." Customary tenure covers 75% of land in most African countries, affecting 90% of land transactions in countries like Mozambique and Ghana. . . . In many of these countries, systems of justice seem to operate almost completely independently of the official state system.[177]

The unified state legal system analytical jurisprudents present as the epitome of law is a relatively recent invention. Through the nineteenth century and into the twentieth century a range of situations existed: power was diffused among local ruling groups; powerful religious rivals to the state exerted legal authority; large private companies exercised legal and governmental powers; and tribal chiefs asserted political and legal authority in many areas throughout Asia, Africa, and the Pacific.[178] Historian Bayly writes, "By the late nineteenth century, most regimes throughout the world were *attempting* to control closely defined territories by means of uniform administrative, legal, and educational structures."[179] The legal effort was stymied by a lack of institutionalized governmental infrastructure, the uneasy coexistence of transplanted state law alongside customary and religious legal regimes, and the fact that throughout the formerly colonized world, state boundaries were drawn with scant attention to preexisting alignments, mashing together communities divided by ethnicity, religion, and/or language, while conversely also separating across territorial borders what were previously unified cultural communities. State consolidation advanced by leaps in the twentieth century, particularly through wars and their aftermath, though not to the same extent everywhere. In Israel today, to offer a final example, in response to the question – "If a contradiction arose between religious law and a state court ruling, which would you follow?" – 97 percent of ultra-Orthodox Jews and 56 percent of Muslims said they would follow their religious law.[180]

---

[177] Leila Chirayath, Caroline Sage, and Michael Woolcock, *Customary Law and Policy Reform: Engaging with the Plurality of Justice Systems* (World Bank Legal Department Paper 2005) 3. For a compelling illustration, see Haider Ala Hamoudi, Wasfi H. Al-Saharaa, and Aqeel Al-Dahhan, "The Resolution of Disputes in State and Tribal Law in the South of Iraq," in Michael Helfland, *Negotiating State and Non-state Law* (New York: Cambridge University Press 2015).

[178] Bayly, *Birth of the Modern World*, supra 254.   [179] Id. 247 (emphasis added).

[180] Tamar Hermann, Ella Heller, Chanan Cohen, Dana Bublil, and Fadi Omar, *The Israeli Democracy Index 2016* (Jerusalem: The Democracy Institute 2016) 84–85, 176, https://en.idi.org.il/media/7811/democracy-index-2016-eng.pdf.

LEGALITY AND FORMALISM AS A PROFESSIONAL
LEGAL CULTURE

An essential component of consolidation of state legal systems has been a body of knowledge, institutions, and practices revolving around legality – collectively constituting a professional legal culture – securing a monopoly position in the construction of state law.[181] "Law," Alan Watson writes, "is above all and primarily the culture of the lawyers and especially of the lawmakers – that is, of those lawyers who, whether as legislators, jurists, or judges, have control of the accepted mechanisms of legal change. Legal development is the product of their culture; and social, economic, and political factors impinge upon legal consciousness only through their consciousness."[182] This is an overstatement. Surrounding social factors pervasively permeate law, as conveyed in Chapter 1, but Watson is correct that the professional legal culture shapes and affects the operation of law.

Jurists' creation of a pan-European Roman law is an unparalleled example.[183] After the collapse of the Roman Empire, Roman law had fallen into disuse in Western Europe, remaining in vestigial forms within local law and canon law.[184] The remarkable revival and spread of Roman law following the rediscovery of Justinian's Code in the final quarter of the eleventh century has been attributed by scholars to several factors. It coincided with papal reforms that extricated the Church from secular authorities, both thereafter using statist elements of Roman law to construct their regimes.[185] It overlapped with the early establishment of universities, particularly at Bologna, which taught Roman law as body of learning.[186] It coincided with a rapid increase in city populations and in long-distance trade.[187] "The new society and economy that began to emerge during the twelfth century required effective methods of dealing with commercial contracts, credit and banking, property transfers, insurance, corporations, municipal government, and particularly in northern Europe, the increasing centralization of royal governments. The *Corpus iuris civilis* offered a system of commercial and municipal law that could be adapted to meet those needs."[188] The hierarchical state and

---

[181] Lawrence Friedman has developed a sophisticated account of legal culture that encompasses both the professional culture as well as general public views toward law. Lawrence Friedman, "Legal Culture and Social Development," 4 *Law and Society Review* 29 (1969). Here I use the term in a looser, shorthand sense to encompass knowledge, institutions, attitudes, and practices of legal professionals.

[182] Alan Watson, *The Evolution of Law* (Baltimore, MD: John Hopkins University Press 1985) 118.

[183] H. Coing, "Roman Law and the National Legal Systems," in *Classical Influences on Western Thought A.D. 1650–1870*, edited by R. R. Bolgar (Cambridge: Cambridge University Press 1977) 30–31.

[184] See Harold J. Berman, *Law and Revolution: The Formation of the Western Legal Tradition* (Cambridge, MA: Harvard University Press 1983) 199–205.

[185] Id. 520–38.   [186] Id. chapter 6.

[187] The European population doubled between 1050 and 1200 and urban populations multiplied by ten. Id. 534.

[188] Brundage, *The Medieval Origins of the Legal Profession*, supra 77.

absolutist authority within Roman law also served the interests of rulers seeking to centralize power.[189]

The diffusion of Roman law was accomplished through the efforts of legal professionals and academic lawyers trained in the Code at universities who brought Roman law concepts, procedures, and forms of legal reasoning to courts across Europe.[190] *Ius commune* was an amalgamation of canon law and Roman law, so called because it was the common law of jurists across Western Europe.[191] Roman law was not positive law enacted by polities, but learned law, which served as ideal reason-based law (*ratio scripta*) invoked to evaluate or supplement positive law, canon law, and customary law.[192] The *ius commune* developed by jurists involved Latin language, highly technical procedures, specific legal provisions, and modes of legal reasoning beyond the ken of most lay people, creating conditions for a monopoly by legal professionals.[193] In France, where customary law was codified, Roman law was used to fill gaps; in Germany, where customary law remained unwritten, lawyers and courts invoked Roman law more comprehensively. Social protests against this trend were voiced loudly in sixteenth-century Germany, when "the arriviste civil lawyers, with their new practices, incomprehensible to laymen, and the fat salaries which they enjoyed, were further identified with the disappearance of the old ways."[194]

Civil codes modeled on Roman law were enacted across the continent. The French Code Civil of 1804 has Roman law elements, and the German Civil Code of 1900 "is profoundly marked by Roman law."[195] "Roman law did live on in the codes themselves, since these took their systematic and conceptual framework from it and also many principles and rules, especially in the fields of contract, succession and testamentary dispositions."[196] A second wave of diffusion occurred through colonization, as mentioned earlier. "In terms of substantive rules, one legacy of Roman law has been a considerable measure of uniformity throughout the legal systems of western Europe, stretching beyond this area into regions which adopted European-based codes."[197] In addition, the Roman law notion *ius gentium*

---

[189] See R. C. van Caenegem, *European Law in the Past and the Future: Unity and Diversity over Two Millennia* (Cambridge: Cambridge University Press 2002) 75–79; A. D. E. Lewis and D. J. Ibbetson, "The Roman Law Tradition," in *The Roman Law Tradition*, edited by A. D. E. Lewis and D. J. Ibbetson (Cambridge: Cambridge University Press 1994) 12.

[190] See generally Lewis and Ibbetson, "The Roman Law Tradition," supra. My discussion of Roman law is indebted to this essay and Stein's book *Roman Law in European History*, supra.

[191] See Van Caenegem, *European Law in the Past and the Future*, supra 13–19.

[192] Berman, *Law and Revolution*, supra 204–05, 532.

[193] See Brundage, *The Medieval Origins of the Legal Profession*, supra chapters 4, 5, and 9.

[194] Peter Stein, *Roman Law in European History* (Cambridge: Cambridge University Press 1999) 92.

[195] Van Caenegem, *European Law in the Past and the Future*, supra 5; the Roman law influence on the Code civil, 3–4.

[196] H. Coing, "Roman Law and the National Legal Systems," in *Classical Influences on Western Thought A.D. 1650–1870*, edited by R. R. Bolgar (Cambridge: Cambridge University Press 1977) 36.

[197] Ibbetson and Lewis, *The Roman Law Tradition*, supra 10.

(universally recognized rules) as well as selected rules from the Code influenced the development of both natural law and international law via the writings of Grotius and others.[198] Roman law thus left an indelible stamp on law and legal thought in various ways across the globe.

Over the same late medieval period, the common law developed in England, with the legal profession exercising a monopoly through complex writ pleadings and legal language (Law French) accessible only to initiates and control of training and admissions to the bar through the Inns of Court. The common law tradition would also subsequently spread around the world with colonization.

A prominent feature of the professional culture of legality is legal formalism. Formalism basically involves adherence to prescriptions. Legal rules are by nature formal in the sense that they are set forth in general terms in advance and dictate outcomes according to their terms. To follow a rule entails doing what the rule requires without factoring in other possible considerations or the consequences that might follow (though decision makers interpreting and applying rules may be subconsciously and consciously influenced by background social attitudes and personal biases). When jurists overlay the inherent formality of legal rules with efforts to logically rationalize and systematize law, the result was an abstract, technical, demanding legal formalism. As Max Weber portrayed German legal science of his day, law "represents an integration of all analytically derived legal propositions in such a way that they constitute a logically clear and internally consistent, and, at least in theory, gapless system of rules under which, it is implied, all conceivable fact situations must be capable of being logically subsumed lest their order lack an effective guarantee."[199] Weber identified logical systemization of law as an advanced stage of legal development involving "systematic elaboration of law and professionalized administration of justice by persons who have received their legal training in a learned and formally logical manner."[200]

The common law system did not claim the same overarching logical systematicity because it is constructed through accretion by judges in individual cases, but it created a different type of formalism that revolved around adherence to the writ system. Formalism of this latter sort was present in Germanic customary law as well as in Roman law, and one can find "all the world over, professional attachment to form for form's sake,"[201] Frederick Pollock remarked.

The tendency of legal professionals to embrace formalism relates to several aspects of legality. General rules are formal by nature. Traditionalism and fixity within law, its conservative cast, anchor and give weight to longstanding rules and doctrines. The rationalization of legal concepts (working out their content and interrelations) and the effort to achieve overarching coherence and consistency generates internal legal imperatives. Additionally, as Bentham, Weber, and

---

[198]   See id. 7, 13–14; Stein, *Roman Law in European History*, supra 13, 94–96, 107–10.
[199]   Weber, *Economy and Society*, supra 656.   [200]   Id. 882.
[201]   Frederick Pollock, *The Genius of the Common Law* (New York: AMS Press [1911] 1967) 17.

many others have pointed out, legal professionals benefit financially by monopolizing law as an artificial formalized system of knowledge, procedures, practices, and modes of reasoning.

Owing to formalistic aspects of law, legal results regularly diverge in content, operation, and outcome from expectations and desires of laypersons. This occurs, Weber says, when "the facts of life are juridically 'construed' in order to make them fit the abstract propositions of law."[202] Consequently, "'lawyers' law' has never been and never will be brought into conformity with lay expectations unless it totally renounces that formal character which is immanent in it."[203]

The social growth and consolidation of state law, in sum, has included the entrenchment of a body of legal language, knowledge, institutions, practices, methods and modes of action, legal formalism, demands for internal consistency and coherence, created and perpetuated by jurists – the purveyors of the legal system. Learning the law and learning to conduct legal activities entails undergoing indoctrination into a shared overlapping complex of legal meaning and practices, enabling lawyers to "see things ... through law spectacles," as Karl Llewellyn put it.[204] Lawyers and judges engaging in legal tasks think within the shared legal meaning system of the professional legal culture, though they don law spectacles with differently colored tints reflecting their different background views and values (surrounding social influences thereby seep into law).[205]

Most areas of modern knowledge, not law alone, have undergone high degrees of specialization, rendering them impenetrable to outsiders. The difference is that law courses through the society, economy, and polity in ways that unavoidably affect people's lives. Social issues, disputes, and influences pass through legal filters, often thereby transformed when brought into legal arenas. State legal systems are not fully transparent mirrors of society (and especially are not mirrors when legal regimes have been transplanted from elsewhere), but rather they are institutionalized systems encrusted by the professional legal culture that constructs legal products within its own terms.

THE THICKENING OF STATE LAW

Law has traveled an enormous distance in the past 10,000 years of human social development, gradually for the bulk of this period, then by bounds in the past several centuries. The United States is illustrative. To work as a lawyer in mid-eighteenth-century America, a person read law books and learned the craft in

---

[202] Id. 885   [203] Id.
[204] Karl Llewellyn, *The Common Law Tradition* (Boston: Little Brown 1960) 19–20.
[205] For a detailed explication of law as a system of shared meaning, practices, and institutions, See Brian Z. Tamanaha, *Realistic Socio-legal Theory: Pragmatism and a Social Theory of Law* (Oxford: Clarendon Press 1997) 142–52, 167–75.

apprenticeships; most were not fully employed as professional lawyers, but worked as planters, clerks, or merchants who engaged in legal tasks on the side.[206] A handful of law schools trained small numbers of students.[207] Law books were few in number, and those that existed were from England.[208] Many state judges in lower and higher courts were laymen without legal training, usually from prominent families.[209] Judicial decisions were based on cultural and Christian norms,[210] the community sense of justice or right declared by judges, common law doctrines carried over from England, and local ordinances, regulations, and legislation. Judges would sit on both trial and appellate levels, riding on horseback through the circuit hearing cases.[211] At the beginning of the nineteenth century, there were no regularly published reports of written opinion of state courts, no treatises on American law, and no legal journals.[212] Nascent forms of bureaucratic administration with legal rules and procedures took shape in the early nineteenth century.[213]

Then came, slowly at first, escalating dramatically in the final decades of the nineteenth century in sync with urbanization, the differentiation and solidification of government organizations and the state and federal legal systems. Up through the second half of the nineteenth century, judges collected fees from cases, prosecuting attorneys were paid for convictions, "tax ferrets" were paid percentages of tax evasions they reported, police received rewards for recovering property, jailors collected fees from inmates for privileges, among other examples in which individuals who carried out government and legal activities were paid by fees and bounties.[214] Direct payment for services was gradually abolished, replaced with the payment of regular salaries tied to offices, followed by the implementation of a merit-based civil service system for public employees with legal protections against interference in the execution of their public functions.[215]

Coinciding with these developments was the positivist view that law could be declared by legislative fiat and, along with it, a view of law as an instrument for solving the problems of industrializing, urban society,[216] as well as to secure personal

---

[206]   Lawrence M. Friedman, *The History of American Law* (New York: Touchstone 1985) 98–100.
[207]   Id. 318–22.   [208]   Id. 102.   [209]   Id. 125–27.
[210]   On references to Christianity in early U.S. common law, see Calvin Woodward, "The Limits of Legal Realism: An Historical Perspective," 54 *Virginia Law Review* 689, 691–94 (1968).
[211]   Friedman, *The History of American Law*, supra 140–41.
[212]   For an overview of the growth of legal publications in the nineteenth century, see Richard A. Danner, "More than Decisions: Reviews of American Law Reports in the Pre-West Era," http://papers.ssrn .com/sol3/papers.cfm?abstract_id=2622299&download=yes.
[213]   For a concise overview of the evolution of administrative law, see Jed Handelsman Shugerman, "The Legitimacy of Administrative Law," 50 *Tulsa Law Review* 301 (2015).
[214]   Nicholas R. Parillo, *Against the Profit Motive: The Salary Revolution in American Government, 1780–1940* (New Haven, CT: Yale University Press 2013) 1.
[215]   An overview of these developments is Jon D. Michaels, "Running Government like a Business … Then and Now," 128 *Harvard Law Review* 1152 (2015).
[216]   William J. Novak, "The Legal Origins of the Modern American State," in *Looking Back at Law's Century*, edited by Austin Sarat, Bryant Garth, and Robert A. Kagan (Ithaca, NY: Cornell University Press 2002) 265–67.

and group interests. Legislatures were willing "to legislate in ways that would deliberately change the societies they governed," including regulating health, morals, economic activities, and the education of citizens.[217] Administrative agencies were created – among them the Interstate Commerce Commission, Department of Interior, Department of Justice, Treasury Department, Food and Drug Administration, etc. – and given legal powers to carry out designated tasks.[218]

Greater active creation and use of law and rapidly expanding economic activities were accompanied by many more lawyers and legal institutions.[219] "The number of lawyers in the United States grew from an estimated 39,000 in 1870 to 161,000 by 1930; and as one might expect, the number of degree-granting law schools with a three-year course of study grew from seven in 1890 to more than 170 in 1931."[220] State and national bar associations formed to establish standards for the legal profession, anxious to restrict access to the bar, raise the reputation of the bar, and enhance the quality of legal services.[221] The number of lawyers reached 1 million in 2000,[222] with 200 law schools churning out more than 40,000 new graduates annually. Starting with zero law journals in the United States in 1800, increasing to around 120 law journals by 1960, there were more than 600 law journals collectively publishing thousands of articles annually by 2000.[223]

City, state, and federal courts are organized as bureaucratic hierarchies with separate trial, appellate, and high courts served by legally trained judges, supported by administrative staffs. The judiciary has differentiated into juvenile courts, domestic relations courts, small claims courts, housing courts, customs courts, social security courts, immigration courts, tax courts, bankruptcy courts, workman's compensation courts, labor and employment courts, intellectual property courts, and securities claims courts.

The sheer number of government bodies exercising legal capacities is hard to fathom. Local, state, and federal governments altogether comprise about 90,000 separate units. At the local level alone, there are "3,033 counties, 19,492 municipal governments, 16,519 town or township governments, 37,381 special district governments";[224] there are 18,000 local and state police agencies, supplemented by a host of separate federal police agencies; a total of 1,500 local, state, and federal prisons, along with privately run prisons, collectively houses more than 2 million prisoners.[225] The federal executive branch contains more than 130 agencies and

[217] Parillo, *Against the Profit Motive*, supra 31.
[218] Novak, "Legal Origins of the Modern American State," supra 264–65.
[219] James Willard Hurst, *The Growth of American Law: The Law Makers* (Boston, MA: Little Brown 1950) 70–74, 185–89.
[220] Novak, "The Legal Origins of the Modern American State," supra 263.
[221] Friedman, *History of American Law*, supra 29–43.
[222] Lawrence M. Friedman, *American Law in the 20th Century* (New Haven, CT: Yale University Press 2002) 8, 29.
[223] See John G. Browning, "Fixing Law Review," *Inside Higher Education*, November 19, 2012, at www.insidehighered.com/views/2012/11/19/essay-criticizing-law-reviews-and-offering-some-reform-ideas.
[224] Novak, "The Myth of the 'Weak' American State," supra 765.   [225] Id.

commissions, and states add many more; there are ninety-four federal judicial districts, as well as an uncounted profusion of state courts.[226] Though precise figures are hard to come by, at the state level alone, nearly 50 million newly filed or reactivated civil and criminal cases exist in a given year (not counting a similar number of traffic and local ordinance violations).[227] Federal district courts see 370,000 new civil and 80,000 new criminal filings each year, along with more than 900,000 bankruptcy filings.[228] Legal services constitute about 2 percent of the nation's Gross Domestic Product, more than $250 billion.[229]

"The twentieth century was the century of the 'law explosion,'" exclaims legal historian Lawrence Friedman. "The sheer size and scale of the legal system grew fantastically."[230] As one indication, the Code of Federal Regulations exploded from nearly 23,000 pages in 1960, to almost 55,000 in 1970, to more than 174,000 pages in 2012.[231] "Meanwhile, every state, city, and town, as well as the federal government, is busy churning out new laws, ordinances, and rules. The books of reported cases, federal and state, are also growing faster than ever before; there are thousands and thousands of volumes on the shelves of the law libraries, and millions of bits and bytes in cyberspace."[232]

The robust thickening of law in the United States has not occurred to the same extent everywhere. Societies in the Global North are on the same trajectory. Many societies in the Global South have far less-developed state legal systems: far fewer lawyers, fewer institutions for training lawyers, less legal material and less developed legal knowledge, and fewer courts. With a population of 7.5 million, for example, Rwanda at the turn of the twentieth century was served by about fifty lawyers, twenty prosecutors, and fifty newly recruited judges;[233] Malawi had 300 lawyers for 9 million people.[234] State law does not develop in isolation – it requires supportive social factors, including academic institutions for training, sufficient economic

---

[226] Id.

[227] State Court Caseload Statistics, Bureau of Justice Statistics, www.bjs.gov/index.cfm?ty=tp&tid=30. See also Marc Galanter, "The Vanishing Trail: An Examination of Trials and Related Matters in Federal State Courts," 1 *Journal of Empirical Legal Studies* 459, 507, 512 (2004).

[228] See Judicial Business 2014, U.S. Courts, www.uscourts.gov/statistics-reports/judicial-business-2014.

[229] Rachel M. Zahorsky, "Law Stagnation May Have Started Before the Recession – And It May be a Sign of Lasting Change," *ABA Journal*, July 1, 2011, B www.abajournal.com/magazine/article/paradigm_shift/. Estimates of the dollar value of legal services vary between $250 billion and $290 billion depending on the year and the source.

[230] Friedman, *American Law in the Twentieth Century*, supra 7.

[231] See Wayne Crews and Ryan Young, "Twenty Years of Non-stop Regulation," *The American Spectator*, June 5, 2013, http://spectator.org/articles/55475/twenty-years-non-stop-regulation#!; Robert Longley, "Federal Regulations," *About News*, http://usgovinfo.about.com/od/uscongress/a/fedregulations_2.htm.

[232] Friedman, *American Law in the Twentieth Century*, supra 7.

[233] Laure-Helene Piron, "Time to Learn, Time to Act in Africa," in *Promoting the Rule of Law Abroad*, edited by Thomas Carothers (Washington, DC: Carnegie Endowment 2006) 275.

[234] 291.

resources to fund legal institutions, and supportive public attitudes committed to legality, among many other conditions.

THE SOCIAL EVOLUTION OF LAW

Law is a social growth that has changed in form and function in the course of human history. Early on, when humans lived in hunter-gatherer bands, law at its most rudimentary established protections and restrictions relating to property, persons, family unions, and sacred matters – the basics necessary for physically vulnerable, comfort-seeking, social-sexual beings with cooperative-competitive tendencies to live together, procure adequate food and shelter, survive, reproduce, and create a collectively cohesive and meaningful existence.

When communities settled and markedly increased in size, forming complex chiefdoms and early states, additional institutions coalesced as an aspect of social complexity, adding structure and organized force to law, creating legal systems tied to the polity. This involved a phase transformation after which law acquired a different form and set of capabilities, most importantly organized tribunals and coercive enforcement. Legal systems continued the basic functions of law maintaining social intercourse just mentioned, while also structuring and enforcing social, economic, and political hierarchy, and enhancing the power of the polity and the legal system itself. States that became empires utilized law as a coercive mechanism to enforce imperial domination and advance imperial economic interests.

In the modern period, with legal institutionalization and entrenchment coinciding with the multiplication of organizations in society generally, and with the growth and consolidation of government organizations in particular, a second-phase transformation has occurred. Law is created at will and has become a multifunctional instrument backed by organized coercion to advance the purposes of government organizations and social, economic, and political interests that influence them. Legal professionals are the handmaidens of specialized legal knowledge and practices and gatekeepers through whom the state legal apparatus operates. The implications of these developments for law and society are elaborated in the next chapter. An additional extension of law as a social growth, taken up in Chapter 6, involves organizations and regulatory regimes dealing with interaction between and across polities.

When laid out in chronological order, it looks like a historical trajectory, with later stages replacing earlier. That is misleading. Residuals, variations, and legacies of earlier forms of law can be found around the world today, interacting with other forms of law present in the same social space. Law exists in multiple coexisting and interpenetrating forms. There is no reason to think we have reached a final stage or endpoint of legal change or that every society is on a uniform and inevitable trajectory of legal development. Law is subject to historical and social influences, is highly variable, and is continuously in the making.

5

Law in the Age of Organizations

Theories of law have failed to account for fundamental changes that have taken place in law and society with the rise of organizations. Ed Rubin observed a quarter century ago that H. L. A. Hart's theory of law is inconsistent with a great deal of legislation and administrative law,[1] though legal theorists have paid no heed. Here I present a theory of law more fitting to modern law. Theories of law propounded by Lon Fuller and H. L. A. Hart, and most jurisprudents, revolve around rule systems of social ordering, but state law does much else that does not fit this characterization. To provide a more refined perspective, I distinguish law as core rules of social interaction from government uses of law, and I identify three subtypes of the latter. Then I elaborate the differences and interaction between these two orientations, in particular engaging with Hayek's notion of background legal rules. Following these theoretical clarifications, I show how the combined result of uses of law in connection with organizations and instrumental uses of law by government gives rise to a relatively fixed legal fabric within society. Then I portray courts as organizations that process cases, a markedly different perspective from standard legal theory discussions of judging. Finally, I explain how this view of law points to a clarification of the status of Hart's theory and theories of law by analytical jurisprudents generally.

A SOCIETY OF ORGANIZATIONS THROUGH LAW

Organizations rapidly ascended in the course of the nineteenth century and proliferated in the twentieth century. Urbanization coincided with and propelled the multiplication of organizations. "In 1900, about 12–15 percent of humankind lived in cities; by 1950, some 30 percent did; but by 2001, more than half did."[2] "The developed world is now about 80% urban and this is expected to be true for the

---

[1] Edward L. Rubin, "Law and Legislation in the Administrative State," 89 *Columbia L. Rev.* 369 (1989). Rubin's analysis of legislation and administrative law is illuminating. The theory I sketch is pitched at a higher level of generality than his more detailed breakdown of legislation.

[2] J. R. McNeill & William H. McNeill, *The Human Web: A Bird's-Eye View of World History* (New York: W.W. Norton & Co. 2003) 282.

entire planet by around 2050."[3] Organizations sustain life in modern cities: "Dependence on heat and light supplied by electricity, on plumbing linked to water supply systems, on automobiles and on the unobstructed roadways they require, on telephonic communications, on regular garbage collection and disposal, to mention only the most obvious examples long antedating the products of recent electronic technology, binds people to myriads of others in far-flung system networks."[4] The vast bulk of this is conducted through organizations. People in cities are born in organizations, supplied food by organizations, educated in organizations, employed in organizations, entertained by organizations, and buried by organizations when they die. We live in "a society of organizations," "the key phenomenon of our time."[5]

Organizations typically are structured as bureaucracies,[6] which consist of functionally differentiated offices held by people engaging in particular tasks, arranged in hierarchical layers with higher offices exercising power over lower ones, collectively functioning in a coordinated fashion to carry out purposes.[7] "The principle of hierarchical office authority is found in all bureaucratic structures: in state and ecclesiastical structures as well as in large party organizations and private enterprises," Max Weber observed. "It does not matter for the character of bureaucracy whether its authority is called 'private' or 'public.'"[8] Organizations operate through internal rules and regulations and standard practices and procedures, from the start and length of the workday, to what to wear and how to comport oneself, to what tasks to carry out, to modes of communication with others. Informal norms and cultures, sometimes contrary to and more powerful than stated formal rules, significantly shape what people within organizations do and condition the operation of formal arrangements. Hence, the same formal rules play out differently within different organizational cultures.

The social growth and consolidation of state law described in the preceding chapter was part and parcel of the social growth and consolidation of bureaucratic organizations within society more generally. The shift to regular payment tied to offices, growth of legal education institutions, specialization of legal knowledge, creation of specialized courts, and so on, were not unique to state law but aspects of commensurate developments across society. Governments, educational institutions, private corporations, and religions and churches all underwent the same kinds of

---

[3]   Luis Bettencourt and Geoffrey West, "A Unified Theory of Urban Living," 467 *Nature* 912, 912 (2010).

[4]   Dennis H. Wrong, *The Problem of Order: What Unites and Divides Society* (Cambridge, MA: Harvard University Press 1994) 233.

[5]   Charles Perrow, "A Society of Organizations," 20 *Theory and Society* 725, 725 (1991).

[6]   This discussion draws on Max Weber, *Economy and Society*, vol. 2, edited by Guenther Roth and Claus Wittich (Berkeley: University of California Press 1968) 956–59.

[7]   S. R. H. Jones, "The Organization of Work: A Historical Dimension," 3 *Journal of Economic Behavior and Organization* 117 (1982). On the competitive advantages of managerial hierarchies, integrated capabilities, and organizational learning, see Alfred D. Chandler, "Organizational Capabilities and the Economic History of the Industrial Enterprise," 6 *Journal of Economic Perspectives* 79 (1992).

[8]   Weber, *Economy and Society*, supra 957.

bureaucratic consolidation, formalization, and specialization in the course of the nineteenth and twentieth centuries.[9]

Law serves multiple pivotal roles in organizations. Many government agencies, businesses, and other types of organizations are created through enabling acts. Their form, function, existence, and activities are shaped by and through law. Contracts between organizations and their employees construct internal employment relationships, and organizations engage in external transactions through contracts with suppliers of goods and services, customers, and sources of financing (investors, lenders). Organizations exercise property rights in the acquisition, preservation, and disposition of assets. Legal personality allows entities to sue and be sued, to commit crimes and torts, to exercise rights like free speech, to be like a natural person in these and many other respects.

Business corporations in particular have been influenced by law and have influenced law in turn. Previously created by legislative act one at a time, general incorporation laws passed across the United States in the mid-nineteenth century paved the way for their rapid multiplication.[10] The legal treatment of corporations is tailored to make them advantageous economic vehicles. Limited liability caps the financial exposure of owners, shielding them from responsibility for debts, torts, contract breaches, or other actions of the corporation. Separate legal personhood allows the corporation to function independently of owners, sequestering its assets from owners, enabling corporations to make commitments and borrow more easily.[11] Regulated stock markets have been created to allow share owners to withdraw their financial investment without disrupting the corporation. In response to the growing presence, power, and influence of business corporations, reams of state and federal regulatory regimes have been constructed, including corporate law, securities regulations, banking and finance laws, labor and employment laws, and consumer protection laws, among others. Large corporations and large government are joined at the hip.

JURISPRUDENTIAL BLINDNESS TO ASPECTS OF STATE LAW

Legal theorists typically characterize law as a rule system maintaining social order. Lon Fuller described law as "the enterprise of subjecting human conduct to the

---

[9] A superb account of the bureaucratic consolidation and formalization of religious organizations around the world is provided in C. A. Bayly, *The Birth of the Modern World 1780–1914* (Oxford: Blackwell 2004) chapter 9.

[10] See generally Willard Hurst, *The Legitimacy of the Business Corporation in the Law of the United States 1870–1970* (Charlottesville: University of Virginia Press 1970). William G. Roy, *Socializing Capital: The Rise of the Large Industrial Corporation in America* (Princeton, NJ: Princeton University Press 1997). Margaret M. Blair, "Locking in Capital: What Corporate Law Achieved for Business Organizations in the Nineteenth Century," 51 *UCLA L. Rev.* 387 (2003).

[11] See Henry Hansmann, Reinier Kraakman, and Richard Squire, "The New Business Entities in Evolutionary Perspective," [2005] *University of Illinois L. Rev.* 5, 11 (2005).

governance of rules."[12] The "first desideratum," he wrote, is that "there must be rules."[13] His eight elements of legality are based on rules: general, public promulgation, not retroactive, comprehendible, not contradictory, not impossible to comply with, stable, and carried out as stated.[14] H. L. A. Hart similarly identified "the principal functions of the law as a means of social control"; "law is used to control, to guide, and to plan life out of court."[15] His concept of law, as mentioned earlier, combines primary rules of obligation that apply to social groups and secondary rules that involve recognizing, changing, and applying primary rules.[16] Hart corrected Austin's position that law consists of obligatory commands of the sovereign, showing that power-conferring rules (secondary) are not like obligatory rules (primary), and legal systems operate through the union of both.[17] Secondary rules "may all be said to be on a different level from the primary rules, for they are all about such rules; in the sense that while primary rules are concerned with the actions that individuals must or must not do, these secondary rules are all concerned with the primary rules themselves."[18]

Thus centered on the role rules play in social order, legal theorists strive to identify what makes law distinct from other normative systems, like customs and morality; and when doing so, they also look at other types of rule systems like games or sports leagues. "When asking about the nature of law," Scott Shapiro writes, "we want to know which properties law necessarily possesses in virtue of being an instance of law and not a game, social etiquette, religion, or some other thing."[19]

To see why this leaves out much of law, one must first know what rules are. Put concisely, rules are binding prescriptions stated in general terms in advance. Rules are "necessarily general," specifying what must be done in types or classes of situations.[20] This is in contrast to particular orders, on one hand, and to untrammeled discretion, on the other. A police officer who shouts "Stop!" is not issuing a general rule, but giving an order in a particular context. Generality is a feature of rules.[21] Another feature is that they are obligatory. The binding effect of a rule precludes the exercise of discretion. "Do what you think is wise" is not a rule because a rule dictates what must be done. Rules help produce uniformity, predictability, and social coordination because people know in advance what will happen in situations addressed by the rule.[22] Filling out his account, alongside rules Hart added obligatory principles and standards.[23]

---

[12]   Lon Fuller, *The Morality of Law*, rev. ed. (New Haven, CT: Yale University Press 1964) 96, 122.
[13]   Id. 46.   [14]   Id. 38–39.
[15]   H. L. A. Hart, *The Concept of Law* (Oxford: Clarendon Press 1961) 39.   [16]   Id. 78–79.
[17]   Id. 237.   [18]   Id. 92.
[19]   Scott Shapiro, *Legality* (Cambridge, MA: Harvard University Press 2011) 9–10.
[20]   Frederick Schauer, *Playing by the Rules: A Philosophical Examination of Rule-Based Decision-Making in Law and in Life* (Clarendon: Oxford University Press 1991) 18.
[21]   Hart, *Concept of Law*, supra 21.   [22]   Schauer, *Playing by the Rules*, chapter 7.
[23]   Hart, *Concept of Law*, 121.

Now think about enabling acts. They are performative devices that give birth to entities like corporations and government agencies. The creation of an entity is not itself a rule and is not about social ordering. It involves the capacity to possess things, exercise powers, engage in transactions, and pursue objectives – to act in the world.

Supporters of Hart might argue his account of power-conferring rules can account for enabling acts.[24] Certain power-conferring rules allow people to create legal arrangements. "The power thus conferred on individuals to mould their legal relations with others by contracts, will, marriages, &c., is one of the great contributions of law to social life,"[25] Hart wrote. But this does not capture what enabling acts accomplish. Here is a New Jersey Act of incorporation from 1791:

> Sec. 1. *Be it Enacted by the Council and General Assembly of this State, and it is hereby Enacted by the Authority of the same,* That all those Persons who have already subscribed, and who, according to the terms hereafter mentioned, shall subscribe for the Purpose of establishing a Company for carrying on the Business of Manufactures in this State, their Successor and Assigns, shall be and they are hereby incorporated by the Name of "The Society for establishing useful Manufactures," and by the same Name, they and their Successors and Assigns are hereby constituted a Body Politic and Corporate in law and shall be able and capable to acquire, purchase, receive, have, hold and enjoy any Lands, Tenements, Hereditaments, Goods and Chattels, of what Kind or Quality soever[.][26]

Subsequent provisions of the Act spell out various powers, requirements, and restrictions on the corporation, many of which involve power-conferring or obligatory rules consistent with Hart's analysis. But the very heart and point of the Act, Section 1, is not a rule and is not about molding relations with others. The operative language *"hereby incorporated"* and *"hereby constituted* a Body Politic and Corporate in law" literally brings the corporation into existence. Contracts, wills, and marriages – constructed through Hart's power-conferring rules – are legal arrangements that facilitate social ordering, but do not themselves engage in actions, whereas corporations are *actors* subject to rules of social ordering.

A plethora of laws issued by legislatures are not general rules and are not involved in social ordering: laws designating memorials, appointing public officials, purchasing or selling federal land or buildings, extending unemployment insurance, abolishing or restructuring an agency, promoting dental health – and a limitless list of routine bills.[27] Budget laws are guidelines for planning purposes; appropriations laws are directions to allocate funds. The parliament of the United Kingdom has passed thousands of "private and personal acts" directed at individuals or

---

[24] Hart, *Concept of Law*, 27–33.   [25] Id. 28.

[26] New Jersey Laws, 16 session, I sit, Chapter 356 (1791) 730, available at http://njlaw.rutgers.edu/cgi-bin/diglib.cgi?collect=njleg&file=016&page=0730&zoom=120.

[27] A Library of Congress website database on legislation shows the extraordinary range of matters covered in statutes. See Library of Congress, Guide to Law Online, www.loc.gov/law/help/guide.php.

corporations that are not general rules[28] – including several hundred legislative acts granting divorces.[29] The Interstate Commerce Commission Termination Act was not a general rule setting forth binding prescriptions,[30] but a declaration that extinguished the ICC. Legislative acts that utter "hereby" often signal direct and immediate legal effect (likewise "establish," "designate," "abolish," "dissolve," "create," etc.). Many legislative acts are statements of policy goals, declarations or designations, symbolic utterances, performative statements that accomplish things, and more. Legislatures are organizations with the power to create law at will and this power is utilized in numerous ways for inexhaustible purposes.

Take the Homeland Security Act of 2002,[31] which created and organized a new federal department, gave it powers and transferred powers from other existing agencies, established specific offices, reorganized the hierarchy and lines of authority among several federal departments, among many other actions. Title I begins with a legal declaration that brings it into being: "There is established a Department of Homeland Security, as an executive department of the United States within the meaning of title 5, United States Code."[32] Provisions changing departments and creating new offices are not rules or orders – the legal declaration immediately accomplishes its stated objective. Significant parts of the Act involve primary and secondary rules, but significant parts do not. (One provision, for instance, designates a trust in the name of a slain CIA officer to benefit relatives of fallen service members.[33])

Or consider the Iran Threat Reduction and Syria Human Rights Act of 2012,[34] which is neither a general rule nor about social or governmental ordering. The Act directs that financial assets of an Iranian bank held frozen in a New York bank account be available to satisfy a judgment for plaintiffs in a specific case in U.S. District Court. In response, the bank asserted it is inappropriate for Congress to enact a non-general rule "for a single pending case – identified by caption and docket number."[35] The U.S. Supreme Court rejected this "flawed" argument, "for it rests on the assumption that legislation must be generally applicable, that 'there is something wrong with particularized legislative action.'"[36] Although legislatures "usually act through laws of general applicability, that is by no means their only

---

[28] See "Chronological Table of Private and Personal Acts (1539–2006)," National Archives, www .legislation.gov.uk/changes/chron-tables/private.

[29] "Obtaining a Divorce," Parliament.uk, www.parliament.uk/about/living-heritage/transformingsociety/ private-lives/relationships/overview/divorce/.

[30] ICC Termination Act of 1995, Public Law 104–88, 109 Stat. 803, 1995-12-29.

[31] Homeland Security Act of 2002, Public Law 107–296, 116 Stat. 2135, www.dhs.gov/xlibrary/assets/ hr_5005_enr.pdf.

[32] Id. Section 101 (a) Establishment, 116 Stat. 2142.

[33] Id. Section 601 (b) Designation of Johnny Michael Spann Patriot Trusts, 116 Stat 2216.

[34] Iran Threat Reduction and Syria Human Rights Act of 2012, H.R. 1905, Public Law 112–158.

[35] *Bank Markazi, aka Central Bank of Iran v. Peterson*, et al., 578 U.S. ___ (2016), slip opinion 19, www.supremecourt.gov/opinions/15pdf/14-770_906b.pdf.

[36] Id 20.

legitimate mode of action," the Court held. "Private bills in Congress are still common. . . . Even laws that impose a duty or liability upon a single individual or firm are not on that account invalid."[37]

Hart's theory of law was constructed on the assumption that legal systems utilize a system of rules to administer rules for social ordering. This captures a lot of law. But nothing requires that law must meet his criteria. The power to declare law creates institutional facts that count as "law" without regard to the form they take or their purpose or function as long as legal officials recognize them as valid "law." (Or to state the point in Hart's own terms: rules of recognition typically do not specify that law must consist of obligatory rules of social ordering, or rules administering those rules.) State law can take any form and can be used to do anything for any purpose legal officials choose. Significant amounts of what is recognized as law today are not primary rules because they do not consist of rules and/or do not involve social ordering; some instances might be considered free-standing power-conferring rules within government organizations unattached to primary rules, but Hart dictates that "secondary rules *are all concerned with* the primary rules themselves."[38]

Hart imposed this tight connection because he was focused on how the legal system is constituted and works in relation to social order, thinking less about the many varied uses of legal mechanisms within and by government organizations. As Rubin observes in his critique of Hart, "a great deal of legislation regulates the behavior of government agencies, not the conduct of private persons."[39] Hart's theory can accommodate this critique by recognizing that law operates in two realms of social ordering: private persons and government organizations.[40] My critique is further that significant aspects of contemporary law do not involve rules and do not involve social ordering.

Perhaps with ingenuity and drastic reductionism many of these legal enactments might be re-described to fit Hart's account. But Hart himself argues "reductionist legal theories" that obscure too much about law should be avoided, citing this as grounds to reject Kelsen's reduction of law to rules directed at government officials.[41] In the same spirit, I contend Hart himself obscured the diverse forms and uses of law within contemporary government that cannot be captured by his dual rule system focused on social ordering.

MANAGERIAL ORGANIZATIONS WIELDING LAW

Administrative agencies have never fit the paradigm of law as a system of rules for social ordering. Agencies are created, structured, and funded through law and exercise legal powers to achieve designated purposes. They make policy decisions,

---

[37] Id. 21. The Court quotes with approval *Plaut v. Spendthrift Farm, Inc.*, 514 U.S. 211, 239 (1995).
[38] Hart, *Concept of Law*, supra 92 (emphasis added).
[39] Rubin, "Law and Legislation in the Administrative State," supra 375.   [40] Id. 380.
[41] Hart, *Concept of Law*, supra 238–39; 35–41.

design and effectuate programs, exercise discretion, carry out investigations, issue legally binding regulations with civil and criminal penalties, prosecute or refer cases for prosecution, and conduct adjudication. Lon Fuller recognized that administrative agencies do not conform to his account of law. "In recent history," he observed, "perhaps the most notable failure to achieve general rules has been that of certain of our regulatory agencies, particularly those charged with allocative functions."[42] He acknowledged that the issues they confront are complex and fluid, involve multiple interacting factors (are polycentric), and require expertise, discretion, research, negotiation, and experimentation, with freedom to change course when necessary.[43]

Fuller drew a contrast between "two forms of social ordering that are often confounded."[44] "One of these is *managerial direction*, the other is *law*."[45] The former involves orders from superiors that inferiors apply to serve the former's purposes, whereas with the latter citizens follow legal rules while pursuing their own affairs. "The rules of a legal system [in contrast to a managerial system] normally serve the primary purpose of setting the citizen's relations with other citizens and only in a collateral manner his relations with the seat of authority from which the rules proceed."[46] His contrast is problematic at the outset, however, because virtually *all* government entities – including executives, legislatures, courts, agencies, and others – are managerial organizations that utilize legal mechanisms in their operations. By setting up managerial direction as the antipode of law, he had difficulty accounting for varied uses of law within government organizations.

An example of protean managerial uses of law is the Federal Reserve Bank (Fed).[47] The Federal Reserve Act of 1913, modified by subsequent legislation, created a central bank that sets interest rates, controls the money supply, and supervises and regulates banks, among other activities.[48] The main bodies of the Federal Reserve System are the Board of Governors, the Federal Open Market Committee, and twelve regional Federal Reserve Banks directed by their own boards of governors. Nationally commissioned private banks are legally required to hold shares in regional Federal Reserve Banks and have voting rights on the election of its board members. The president appoints the chair and members of the Board of Governors

---

[42] Fuller, *Morality of Law*, supra 46–47.

[43] Fuller contrasts decisions suited to judging against the types of decisions administrative agencies make, which are better suited to negotiation and managerial discretion. Lon Fuller, "The Forms and Limits of Adjudication," 92 *Harvard L. Rev.* 353 (1978).

[44] Fuller, *Morality of Law*, supra 207.   [45] Id. 207.   [46] Id. 207–08.

[47] For an overview of the powers and activities of the Federal Reserve, see *The Federal Reserve System Purposes and Functions*, 5th ed. (Federal Reserve 2005), www.federalreserve.gov/pf/pdf/pf_1.pdf; The Structure of the Federal Reserve, federalreserveeducation.org, www.federalreserveeducation.org/about-the-fed/structure-and-functions; and general information, Board of Governors of the Federal Reserve System, www.federalreserve.gov/.

[48] See Mission, Board of Governors of the Federal Reserve System, www.federalreserve.gov/aboutthefed/mission.htm. A concise description of the Fed is Neil Irwin, "Nine Questions about the Federal Reserve You Were too Embarrassed to Ask," *Washington Post*, September 18, 2013, www.washingtonpost.com/blogs/wonkblog/wp/2013/09/18/9-questions-about-the-federal-reserve-you-were-too-embarrassed-to-ask/.

to staggered terms. The chair and board members do not take instructions from and cannot be fired by the president or Congress.

The Fed's mandate is to seek full employment, low inflation, and a stable financial system. Among its activities, the Fed serves as a bank for other banks, while at the same time it regulates those banks. To affect the money supply, the Fed loans money to banks at an interest rate it sets, it buys and sells government securities, and it establishes the minimum amount banks must hold in reserve.[49] The Fed is also responsible for circulating currency printed at the U.S. Treasury Department (stamped "legal tender" and "Federal Reserve Note"), which it distributes to banks withdrawing cash from accounts at regional Federal Reserve Banks.[50] Member banks are paid dividends on their shares at statutorily fixed rates. Any profits the Fed earns from its activities are deposited in the Treasury. The Federal Reserve System has 20,000 employees, owns more than $2 billion in real estate, and has more than $3.5 trillion on its books.[51] It earned a profit of $100 billion in 2015.[52] The chair participates in regular meetings with heads of central banks of other advanced capitalist countries (the Basel Committee) to coordinate regulatory requirements and enforcement actions across nations. During the financial crisis of 2008, the Fed took actions outside its legal authority when propping up failing non-bank companies,[53] and when it seized a controlling equity stake in insurance giant AIG.[54] In terms of the standard divide between public and private, the Fed is neither one nor the other, but a combination of both. This hybrid creature with immense power to influence the national and global economy is wrought by law, operates through law, and wields law in its activities.

No existing theory of law adequately accounts for government entities that utilize legal mechanisms in myriad ways in their activities.[55] A theory of law that fails to account for this is inadequate to contemporary law.

---

[49] Each increases the money supply in a different way tied to lending. First, issuing a loan in effect creates money because the borrower obtains money while the lender counts the amount due as an asset, and a low discount rate encourages banks to borrow more and loan it out, thereby increasing the money supply. Second, when the Fed buys government securities like Treasury bills, the amount it pays is deposited in a bank, which loans it out. Third, the Fed can adjust the amount banks are required to hold on reserve, which determines how much they can loan out.

[50] See "How Currency Gets in Circulation," Federal Reserve Bank of New York, www.newyorkfed.org/aboutthefed/fedpoint/fedo1.html.

[51] Irwin, "Nine Questions about the Federal Reserve You Were too Embarrassed to Ask," supra.

[52] Tyler Durden, "The Cozy Relationship between the Treasury and the Fed," February 2, 2016, *Zero Hedge*, http://www.zerohedge.com/news/2016-02-04/cozy-relationship-between-treasury-and-fed.

[53] Eric A. Posner, "What Legal Authority Does the Fed Need During a Financial Crisis?" University of Chicago Working Paper, January 22, 2016, http://papers.ssrn.com/sol3/Papers.cfm?abstract_id=2723524.

[54] See Recent Case Note, "*Starr International Co. v. United States*: Court of Federal Claims Holds that Government Acquisition of Equity Share in AIG Effected an Illegal Exaction," 129 *Harvard L. Rev.* 859 (2016).

[55] Jeremy Waldron is picking up a different aspect of the same issue when he protests against conceptions of the rule of law that neglect public law. Jeremy Waldron, "The Rule of Law in Public Law," in

TWO ORIENTATIONS OF LAW

Let us again distinguish two orientations (introduced in Chapter 2): 1) law as fundamental rules of social intercourse, and 2) law in connection with government objectives.[56] The second orientation is divided into three types: laws that secure the power of the state; laws that internally arrange and facilitate the affairs of government organizations; and laws that advance government initiatives in the social arena. These are not separate domains – the two orientations of law intersect, interpenetrate, and interact.

A. *Legal rules of social intercourse.* Law serves a fundamental role in coordinating social behavior and responding to conflicts between actors (individuals and entities). Legal rules on property, personal injuries, binding agreements, labor, spousal relations, and offspring address the basic conditions of human social interaction. Adam Smith, David Hume, H. L. A. Hart, Friedrich Hayek, and many others have described these as fundamental legal components of order in human social groups.[57] All societies have rules on these matters, though they vary greatly depending on cultural and religious values, the economic system, the political system, and the level of social complexity. This variation is evident in property rights. Real property in many small-scale societies was collectively owned and woven into kin relations and group identity; it could not be bought and sold by individuals; rights related to use, access, and fruits of the land. Real property rights in modern capitalist societies, in contrast, involve freely alienable individual ownership, making property a financial asset for citizens. In contemporary China, all land is owned by the government (collecting rents), with people holding transferrable use rights.[58] In each case, property rights are tied to social-economic-political aspects.

It cannot be assumed that state legal rules on social intercourse match rules people actually abide on these matters. They coincide when law and society are closely integrated through long coevolution, functioning in a mutually complementary fashion as implicitly assumed background aspects of social intercourse. A divergence may exist, however, when state legal rules and institutions addressing these matters have been imposed or borrowed from elsewhere, or when the state legal system adopts the rules of certain social groups to the exclusion of others, or when pockets of immigrant communities within society adhere to their own rules. In these circumstances, groups within society may abide by their own customary or

---

The Cambridge Companion to Public Law, edited by Mark Elliot and David Feldman (Cambridge: Cambridge University Press 2015).

[56] Friedrich Hayek distinguishes these two perspectives on law in Friedrich Hayek, *Law, Legislation, and Liberty: Rules and Order*, vol. 1 (Chicago: Chicago University Press 1973).

[57] Hart, *The Concept of Law*, supra 189–95.

[58] See Stuart Leavenworth and Kiki Zhao, "In China, Homeowners Find Themselves in Land of Doubt," *New York Times*, May 31, 2016, www.nytimes.com/2016/06/01/business/international/in-china-homeowners-find-themselves-in-a-land-of-doubt.html?_r=0.

religious laws while state law enforces a different set of rules.[59] In many rural areas of the Global South, as mentioned earlier, customary property law still prevails among inhabitants, inconsistent with state law. Similar divergences exist on family law issues and other matters. State law often is not socially efficacious in these situations.

The state legal rules of social intercourse are stable and evolve slowly in piecemeal fashion. They reflect and constitute power dynamics within society. Individuals, entities, and social groups perpetually contest aspects of these rules in executive, administrative, legislative, and judicial arenas. It can be over religious or cultural values, like whether gay marriage should be allowed or how custody of the child of divorce should be determined. It can be over economic or moral issues: whether unfair contracts are enforceable or whether liability for personal injuries should require fault. It can be over moral or social policy issues, like whether criminals should be punished or rehabilitated. All sorts of clashes arise over these rules. Constantly buffeted by economic, political, cultural, and technological factors – with powerful interests having greater though not complete sway – background legal rules undergo gradual piecemeal change though legislation, executive and administrative actions, court decisions, and the everyday activities of lawyers advancing the purposes of clients.

B. *Three uses of law related to government organizations.* The second orientation focuses on uses of law by government entities. One of the defining features of the modern state is the claim to exercise a monopoly of legitimate coercive force through law. Government is not a monolithic actor, but a vast complex of institutions operating at different levels and in different settings, some closely integrated, others loosely associated, others independent, and some at odds with each other. Government organizations come in many forms at different levels of generality, from executive offices, to legislatures, to administrative agencies, to courts, to municipal councils, to prosecutors' offices and opposing defenders' offices, to police offices, to public school systems, to quasi-public entities like Amtrak, to hybrids like the Fed. They are influenced internally by people occupying offices with their own interests, ideas, and objectives, as well as externally by interests seeking to control or shape the activities and objectives they carry out.

Three overlapping uses of law by government organizations can be distinguished. First we must set aside usual assumptions about government as a distinct entity. Instead think of government in basic social terms as complexes of bureaucratic organizations like others in society. Imagine society populated with a multitude of people, a multitude of organizations, and networks of connections between and among them. All organizations require resources, have internal arrangements, and carry out projects. Distinctively among the population of organizations, government organizations utilize the mechanisms of law backed by coercion in its activities.

---

[59] See Brian Z. Tamanaha, "Understanding Legal Pluralism: Past to Present, Local to Global," 30 *Sydney L. Rev.* 375 (2008).

1. One use government makes of law is to empower, support, and protect its own complex of organizations. Legally imposed and enforced taxes, customs, fines, and fees supply revenues the government requires to function. (Other organizations in society must get people to voluntarily hand over revenues they need to function.) Conscription laws supply bodies for labor and self-defense. Laws authorizing searches, arrests, imprisonment, forfeitures of personal property, and taking land enable the government to act forcefully against citizens. Laws authorizing government surveillance and intelligence gathering enable it to monitor behavior. Laws that criminalize lying to government officials force people to be forthcoming on demand. Heightened penalties against killing or kidnapping government officials deter and punish attacks against personnel. Laws against spying and sedition help suppress opposition. Curfews and martial law enable the government to tighten control and exert armed force. Immunities for government organizations and their personnel protect its resources and free officials from concerns about personal liability for inflicting harms. In these and other ways law is used to bolster government organizations, giving them powers other organizations do not enjoy, backed by threat of coercive force.

Many of these legal actions are explicitly justified as necessary to allow the government to carry out its social ordering functions, linking to the first orientation of law, or to further the public good, linking to the third government use of law (taken up in a moment). Whether these claims are true is a contingent matter that depends on a given state legal system and the situation at hand. "When men are in the position of governors they cannot escape seeing the justice on the side of their own special interests when these interests conflict with those of the rest of the community," wrote Morris Cohen. "The governments almost always think it necessary to keep and to perpetuate their power."[60] Political scientist Charles Tilly characterized "state making as organized crime" because in many instances it operates like an extortion racket that coercively takes money from citizens with promises of protection, while using the money in other ways.[61] The primary orientation of the state legal apparatus in Syria and North Korea today is above all else to maintain the regime in power. These are extreme examples, but this orientation is present to one degree or another in every state legal system.

2. The second use involves the structuring and internal operation of government – to establish, organize, facilitate, communicate, and in other ways run its operations. This category includes everything from constitutional provisions structuring government, to election laws and civil service laws for public offices, to enabling acts creating agencies, to appropriation laws directing funding. This use constructs the

---

[60] Morris Cohen, "The Basis of Contract," 46 *Harvard L. Rev.* 553, 560 (1936).

[61] See Charles Tilly, "War Making and State Making as Organized Crime," in *Bringing the State Back In*, edited by Peter Evans, Dietrich Rueschemeyer, and Theda Skocpol (Cambridge: Cambridge University Press 1985).

general polity and well as specific governmental organizations. Law's declarative, performative, directive, and communicative capacities are utilized by government organizations to effectuate tasks that all organizations handle. All bureaucratic organizations have structures, issue directives, orders, plans, and guidelines, communicate between units, utilize rules, practices, and procedures, and so forth – this is bureaucratic rationality in operation. What are called "budget" and "appropriation" laws in government are parallel to "budget plans" and spending "directives" or "authorizations" in private corporations. Legislation creating or rearranging government departments is akin to corporate reorganizations.

Executives, legislatures, agencies, courts, police, and other government organizations use law in their operations in numerous ways. Government organizations use law for these tasks because it is a handy, versatile mechanism for getting things done. Law is especially useful across functionally differentiated government organizations, as when a legislature creates, charges, funds, structures, restricts, and exercises oversight over an agency. Because courts declare law and work largely with legal materials, they utilize law in their internal operations more so than most other government organizations. A few examples include procedural rules, jurisdictional rules, evidence rules, admissions to the bar, and professional rules for lawyers and judges. What lawyers see as legal rules in this context are at bottom operational rules for courts as organizations carrying out their assigned tasks.

3. A third use government makes of law is to pursue initiatives and achieve objectives in the social arena. Government initiatives typically are justified in the name of the public welfare or common good, pursuing agendas fought over by competing interests and social groups. This use of law spans the gamut of governmental activities, from criminalizing drugs and pornography, to creating and regulating corporations, to setting the terms of labor organizing and employment conditions, to establishing a social welfare system, to providing an education system, to issuing health, sanitation, and safety regulations, to developing and maintaining transportation, communication, water, sewage, and electrification infrastructures, to preserving the environment, to guarding the border, and many more undertakings. Taxes are a common legal means to achieve goals, like high gasoline taxes to reduce driving, cigarette taxes to inhibit smoking, or a penalty tax to coerce people to procure health insurance. This is legal instrumentalism – the active use of law to achieve objectives that increased during the course of the nineteenth century and became ubiquitous in the twentieth century.

The first use of law is about securing the power of government organizations; the second is about their internal structuring and operations; the third facilitates the achievement of objectives in the social arena. These three uses of law are not mutually exclusive categories, again, merely different angles. More than one use is commonly at play in the same context. Taxes obtain revenues for government organizations (first use), while designed in ways that instrumentally further objectives like redistribute wealth or create positive or negative incentives for social behavior (third use). Obligatory conscription enhances the power of governments by forcing people to serve in the armed forces (first use) as a means to defend the nation from perceived external threats (third use). Congress created the Fed and gave it legal powers (second use) to regulate banks and stabilize the financial system (third use).

Seeing law in terms of these two orientations, and the three versions of the second, allows a more comprehensive and refined understanding of how contemporary governments utilize law. Hart's primary and secondary rules center on the legal system engaged in social ordering and fully captures the first orientation of law as rules of social intercourse. His scheme also picks up significant aspects of government uses of law to support its own power (first use) and regulatory regimes that advance government projects (third use). But Hart's concept of law misses a great deal of how government utilizes law to accomplish things by declaration, to direct, to communicate, to undertake symbolic actions, and to carry out various tasks within the operation of government organizations (much of the second use, and aspects of the first and third). By extending his notion of social ordering to also apply to the realm of internal operations of government, Hart's theory can cover parts of the second use, but that still leaves much out.

His account cannot contain all the many varied uses of law because the untrammeled power to declare law renders it a malleable device that can be used in any way whatsoever, including even legal declarations with suprapositive or metaphysical ambitions. Legal officials can recognize the sovereignty of God and the obligatory force of divine legislation, as explicitly set forth in the constitution of Iran,[62] or the existence of rights held by people outside positive law, as stated in the Ninth Amendment of the U.S. Constitution. Article 1 of the German constitution declares: "(1) Human dignity shall be inviolable. To respect and protect it shall be the duty of all state authority. (2) The German people therefore acknowledge inviolable and inalienable human rights as the basis of every community, of peace and justice in the world."[63] Section 1 consists of an obligation imposing provision (albeit with fuzzy content), and Section 2 is a positive law enactment that declares the existence of pre-positive rights binding on all societies. There are no limits to what can be enacted as law, so it also transcends the two orientations I have specified.

---

[62] See Article 2, General Principles, Islamic Republic of Iran Constitution, www.iranonline.com/iran/iran-info/government/constitution-1.html for a Western example recognizing God and binding natural law, Code of Canon Law of 1917, Canon 6 n. 6; Edward N. Peters, *The 1917 Pio-Bendictine Code of Canon Law* (San Francisco, CA: Ignatius Press 2001) 31. See generally Stephan Kuttner, "Natural Law and Canon Law," 3 *Natural Law Institute Proceedings* 83 (1950).

[63] Basic Law for the Federal Republic of Germany, Article 1(1)(2), English translation available at www.gesetze-im-internet.de/englisch_gg/englisch_gg.html#p0015.

SEQUENTIAL EMERGENCE OF ORIENTATIONS, AND THEIR INTERACTION

Jurists may see in the two orientations echoes of the public law–private law distinction, but they do not coincide. The first orientation shares private law's focus on interaction between individuals (natural and legal persons), but it encompasses both civil law and criminal law provisions, which are classed separately in the public law–private law divide. Battery in torts and battery in criminal law are separated as private law and public law, respectively, while both are in the first orientation. Criminal law is classed as public law, whereas here some criminal law provisions are rules of social intercourse (murder, theft) while others are government uses (treason, tax evasion, lying to officials). Professional rules for lawyers are government uses, though they are often left out of both public and private law categories. The two orientations sketched here suggest that the old Roman law public law–private law divide is not the most informative way to examine modern law.

Friedrich Hayek provides one way to mark legal rules of social intercourse in contrast to instrumental uses of law by government (his focus was the third type): the former "merely limits the range of permitted action and usually does not determine a particular action; and what it prescribes [unlike the latter] is never accomplished but remains a standing obligation on all."[64] Another generalization is that legal rules of social intercourse are all "rules" related to social ordering, as Fuller and Hart posited, whereas, while many government uses of law are rules, many are performative declarations, particular directives or orders, discretionary acts, and other non-rule oriented exercises of law, many not related to social ordering. In sum, the former are basic to social intercourse, whereas government uses of law are tied to power, resources, structure, and various actions within government organizations and purposive activities in the social arena.

Legal rules of social intercourse extend back to the earliest human societies, addressing fundamental aspects of life within human social groups. Hunter-gatherer bands had basic laws of property, personal injury, debt obligations (or reciprocal gift-giving), and sexual relations and offspring (and perhaps labor). While the content of these rules varies greatly, having rules of this sort is universal and tied to our nature as human social animals, structuring and maintaining our relations. Background legal rules are not neutral in content or effect: they allocate and preserve resources and social and economic power. In many societies past and present, to offer a common example, husbands have held legal advantages over wives in matters of property, personal violence, sexual conduct, and marital rights.

Government uses of law are tied to the emergence of political-legal institutions. As social groups became more populous and complex, political structures integrated with and backed by legal institutions coalesced; in addition to rules of social

---

[64]   Hayek, *Law, Legislation, and Liberty,* supra 127.

intercourse, layers of law formed to enforce social, economic, and political hierarchies. Examples of the first government use of law – enhancing the power of government and individuals who staff it – trace back to chiefdoms and early states. Adam Smith observed that threats to state power, including treason and desertion by soldiers, are treated most severely, particularly early in a state's development.[65] "Those which immediately affect the state are those which will first be the objects of punishment."[66] Government legal domination in these early arrangements was simultaneously elite domination (rulers, high caste, priests, hereditary aristocracy, wealthy), as no public–private divide existed. Law immediately served government power and directly served the power of elites.

Utilizing law to arrange government affairs and pursue social objectives – the final two uses of law by government – gradually increased from the sixteenth century onward with the consolidation of state institutions.[67] These latter two uses erupted in the modern age as government bureaucracies multiplied and improved their functional capabilities in conjunction with the proliferation and expansion of organizations in society more generally – when governments ballooned in size and scope to deal with the activities of large business corporations, the complex living conditions of mass urban centers, and rapidly growing transnational political and economic activities.

It must be emphasized again that the two orientations are not separate realms – rules of social intercourse are pervasively interpenetrated by government uses of law. Both are constituted within the same complex of legal organizations, subject to the same external influences. And the three government uses of law frequently overlap or coincide. Nonetheless, these distinctions provide a useful framework for analysis that captures discernable differences.

Wartime laws offer a dramatic illustration of government uses of law to achieve objectives and how this intersects with background social rules. In the course of World War I,[68] through legislation, executive ordinances, decrees, and judicial decisions, European governments across the continent engaged in far-reaching legal actions: established price controls, conscripted men for military service, took over factories and coal mines, requisitioned wheat and grain, regulated production and rationed basics like sugar and bread, seized private property, controlled labor hours and pay, declared moratoria on payment of various debts, suspended or deferred commercial contracts, conferred immunities on military personnel from

---

[65] Adam Smith, *Lectures on Jurisprudence*, edited by R. L. Meek, D. D. Raphael, and P. G. Stein (Indianapolis, IN: Liberty Fund 1982) 209.

[66] Id. 130.

[67] Paul Craig presents multiple uses by the English government of law from the sixteenth century on to facilitate government initiatives in health, safety, and trade regulation, flood protection, poor relief, and collection of excise taxes. Paul Craig, "The Legitimacy of U.S. Administrative Law and the Foundations of English Administrative Law: Setting the Historical Record Straight" (June 30, 2016), available at http://papers.ssrn.com/sol3/papers.cfm?abstract_id=2802784.

[68] A terrific collection of articles on wartime law is Michael Lobban and Willem H. van Boom, eds., "The Great War and Private Law," 2 *Comparative Legal History* 163–324 (2014).

debt and rent collection, voided contracts with enemy aliens, seized property of enemy-owned firms and liquidated assets, recognized marriages between women at home and soldiers at the front, abolished the necessity for husbands' permission to allow wives' employment, and engaged in policy analysis in judicial interpretations, among numerous instrumental legal actions, many of which directly affected basic laws of social intercourse.[69]

European governments on both sides of the conflict utilized legal mechanisms in numerous ways to further their war efforts. That wars have contributed mightily to the construction of the modern state is a political science commonplace. Less often recognized is that wartime uses of law bludgeoned beliefs among traditionalist jurists that the legal realm of social intercourse (property and contract rights particularly) could not be interfered with for instrumental reasons. Wartime government uses of law thoroughly affected existing legal rights of property, contract, personal injuries, and family law, implementing a number of legal changes that remained in place following the war, reinforcing the sense that law can be used to do *anything*. Far-reaching instrumental legal activity in such concentrated form was unusual for its time, but the various forms law took and the range of actions illustrated by this episode are now taken for granted.

WHY COMMON LAW IS NOT A SPONTANEOUS ORDER REFLECTING SOCIETY

Because the notion of background legal rules is identified with Friedrich Hayek,[70] it behooves me, as I further elaborate on the two orientations and their connections, to undo his misunderstanding of the common law. Hayek portrayed the common law as a spontaneous ordering of background legal rules that reflect social life.[71] Spontaneous orders like the market are grown "orderly structures which are the product of the action of many men but are not the result of human design."[72] Hayek contrasted spontaneous orders with designed orders, which he associated with instrumental legislation. His argument is that rules of social intercourse contained in the common law are a bottom-up creation of the people (hence good), while instrumental legislation is susceptible to capture or faulty hubristic ideas, prone to failure or causing unanticipated social disruptions (hence bad).

---

[69] These examples are in symposium articles, summarized by Michael Lobban, "Introduction, The Great War and Private Law," 2 *Comparative Legal History* 163 (2014).

[70] See, e.g., Louis Hunt and Peter McNamara, *Liberalism, Conservatism, and Hayek's Idea of Spontaneous Order* (New York: Palgrave Macmillan 2007); Norman Barry, "The Tradition of Spontaneous Order," 5 *Literature of Liberty* 7 (1982); Jerry Z. Muller, "The Limits of Spontaneous Order," in Hunt and McNamara, *Liberalism, Conservatism, and Hayek's Idea of Spontaneous Order*, supra 198–209; Naeem Inayatullah, "Theories of Spontaneous Disorder," 4 *Review of International Political Economy* 319 (1997); Alain de Benoist, "Hayek: A Critique," 100 *Telos* 71 (1998).

[71] Hayek, *Law, Legislation, and Liberty*, supra 13.   [72] Id. 37.

Hayek attributed the notion of spontaneous order to Adam Smith, David Hume, and other Scottish Enlightenment philosophers.[73] Hume asserted that basic legal rules regarding social intercourse evolved without conscious human design owing to their utility. Property law arises, Hume wrote, "gradually, and acquires force by a slow progression, and by our repeated experience of the inconveniences of transgressing it."[74] "In like manner are languages gradually establish'd by human conventions without any promise. In like manner do gold and silver become the common measure of exchange."[75] Like language and money, law arises because it serves social needs and evolves over time in connection with those needs.

The common law is a spontaneous order reflecting society, Hayek claimed, because common law judges make decisions that comport with people's legitimate expectations. "The aims of the rules must be to facilitate that matching or tallying of the expectations on which the plans of the individuals depend for their success."[76] The judge is "bound by generally held views of what is just,"[77] coming to the correct solution by trained intuition, and applying reason to rationalize law within the existing body of legal principles.[78] Developing in this fashion, according to Hayek, the common law specifies general background rules protecting property, enforcing contracts, prohibiting force and fraud, etc., that match social understandings. Identifying his position with historical jurisprudence, he repeats the old saw that judges do not make law, but merely declare law immanent in social customs and values.[79]

This is a highly romanticized view of common law judging. To become part of law, social customs and values must be affirmatively recognized by judges, who are not transparent sieves. In a majestic historical survey of Western legal thought, Donald Kelley comments skeptically about the frequently touted connection between custom and law:

> With the advent of written forms, however, even with the provisio of popular "approval" and "tacit consent," custom lost its primary ties with its social base and came under the control of legal and political authorities. . . . [The] true significance of the transition from "custom" to "customary law" . . . is that once again the legal experts have begun to take over. This indeed is the import of the twelfth-century revival of "legal science," in which custom joins civil and canon law in the arsenal of the "language of power" which jurists come in large part to monopolize.[80]

---

73 Id. 20–24. Ronald Hamowy, *The Scottish Enlightenment and the Theory of Spontaneous Order* (Carbondale: Southern Illinois University Press 1987).

74 Davie Hume, *A Treatise of Human Nature*, edited by L. A. Selby-Bigge (Oxford: Clarendon Press 1958) 490.

75 Id.   76 Hayek, *Law, Legislation, and Liberty*, supra 98.   77 Id. 116.   78 Id. 120.

79 Id. 123.

80 Donald R. Kelley, *The Human Measure: Social Thought in the Western Legal Tradition* (Cambridge, MA: Harvard University Press 1990) 106.

Though substantially influenced by surrounding social views, legal actors do not passively reflect prevailing social customs – they actively construct "customary law" and common law. This is why the professional legal culture elaborated in the preceding chapter must be kept in mind.

Jeremy Bentham eviscerated Blackstone's assertion that the common law was custom descended from time immemorial,[81] dismissing "this miserable sophistry in speaking of the Common Law that is to give a relish to all that froth, all that doting pedants have driveled out upon it in the way of panegyric."[82] Much of the common law is "legal gibberish," he wrote, utterly foreign to people's expectations.[83] Lawyers benefit from excessive legal obscurity, "having for its object the extracting ... out of the pockets of the people, in the largest quantity possible, the produce of the industry of the people."[84] To keep the two apart analytically, Bentham separates customs and usages people follow ("custom *in pays*") versus what judges recognize and enforce as custom, "custom among Judges" ("custom *in foro*").[85] Sociological jurisprudent Eugen Ehrlich makes a parallel separation between *rules of conduct* observed in social associations (what he called "living law") versus *norms for decision* and *legal propositions*, the working legal materials of courts and jurists.[86]

Hayek fails to heed Bentham's and Ehrlich's warning that one cannot assume a correspondence exists between laws recognized by courts and lived customs and social values because law is created within legal institutions. Setting aside the fact that throughout its development the common law has been influenced by legislation,[87] the common law has always been a selective construction by lawyers and courts within the legalistic framework of the professional legal culture. "The common law system is properly located as a customary system of law in this sense," historian A. W. B. Simpson writes, "that it consists of a body of practices observed and ideas received by the caste of lawyers, these ideas being used by them as providing guidance in what is conceived to be the rational determination of disputes litigated before them."[88] It was based on what judges of the king's courts deemed reasonable, disregarding local customs when they saw fit.[89] Judicial claims of "reason" reflected the values and interests of the landed gentry on contested social

[81]   Jeremy Bentham, A *Comment on the Commentaries and a Fragment on Government*, edited by J. H. Burns and H. L. A. Hart (London: University of London Press 1977) 166.

[82]   Id. 201.   [83]   Id. 170, 165–80.   [84]   Id. 509.   [85]   Id. 182–83.

[86]   Eugen Ehrlich, *Fundamental Principles of the Sociology of Law*, translated by Walter L. Moll (Cambridge, MA: Harvard University Press 1936) 121–36.

[87]   See Matthew Hale, *The History of the Common Law of England*, p. 2, www.bdlawservice.com/books/the_history.pdf; Bentham, A *Comment on the Commentaries and a Fragment on Government*, supra 166.

[88]   A. W. B. Simpson, "The Common Law and Legal Theory," in *Folk Law: Essays in the Theory and Practice of Lex Non Scripta*, edited by A. D. Rentlen and A. Dundes (New York: Garland Publishing 1994) 133.

[89]   An informative discussion is Samuel T. Morrison, "Custom, Reason, and the Common Law: A Reply to Hasnas," 2 *NYU Journal of Law & Liberty* 209, 224–30 (2007).

issues.[90] Selected social influences come into the common law within the terms provided by the professional legal culture of knowledge, doctrines, practices, and modes of analysis.

Hume's analogy to language and money reveals a crucial difference Hayek overlooked. Language and customs *are* spontaneously evolved orders. Unlike the common law, no organizations issue declarations that control language or custom or decisively shape the course of their evolution. Money originally evolved without design (probably to pay debts rather than facilitate exchange[91]), but when governments and banks became involved in issuing money, it was no longer a matter of unhampered evolution, but conscious decisions and efforts at control (albeit not entirely successfully). This holds for law as well.

Hayek presents two starkly opposed poles – designed versus spontaneous – but the common law involves a dynamic interaction of both. What gives it the appearance of a spontaneous order is the common law develops through aggregate decisions by a multitude of judges. In addition to regular legislative interventions, however, designs are injected at critical nodes in the process. Appellate judges issue decisions that clarify common law doctrines, provide direction and uniformity, resolve conflicts and create coherence with other doctrines, decide among alternatives, and consider social consequences under the influence of ideological beliefs. Treatises and restatements prepared by jurists select cases and categorize common law subjects, make choices, and organize the whole in a coherent manner, which in turn influences judges. No single person or group designs the entire common law in one swoop, it is true, but legislation taken in the aggregate is also not designed; and just as individual pieces of legislation are designed to achieve social objectives, specific doctrinal areas are constructed by appellate courts with social consequences in mind. Thus the common law has significant elements of design, it is shaped by the legal professionals under the influence of their background views filtered through legal knowledge, practices, and institutions, and it is not an unadulterated mirror of general social views.

Hayek concedes the common law does not always reflect community values:

> But the most frequent cause is probably that the development of the law has lain in the hands of members of a particular class whose traditional views made them regard as just what could not meet the more general requirements of justice. There can be no doubt that in such field as the law on the relations between master and servant, landlord and tenant, creditor and debtor, and in modern times between organized business and its customers, the rules have been shaped largely by the views of one of the parties and their particular interests – especially where, as used to be true in the first two of the instances given, it was one of the groups concerned which almost exclusively supplied the judges.[92]

[90] See Robert Gordon, "Hayek and Cooter on Custom and Reason," 23 *Southwestern University L. Rev.* 453 (1994).
[91] See David Graeber, *Debt: The First 5000 Years* (Brooklyn, NY: Melville House 2011) 59–60.
[92] Hayek, *Law, Legislation, and Liberty,* supra 89.

This concession gives away his position. Hayek downplays these as regrettable aberrations,[93] but they are major areas of law. The common thread is that judges shaped legal doctrines to favor an economically dominant party, which is a common feature of law.

Who occupies the bench and their beliefs and social values has an impact in the making and remaking of the common law. This is well known in the United States, where an open battle wages over who shall be elected to serve on state appellate courts that produce the common law (the same battle occurs over federal judge-ships).[94] From 2000 to 2009, $207 million in total campaign contributions were received by judicial candidates for state high courts; $62.5 million from business groups and $6.7 million from unions.[95] Financial contributors support judges who share their ideological views, expecting that this will be reflected in their legal decisions.

A society with cultural, class, religious, racial, ethnic, occupational, regional, or political divisions – most societies today in one way other another – will inevitably have conflicting views of justice. Powerful groups have more influence on law than less powerful groups. Oliver Wendell Holmes wrote, "Whatever body may possess the supreme power for the moment is certain to have interests inconsistent with others which have competed unsuccessfully. The more powerful interests must be more or less reflected in legislation."[96] He focuses on legislation in this passage, but the influence of powerful groups in society permeates the common law as well.

As Holmes and Rudolph von Jhering observed in the nineteenth century, and many theorists have repeated since, law is the product of struggles between compet-ing views and social interests, often fought in the name of justice and the social good.[97] These contests over law, shaped by power dynamics, ceaselessly take place in all legal arenas, affecting the common law as much as legislation, administrative agency actions, and executive legal actions.[98] The results of this process are stamped into the rules of social intercourse and instrumental government uses of law. While it is useful to separate the two orientations for analytical purposes, it is a mistake to think they are fundamentally different (per Hayek) because all state law is created within the same complexes of legal institutions subject to the same surrounding social influences and dynamics.

---

[93] Id. 100.

[94] See Brian Z. Tamanaha, *Law as a Means to an End: Threat to the Rule of Law* (New York: Cambridge University Press 2006) 172–89.

[95] See James Sample, Adam Skaggs, Jonathan Blitzer, and Linda Casey, *The New Politics of Judicial Elections 2000–2009: Decade of Change* (New York: Brennan Center for Justice 2010) 8; see also Emily Heller, "Business and the Bench: U.S. Chamber of Commerce Scores Big in Backing Judicial Elections Nationwide," 51 *Palm Beach Daily Business Review*, November 9, 2004.

[96] Oliver Wendell Holmes, "The Gas Stoker's Strike," 7 *American L. Rev.* 582, 583 (1873).

[97] See Rudolph von Jhering, *The Struggle for Law* (Westport, CT: Hyperion Press 1979).

[98] See Tamanaha, *Law as a Means to an End*, supra.

THE LEGAL FABRIC OF SOCIETY

Henry Maine famously declared: "Starting, as from one terminus of history, from a condition of society in which all the relations of Persons are summed up on the relations of Family, we seem to have steadily moved towards a phase of social order in which all these relations arise from the free agreement of individuals."[99] "We may say that the movement of the progressive societies has hitherto been a movement from Status to Contract."[100] Maine uttered these words in the mid-nineteenth century, at the height of liberal individualism.

Law in society has since evolved beyond contract to comprise a pervasive, relatively fixed legal fabric. This stable legal fabric is the aggregate product of five factors: the proliferation of organizations using law, the pervasive use of form contracts, the innate standardizing tendencies within law, the instrumental government uses of law, and the interconnectedness of law within society entrenched over time. A few words will be said about each in turn. My exemplar again is the United States, which has traveled far in this process.

To an extent unparalleled in human history, as mentioned earlier, basic needs and wants of people in advanced capitalist cities – housing, food, water, education, work, security, transportation, entertainment, etc. – are arranged within and through organizations. Previously, the bulk of this was accomplished within the family and local community. An indication of this transformation is a wholesale shift in how people obtain their sustenance. In the United States, "Wage dependency covered about 20 percent of the population in 1820, and 80 to 90 percent by 1950."[101] Widespread wage dependency exists in societies dominated by organizations that compensate employees for work rendered. Adam Smith's four stages of subsistence – hunter-gatherer, pastoral, agricultural, and commercial[102] – (or whatever stages one prefers) have given way to a new stage of subsistence obtained through work in organizations. Since organizations conduct their activities through law in multiple ways, the pervasiveness of organizations in society brings the pervasiveness of law.

On the surface, this has the appearance of a contract-based society because contracts are ubiquitous. Organizations of various types, private and public, enter contracts with employees, suppliers of material, distributors, transporters, service providers, investors, lenders, and customers/clients. If contract is understood to mean individuals and entities consensually tailor the terms of their legal arrangements, however, that is not the situation.

Rent an apartment, take out a mortgage, hook up gas and electricity, acquire a credit card, obtain a loan, open a bank account, sign with a phone carrier, download a computer program, enter an employment relationship, purchase goods, attend a sporting event or concert – for these and innumerable other daily transactions, while

[99] Henry Maine, *Ancient Law*, edited by A. Montagu (Tucson: University of Arizona Press 1986) 163–65.
[100] Id. 165.   [101] Perrow, "A Society of Organizations," supra 729.
[102] Smith, *Lectures on Jurisprudence*, supra 14.

price can be haggled and quality and quantity decided, the legal arrangement is *preset*. People bind themselves to form contracts filled with detailed legal language specifying terms and conditions, frequently unread, often without thinking twice about it.[103] The legal arrangements usually cannot be individually tailored through negotiation except by wealthy or powerful parties.

Form contracts are ubiquitous because it is more convenient, more certain, cheaper, and more efficient for organizations to standardize transactions. This is encouraged by routines and uniformity within the bureaucratic rationality of organizations. It is a function of the superior bargaining power of organizations that offer jobs, products, and services on "take it or leave it" contractual terms. Banks offer loans to businesses and individuals with largely preset terms. Insurance companies compel standard liability-limiting terms on insureds. And so it goes with all manner of transactions. Since the vast bulk of economic transactions are channeled through organizations using form contracts, the vast bulk of economic transactions have pre-established legal terms.

The tendency of law itself to settle on, copy, and repeat standard words, phrases, and provisions feeds and reinforces the proliferation of form contracts. This involves the formalization of legal terminology in packets of settled legal meaning.[104] Many legal agreements are cut-and-paste products comprised of previously interpreted and utilized words and phrases. Legal actors repeat technical words and phrases because their implications are relatively known and predictable, and imitation is more cost-effective and less risky than drafting entirely new formulations. Standard templates are common in legal offices for transactions, complaints, motions, briefs, and other legal documents. Legal standardization builds on and incorporates generally fixed aspects of background legal rules, like established rules of property, contract, and torts, and incorporates terms and requirements of various sorts legally imposed by government.

Critics have argued that form contracts are not within the spirit of contracts.[105] Lay people do not understand legal jargon. Employees lack the capacity and freedom to negotiate the details of employment contracts set by employers (and unions). Consumers do not read sales and service contracts they enter, signing away legal rights through waivers of liability and accepting mandatory arbitration should a dispute arise. People have little choice in the matter other than to not take the job or

---

[103] A reporter read the full terms and conditions of every service he used on the internet for a week. It amounted to "146,000 words of legalese." If you do not hit "agree," "it simply bounces you back to the page before, and waits for you to try again." The terms of the agreements tend to be written in broad terms protective of the rights of the company. See Alex Hern, "I Read all the Small Print on the Internet and It Made Me Want to Die," *The Guardian*, June 15, 2015, www.theguardian.com/technology/2015/jun/15/i-read-all-the-small-print-on-the-internet.

[104] See Pierre Bourdieu, "The Force of Law: Toward a Sociology of the Juridical Field," 38 *Hastings Law Journal* 814, 848–50 (1987).

[105] See Margaret Jane Radin, *Boilerplate: The Fine Print, Vanishing Rights, and the Rule of Law* (Princeton, NJ: Princeton University Press 2013) 1.

engage in the transaction at all, and available alternatives frequently impose the same standard terms.

The point here is not to reiterate these common criticisms. Even if objectionable terms were legally prohibited as critics advocate, form agreements would still be ubiquitous and would still be presented on a take-it-or-leave-it basis. The standardization of transactions is characteristic of mass societies in which organizations channel a huge bulk of social intercourse. This was already apparent when Karl Llewellyn astutely remarked in 1931: "the major importance of legal contract is to provide a frame-work for well-nigh every type of group organization and for well-nigh every type of passing or permanent relations between individuals and groups, up to and including states – a frame-work highly adjustable, a frame-work which almost never accurately indicates real working relations, but which affords a rough indication around which such relations vary, an occasional guide in cases of doubt, and a norm of ultimate appeal when the relations cease in fact to work."[106] Morris Cohen identified the growing standardization of contracts as a means to manage the increasing complexity and volume of transactions.[107]

Adding to standardization brought by form contracts and legal repetition, layers of laws and regulations address a vast range of activities, setting minimum terms and restricting options. (These requirements are also often incorporated in form contracts.) Health regulations impose standards for food and drugs; consumer protection regulations impose warranties and protect purchasers from fraud; safety regulations cover the characteristics and operation of trains, planes, automobiles, boats, lawn mowers, and so on; safety and sanitation protections are required in homes, rental properties, hotels, and restaurants; labor laws set rules for collective bargaining and employment laws apply to work conditions; workmen's compensation laws cover injuries suffered at work; licensing requirements apply to innumerable occupations; environmental restrictions apply to pesticide use, particulates released from factories, and so on. The list of legally imposed features and restrictions is endless and constantly added to. Even seemingly individualized situations can be standardized by law. In many states, child support payments are determined according to a preset formula based on income and costs.[108]

With many transactions mostly fixed and uniform owing to standard contract terms and legally imposed requirements, what once were "legal services" tailored individually for clients by legal professionals are now becoming "legal products" sold as commodities.[109] Standardized wills, divorce agreements, patent applications,

---

[106] Karl Llewellyn, "What Price Contract? An Essay in Perspective," 40 *Yale Law Journal* 704, 736–37 (1931).

[107] Cohen, "The Basis of Contract," supra.

[108] See Missouri Supreme Court Rules, 88.01, Presumed Child Support, Civil Procedure Form No. 14, www.courts.mo.gov/courts/clerkhandbooksp2rulesonly.nsf/o/bb1f5facef06aef386256ca60052137f? OpenDocument.

[109] On commoditization of law, see Richard Susskind, *The End of Lawyers?* rev. ed. (Oxford: Oxford University Press 2010).

incorporation forms, apartment leases, and other legal matters can be downloaded for a fee from the internet and filled in without professional assistance.

Entrenching the fixity of the legal fabric is the passage of time and the inter-connectedness of law within society. Long co-evolution within society renders existing legal doctrines into normalized aspects of social interaction.[110] Routine affairs build on top of and around laws (though social actors may also ignore law or rearrange their actions to circumvent it). Mortgages, for instance, developed over the course of several centuries in English law via the interaction of statutes promoting selected economic interests with evolving common law property doctrines.[111] Mortgages now occupy a pivotal place in real property financing and can be modified in various ways, but cannot be abolished without wreaking economic havoc. The same is true of many other long-standing legal arrangements – in principle alterable entirely, but in practice not. Law and surrounding social and economic relations become mutually anchored and relatively fixed though lengthy coexistence.

These five factors collectively have given rise to a legal infrastructure addressing large domains of social interaction. The rules of social intercourse are intertwined with instrumental uses of law by government within this legal fabric and social and economic transactions build on and take place against this infrastructure. Competing social interests engage in contests to influence what legislatures, executives, courts, and agencies legally enforce, thereby adding to or altering the legal fabric, knitting new parts and reknitting old, though stable and relatively fixed in the aggregate.

COURTS AS ORGANIZATIONS

All state institutions with legal functions – police, prosecuting agencies, legislatures, prisons, and others – are organizations that can be analyzed in terms of their designated purposes. Here I focus on courts as organizations. Anglo-American jurisprudents accord a great deal of attention to judges and judging, but rarely do they analyze courts as organizations. The iconic image of a court in legal theory is an enrobed judge presiding on the bench issuing rule-based decisions to decide cases. That image, most fitting for appellate judges, is not the main task of most judges. Lower court judges work primarily as docket managers working their way through the constant flow of incoming cases as quickly as possible consistent with their role obligations (be fair, be unbiased, apply the law, be professional, be efficient, carry their fair load). Judges expeditiously process cases in several ways: disposing of cases early on (dismissal for lack of jurisdiction, failure to state a claim, summary judgment, etc.); stamping agreements reached by the parties (plea bargains, settlements,

---

[110]   See Pierre Bourdieu, "The Force of Law: Toward a Sociology of the Juridical Field," 38 *Hastings Law Journal* 814, 843–48 (1987).

[111]   See A. W. B. Simpson, *A History of the Land Law*, 2nd ed. (Oxford: Oxford University Press 1986) 141–43.

no fault divorces, etc.); or sending cases to other venues for processing (mediation, arbitration).[112] And that is largely how courts in the United States operate. A familiar though overlooked sign of courts as bureaucracies is that law clerks carry out significant judicial responsibilities, including drafting judicial opinions.[113] Courts are organizations that process cases. *That* is their primary purpose.

Trials are resource consuming and impede the processing of cases. The number of cases resolved by trial has fallen steadily for decades in both federal and state courts, dubbed "the vanishing trial" by Marc Galanter.[114] In 1960, 11.5 percent of federal civil cases were resolved by trial, compared to 1.8 percent in 2002; the percentage has since further declined to 1.1 percent.[115] Criminal dispositions by trial in federal courts have declined from 15 percent in 1962 to under 5 percent in 2002.[116] Bankruptcy cases terminated by trial have fallen from 16.4 percent in 1982 to 4.8 percent in 2002.[117] "Although virtually every other indicator of legal activity is rising," he observes, "trials are declining not only in relation to cases in the courts but to the size of the population and the size of the economy."[118] Both the percentage and the absolute number of cases resolved by trial have declined. In addition, federal trial judges have exhibited a steady decline in the number of hours presiding on the bench, currently averaging less than two hours per day.[119] In higher courts, many appellate cases are decided without oral arguments and without published opinions or any written opinion at all.[120] The U.S. Supreme Court now decides about seventy-five cases annually, less than half the number of cases it decided in the 1980s and earlier.[121]

The explanation for these general trends does not appear to be that courts are overworked from heavier caseloads. Two decades ago, with fewer judges and far less money, Galanter points out, federal courts conducted more than double the number of civil trials.[122]

So what explains the decline? Judges operate with a managerial mentality encouraged in judicial meetings and training seminars.[123] The Civil Justice Reform Act Congress passed in 1990 urged judges to find ways to reduce expenses and streamline

---

[112] See Trevor C. W. Farrow, *Civil Justice, Privatization, and Democracy* (Toronto: University of Toronto Press 2014). Trevor provides an in-depth study of this phenomenon in Canada, mentioning parallels in the United States.

[113] See Joseph Vining, "Justice and the Bureaucratization of Appellate Courts," 2 *Windsor Yearbook of Access to Justice* 3, 7–8 (1982).

[114] See Marc Galanter, "The Vanishing Trial: An Examination of Trials and Related Matters in Federal and State Courts," 1 *Journal of Empirical Legal Studies* 459 (2004).

[115] See Hans A. von Spakovsky, "The Unfair Attack on Arbitration: Harming Consumers by Eliminating a Proven Dispute Resolution System," Legal Memorandum, The Heritage Foundation, July 17, 2013, http://report.hertage.org/lm97.

[116] Galanter, "The Vanishing Trial," supra 492–93.   [117] Id. 498.   [118] Id. 460.

[119] See Jordan M. Singer and William G. Young, "Bench Presence 2014: An Updated Look at Federal Court Productivity," 48 *New England Law Review* 565, 566–67 (2014).

[120] Galanter, "The Vanishing Trial," supra 529.

[121] See Deena Shanker, "The U.S. Supreme Court decides less than half as many cases as it did 40 years ago – and that's just fine," *Quartz*, July 5, 2015, http://qz.com/443100/supreme-court-decisions/.

[122] Galanter, "The Vanishing Trial," supra 519.   [123] Id. 519–20.

the process, including promoting pretrial settlements and authorizing judges to "refer appropriate cases to alternative dispute resolution programs."[124] Judges' ability to dismiss cases has been enhanced in federal courts through heightened pleading requirements that require plaintiffs to show a plausible right to relief prior to an opportunity for discovery.[125] "As adjudication is diffused and privatized," Galanter observes, "what courts do is changing as they become the site of a great deal of administrative processing of cases, along with the residue of trials in high stakes and intractable cases."[126] When plowing through the continuously refilling stack of cases on their desk, judges dismiss cases at the outset, encourage and pressure parties to settle, or send them to arbitration, seeing only a vanishingly small number through trial.[127]

A cost-effective way to manage cases is to keep them out of court to begin with. Congress enacted the Federal Arbitration Act (1925) to encourage businesses to resolve disputes among themselves in arbitration, but in the past two decades corporations have systematically incorporated mandatory arbitration clauses in their contracts with employees and consumers. Credit cards, brokerage agreements, and cell phone contracts require arbitration. Mandatory arbitration is also common in insurance disputes and employment discrimination and retaliation claims. Arbitration clauses are required by nursing homes, educational institutions, medical clinics, automobile companies, and funeral homes, and continue to spread.[128] Judges have facilitated these contractually imposed denials of access to courts by upholding the validity of mandatory arbitration clauses and routinely upholding arbitration decisions.[129] Civil justice is being privatized because corporations prefer it and it lightens demands on courts.[130] Business for private arbitration companies is rapidly increasing, with the American Arbitration Association indicating 200,000 annual filings in 2012, up from 150,000 in 2007.[131]

Delay, costs, and the involvement of lawyers also discourage cases from court. In federal court, the median length of time from filing a complaint to trial is 23.6

---

[124] Civil Justice Reform Act of 1990, 28 U.S.C. Sections 471–82, Section 473(a)(6).

[125] See *Ashcroft v. Iqbal*, 556 U.S. 662 (2009); *Bell Atlantic Corp. v Twombly*, 550 U.S. 544 (2007).

[126] Galanter, "The Vanishing Trial," supra 531.

[127] For a demonstration of the deleterious consequences of this decline, see Robert P. Burns, *The Death of the American Trial* (Chicago, IL: Chicago University Press 2009).

[128] See Jessica Silver-Greenberg and Michael Corkery, "In Arbitration, a 'Privatization of the Justice System,'" November 1, 2015, *New York Times*, www.nytimes.com/2015/11/02/business/dealbook/in-arbitration-a-privatization-of-the-justice-system.html?hp&action=click&pgtype=Homepage&module=first-column-region&region=top-news&WT.nav=top-news&_r=0.

[129] See American Express Co. Italian Colors Rest., 133 S. Ct. 2304 (2013); AT&T Mobility LLC v. Concepcion, 131 S.Ct. 1740 (2011).

[130] A detailed study of this diffusion revealing its adverse legal and social implications is Judith Resnick, "Diffusing Disputes: The Public in the Private of Arbitration, the Private in Courts, and the Erasure of Rights," 124 *Yale Law Journal* 2804 (2014).

[131] Id. 2936.

months, compared to an average 6.9 months from a request for arbitration to final award.[132] Attorneys' fees and legal proceedings (pretrial motions, discovery, investigation, experts) are costly, prohibitive in cases with monetary value below a few thousand dollars or for people with limited resources. Merchants or members of small communities involved in disputes often prefer to resolve matters consensually among themselves rather than go to court.[133] As Galanter observes, in "many instances the participants can devise more satisfactory solutions to their disputes than can professionals constrained to apply general rules on the basis of limited knowledge of the dispute."[134]

Lack of money is a major factor inhibiting access to courts. More than a million Americans each year are unable to afford or obtain appointed lawyers in civil cases, including life-affecting matters like eviction proceedings, child custody proceedings, and child support proceedings.[135] People in these situations represent themselves or do not show up, losing by default. People who suffer injuries or property damage caused by others may be covered by insurance (if the parties involved have policies), but insurance companies protect their own economic interests and disagreements over coverage requires legal assistance. The image of two parties battling in court armed with lawyers protecting their legal rights is not a reality for many people of ordinary means.[136]

Criminal cases involve different factors, but here as well a high percentage of cases settle through plea agreements. In the 1920s, 70 percent of convictions were obtained through guilty pleas.[137] In recent years, about 94 percent of convictions in state court and 97 percent in federal court are guilty pleas.[138] Criminal defendants who plead guilty are rewarded with more lenient outcomes, while those who demand a trial and are subsequently found guilty suffer significantly worse penalties. A substantial majority of criminal defendants lack financial resources to retain lawyers,[139] and many plead guilty without the assistance of

---

[132] Von Spakovsky, "The Unfair Attack on Arbitration," supra 7.

[133] See Stewart Macaulay, "Non-contractual Relations in Business: A Preliminary Study," 28 *American Sociological Review* 55 (1963); Robert Ellickson, *Order Without Law: How Neighbors Settle Disputes* (Cambridge, MA: Harvard University Press 1994).

[134] Marc Galanter, "Justice in Many Rooms: Courts, Private Ordering, and Indigenous Law," 19 *Journal of Legal Pluralism* 1, 4 (1981).

[135] See Legal Services Corporation, Documenting the Justice Gap in America: The Current Unmet Civil Legal Needs of Low-Income Americans (September 2009), www.lsc.gov/sites/default/files/LSC/pdfs/documenting_the_justice_gap_in_america_2009.pdf.

[136] Attorneys will bear the cost of bringing tort cases with large potential recoveries and a solid chance of success because their compensation is a percentage of the recovery.

[137] See Albert W. Alschuler, "Plea Bargaining and Its History," 79 *Columbia L. Rev.* 1, 26 (1979).

[138] See Anne R. Traum, "Using Outcomes to Reframe Guilty Plea Adjudication," 66 *Florida L. Rev.* 823, 854 (2014); Lucian E. Dervan and Vanessa A. Edkins, "The Innocent Defendant's Dilemma: An Innovative Empirical Study of Plea Bargaining's Innocence Problem," 103 *Criminal Law and Criminology* 1, 6 (2013).

[139] See Bureau of Justice Assistance, Contracting for Indigent Defense Services: A Special Report (2000), U.S. Department of Justice, www.ncjrs.gov/pdffiles1/bja/181160.pdf.

lawyers.[140] State-funded or appointed lawyers are underpaid and overburdened, with insufficient time to allocate to each defendant.[141] As with judges, defense lawyers and prosecutors are themselves wading through piles of cases and have strong incentives to dispose of as many as possible through plea agreements. In combination with other aspects of the criminal justice system – including punitive laws and sentencing owing to anti-crime rhetoric and attitudes by politicians and judges – this results in the highest prison population and second highest rate of incarceration in the world.[142]

An exceedingly small percentage of cases make it through trial, mainly: criminal cases where the defendant insists on innocence or faces a severe penalty no matter what happens; high-value civil cases with no clear outcome; and highly motivated cases in which cost is a secondary concern, like child custody cases or public interest litigation. In jury trials, judges act as trial managers with the primary task of ensuring an orderly presentation of evidence.

The managerial role of judges is especially evident in litigation brought by parties seeking to use courts to effectuate social and political change in matters ranging from environmental protection, to prison reform, to educational reform – instrumental uses of law through the vehicle of courts. Unlike the usual bilateral litigation structure, multiple parties are involved in public interest litigation representing different interests and points of view. Judicial decisions involve significant public policy questions. The remedy sought often is not compensation for past injury, but instead consists of legislative-like detailed decrees formulated by the parties that require government actions or reforms, with courts thereafter maintaining oversight for lengthy periods.[143] These cases depart so substantially from the standard image of judges applying law that a knowledgeable observer remarked, "the proceeding is recognizable as a lawsuit only because it takes place in a courtroom before an official called a judge."[144]

In Lon Fuller's antithesis between managerial direction versus law as rules, it turns out that courts are case-processing organizations in which judges operate much of the time in a managerial mode.[145] Fuller would be aghast.

---

[140] See "Five Problems Facing Public Defense on the 40th Anniversary of *Gideon v. Wainwright*," National Legal Aid and Defender Association, www.nlada.org/Defender/Defender_Gideon/ Defender_Gideon_5_Problems.

[141] See Tina Peng, "I'm a Public Defender. It's Impossible for Me to Do a Good Job Representing My Clients," *Washington Post*, September 3, 2015, www.washingtonpost.com/opinions/our-public-defender-system-isnt-just-broken–its-unconstitutional/2015/09/03/aadf2b6c-519b-11e5-9812-92d5948a40f8_story.html.

[142] See *World Prison Brief Database*, Institute for Criminal Policy Research, Birkbeck, University of London, www.prisonstudies.org/highest-to-lowest/prison-population-total.

[143] These implications are detailed in Ross Sandler and David Schoenbrod, *Democracy by Decree: What Happens When Courts Run Government* (New Haven, CT: Yale University Press 2003).

[144] Abraham Chayes, "The Role of the Judge in Public Law Litigation," 89 *Harvard L. Rev.* 1281, 1303 (1976).

[145] See Jonathan T. Molot, "How Changes in the Legal Profession Reflect Changes in Civil Procedure," 84 *Virginia L. Rev.* 955 (1998).

Courts depend on private forums to carry a major load of legal disputes. This is part of a broader trend in society of government organizations relying on private actors to complete public functions. Large universities have their own gun-carrying police departments, commingling private funding and priorities with public power to arrest and maintain order. Police departments work closely with private security forces at colleges, shopping malls, residential enclaves, and public venues like sports stadiums and concert halls; privately run prisons house criminals sentenced by courts; private contractors work alongside the military. Regulation of the environment, the internet, and other domains involve the participation, expertise, and monitoring by private actors.[146] Google, for instance, enforces the European Union's "right to be forgotten on the Internet" law, passing judgment on more than 400,000 cases in the first two years, which the European Union does not have the technological or institutional capacity to handle.[147]

At the same time private organizations are shouldering a greater load of legal functions, they have come to incorporate within their own operations legal norms like due process and formal decision making, taking on legal characteristics through imitation or out of concern to avoid liability.[148] Legal procedures, functions, and modes of operation are thus diffusing outward from governmental legal organizations and being picked up by private organizations. In turn, courts regularly defer to or accept formal arrangements within organizations as sufficient to meet legal requirements.[149] "Through this interplay, the boundaries of these fields [organizations and law] tend to blur, and their logics tend to merge."[150]

The problems of modern mass societies are too complex and numerous for government legal organizations to manage alone. Technological advancements promise further far-reaching changes in law to deal with these problems. A primitive first step was policing by automated cameras at stop lights. Now mass surveillance for national security purposes as well as for basic police work is done by computer algorithms searching big data comprised of all accessible digital information.[151] Electronic searches of documents for criminal and civil cases (e-discovery, document review) are increasingly common. Artificial intelligence has the capacity to carry out regulatory

---

[146] See Orly Lobel, "The Renew Deal: The Fall of Regulation and the Rise of Governance in Contemporary Legal Thought," 89 *Minnesota Law Review* 342 (2004). For refinements of Lobel's claims, see Bradley C. Karkkainen, " 'New Governance' in Legal Thought and in the World: Some Splitting as Antidote to Overzealous Lumping," 89 *Minnesota Law Review* 471 (2004).

[147] Mark Scott, "Europe Tried to Rein in Google. It Backfired." *New York Times*, April 18, 2016, www.nytimes.com/2016/04/19/technology/google-europe-privacy-watchdog.html?_r=0

[148] See Lauren B. Edelman, "Legal Environments and Organizational Governance: The Expansion of Due Process in the Workplace," 95 *American Journal of Sociology* 1401 (1990).

[149] Lauren B. Edelman, Linda H. Krieger, Scott R. Eliason, Catherine R. Albiston, and Virginia Mellema, 117 *American Journal of Sociology* 888 (2011).

[150] Id. 900.

[151] See Elizabeth E. Joh, "The New Surveillance Discretion: Automated Suspicion, Big Data, and Policing," 10 *Harvard Law and Policy Review* 15 (2016).

compliance and enforcement.[152] A machine-learning algorithm has achieved a high success rate in predicting outcomes for open questions of tax law applied to specific situations.[153] Once outcomes can be predicted, the next step is algorithms that render legal decisions. This is an early stage of mining the potential of extraordinary computing power and massive information, with unknown transformative effects for law and society certain to come.

VARIATION OF LEGAL FABRIC AND ORGANIZATIONS ACROSS SOCIETIES

Social interaction is enhanced by trust the legal fabric provides in urban societies where people daily move among a multitude of strangers.[154] In simpler societies, trust was ensured by face-to-face relationships and reputation, whereas in advanced capitalist societies dominated by organizations, it is provided by the legal fabric. The legal fabric thus is critical to life in modern cities. A vast ocean of transactions and interaction takes place against the backdrop of this legal fabric. It is conceivable that the legal fabric produces more certainty in expected legal outcomes, helping prevent problems, promoting settlements, and rendering access to legal forums less necessary when problems do arise, though whether any of this is true has not been empirically confirmed. When things go wrong, many people are legally obliged to go to private forums to seek redress, or lack the financial wherewithal to enforce their legal rights in court. The use of courts in the United States is rationed by ability to pay with a high price for access. People who cannot procure lawyers must represent themselves or absorb their losses. For a significant portion of the U.S. populace, this combination amounts to reams of law *ex ante* coinciding with constrained access to law *ex post*.

Societies vary in the relative extent to which state law creates a legal fabric, the scope of its coverage, and access to courts when problems arise. All advanced capitalist societies have legal fabrics comparable in solidity and scope to the United States. They too are populated with innumerable organizations that utilize standardized contracts, and they too have extensive, government-imposed legal requirements covering all manner of interactions. Most of these countries deliver legal aid in civil and criminal cases to people who cannot afford it at levels superior to the United States, though cost is a pressing issue.[155] In the United Kingdom,

---

[152]   Banking Tech, "Artificial Intelligence Set to Transform Regulatory Compliance," *Banking Technology*, September 19, 2016, www.bankingtech.com/566622/artificial-intelligence-set-to-transform-regulatory-compliance/.

[153]   Benjamin Alarie, Anthony Nibless, and Albert Yoon, "Using Machine Learning to Predict Outcomes in Tax Law," 58 *Canadian Business Law Journal* 231 (2016).

[154]   See Karl Llewellyn, "What Price Contract?" supra 718–21. On the importance of trust, see Paul Seabright, *The Company of Strangers: A Natural History of Economic Life*, rev. ed. (Princeton, NJ: Princeton University Press 2010).

[155]   For a detailed survey of European legal aid, see, e.g., Maurits Barendrecht, et al., "Legal Aid in Europe," HIIL (2014), www.hiil.org/data/sitemanagement/media/Report_legal_aid_in_Europe.pdf. The United States scores poorly in "affordability and access," with a score of 0.47, significantly below

a recent report issued by the judiciary found, "the single, most pervasive and intractable weakness of our civil courts is that they simply do not provide reasonable access to justice for any but the most wealthy individuals[.]"[156] The solution advocated in the report is an online court system that allows people to file and process claims without the participation of lawyers. Many countries across the globe identify attorneys' fees as a major problem for public access to court.[157]

Outside of advanced capitalist societies, the state legal fabric can be frayed or patchy. When state organizations and the legal system function poorly, instrumental government uses of law are more limited (focused on state power). Residents of shantytowns in mega cities around the globe lack legal title to their property, the policing system can be corrupt or ineffective, residents work in underground economies outside contract law, courts are costly, distant, and inefficient, legal assistance is unavailable or too expensive.[158] In rural areas, customary law or religious law often provide rules of social intercourse people follow, with little or no state legal fabric present.

FROM HART TO SOCIAL LEGAL THEORY

Despite very different appearances, the theory of law I sketch is congruent with Hart's analysis, though we diverge at points. On the first page of *The Concept of Law* he states, "Notwithstanding its concern with analysis the book may also be regarded as an essay in descriptive sociology."[159] His assertion has been widely dismissed on grounds that little in the text is sociological, but it is accurate. Hart views law as a social phenomenon, and he analyzes law's various relations to morality, social necessities, social functions, and so forth. My approach also combines analysis and descriptive sociology, though I resort far more to social science than he does.

When setting out his distinction between primary rules of social obligation and power-conferring secondary rules, Hart noted, "A full detailed taxonomy of the varieties of law comprised in a modern legal system, free from the prejudice that all *must* be reducible to a single simple type, still remains to be accomplished."[160] The two orientations I distinguish between rules of social intercourse and government uses of law, and the three subtypes of the latter, is a more detailed breakdown of varieties of modern law, elaborating aspects he missed.

Hart's enduring contribution to jurisprudence was to ground the existence of law ultimately in collective recognition.[161] The "rule that what the Queen in Parliament

---

other developed countries. See The World Justice Project, Rule of Law Index 2015, United States Country Profile, p. 152.

[156] Lord Justice Briggs, Civil Courts Structure Review: Interim Report, December 2015, 5.23, p51, www.judiciary.gov.uk/wp-content/uploads/2016/01/ccsr-interim-report-dec-15-final1.pdf; Lord Justice Briggs, Civil Courts Structure Review: Final Report, July 2016, www.judiciary.gov.uk/wp-content/uploads/2016/07/civil-courts-structure-review-final-report-jul-16-final-1.pdf.

[157] World Justice Project, Rule of Law Index 2015, supra 45.

[158] For a comparative overview showing a range of variation, see The World Justice Project, supra.

[159] Hart, *Concept of Law*, supra v. [160] Id. 32. [161] Id. 102–07.

enacts is law" is true simply because courts, government officials, and citizens in the United Kingdom socially accept it.[162] Building on this social recognition, legal officials collectively recognize criteria for legal authority, validity, change, application, and execution to produce and carry out obligatory legal rules that apply to social behavior. My understanding of law as a social institution incorporates these Hartian insights.

The main initial difference lies in our contrasting frameworks. Hart's objective was to produce a theory of law based on the essential characteristics of state law. This focus is certainly justified and his results are illuminating. The theory of law I develop does not isolate on state law because law is inextricably tied to and conditioned by surrounding factors. Societies consist of unique constellations of cultural, social, economic, political, material, ecological, and technological influences that shape law and are shaped by law. Societies evolve in the course of history, with law an integral aspect of this process. Combining these two propositions leads to looking at law *within* societies, including multiple forms of law, as they change over time. Thus I go in directions he did not explore.

A holistic view highlights aspects of modern law ignored by analytical jurisprudents, among which, versatile government uses of law, public-private commingling of legal institutions and functions, courts operating as organizations, and the background legal fabric. While none of this can be considered necessary features of law for all times and places, state law has evolved this way.

Where we directly join issue involves implications that follow from Hart's account of social recognition as the ultimate basis of law, and on the status of his theory of law. One of Hart's seminal insights is that law ultimately rests on conventional social acceptance. When he characterized law as a system of secondary rules (power-conferring) and primary rules (obligation) for social ordering, however, he *presupposed* criteria of law's form and function without considering that nothing requires rules of recognition to incorporate these criteria. The criteria of law are contingent and depend on the particular socially recognized manifestations of law at issue. Law can be anything, can take any form and serve any function, legal officials and/or people conventionally recognize.

The lesson to be drawn is that Hart's theory at bottom consists of a set of abstract generalizations about state law in highly legalized, advanced, capitalist nations. They do not capture everything about state law in these countries (missing aspects of government uses of law that are not about rules or social ordering), they do not account for variations in countries with less developed state legal institutions, and they do not account for forms of law other than state law.

---

[162]   Id. 104.

6

What Is International Law?

International law is a particular social-historical legal tradition that emerged and spread over time to deal with matters between and across polities. Obvious as this statement may appear, its full implications point to a thorough reconstruction of theoretical accounts of international law. Theories of international law suffer from conceptual and ideological barriers. The conceptual barrier is a theoretical framework tracing back to Jeremy Bentham that distorts perceptions by situating domestic law and international law as separate, parallel systems and categories. The ideological barrier is rooted in the deep normative commitment among generations of international jurists (at least until relatively recently) to construct an all-encompassing international legal system, perpetuating a false vision of the place of international law and how it relates to domestic law and to transnational regulation. Dismantling these barriers allows a sounder understanding of international law.

Part I of this chapter recounts how Bentham inadvertently created an enduring set of theoretical problems. Part II describes international law as a specific social-historical legal tradition, showing its European origins and diffusion with imperialism, and exposing three slants in international law. Part III broadens the lens to sketch the history of interaction between and across polities and how this has been managed in the past and present, detailing contemporary efforts to deal with this interaction through organizations and transnational law and regulation. With this background in place, Part IV elaborates a series of theoretical clarifications. First, I unravel several confusions that result from construing state law and international law as parallel categories and conflating system with category. Then I explain why international law is a genuine form of law, though not a unified hierarchical system. Contrary to common perceptions, furthermore, I show that state law and international law are not and have never been separate systems. Finally, I clarify the relationship between international law and transnational law and regulation. Aspects of this theoretical reconstruction may initially appear surprising, but they follow from the insight that international law is a social-historical tradition.

PART I. BENTHAM'S VEXATIOUS LEGACY

International jurists still battle the ghost of Jeremy Bentham. In a few brief assertions at the end of a lengthy book on law in general, written in 1789, Bentham proposed "international law" as a more apt label than the then current "law of nations," because the latter, he thought, confusingly suggests national law.[1] International law involves "the mutual transactions between sovereigns," he asserted. "Transactions which may take place between individuals who are subjects of different states" are domestic law.[2] This new label and understanding quickly took hold. Robert Phillimore's influential 1854 *Commentaries upon International Law* begins, "The necessity of mutual inter-course is laid in the nature of States. ... The intercourse of Nations, therefore, gives rise to International Rights and Duties, and these require an International Law for their regulation and enforcement."[3] The classic *Law of Nations* by J. L. Brierly proclaims: "The Law of Nations, or International Law, may be defined as the body of rules and principles of actions which are binding upon civilized states in their relations with one another."[4]

Bentham's conception of the field was narrower than prevailing views when he wrote.[5] "More or less inadvertently, Bentham changed the boundaries of the field he sought to define."[6] In the eighteenth century, law of nations was commonly thought to include three categories: the law of traders or merchants from different locales, maritime and admiralty law, and legal relations between states (including diplomatic immunities, treaties, and customary rules of war and peace).[7] Consistent with this broader view, Blackstone defined law of nations to encompass "intercourse which must frequently occur between two or more independent states, and the individuals belonging to each";[8] he identified a range of subjects, including "civil transactions and question of property between the subjects of different states,[9] "the law merchant, which is a branch of the law of nations," bills of exchange, shipwrecks and prizes at sea, treatment of diplomats, piracy, and a few others.[10]

By limiting his conception to state-to-state matters, Bentham excluded transactions between individuals of different states – business affairs, recognition of foreign

---

[1] See Jeremy Bentham, *An Introduction to the Principles of Morals and Legislation*, edited by J. H. Burns and H. L. A. Hart (University of London: Athlone Press 1970) 296.

[2] Id.

[3] Robert Phillimore, *Commentaries upon International Law* (London: William Benning and Co 1854) v.

[4] J. L. Brierly, *The Law of Nations*, 6th ed. (Oxford: Clarendon Press 1963).

[5] An informative analysis of Bentham's views is M. W. Janis, "Jeremy Bentham and the Fashioning of 'International Law,'" 78 *American Journal of International Law* 405 (1984).

[6] Janis, "Jeremy Bentham and the Fashioning of 'International Law,'" supra 410.

[7] See Edwin D. Dickinson, "The Law of Nations as Part of the National Law of the United States," 101 *University of Pennsylvania L. Rev.* 26, 26–34 (1952).

[8] William Blackstone, *Commentaries on the Laws of England*, Book Four (Oxford: Oxford University Press [1765–69] 2016) 44.

[9] Id. 45.   [10] Id. 44–45.

judgments, divorce and child custody, etc. – all relegated to domestic law. Joseph Story in the 1830s coined the term "private international law" to cover these matters, as distinct from "public international law" addressing legal arrangements between states.[11] This division split the field, in effect ejecting private international law. Also known as "conflicts of law" or "choice of law," private international law was designated domestic law.[12] Prominent early twentieth-century international law scholar Lassa Oppenheim found it "necessary to emphasize that only the so-called public International Law, which is identical with Law of Nations, is International Law, whereas the so-called private International Law is not, at any rate not as a rule."[13]

Perennial complaints have issued from international lawyers lamenting the flawed public–private international law demarcation. It fails for multiple reasons: international courts render decisions on choice of law issues, articulating rules that are not domestic law; the private international law principle of comity is tied to maintaining peaceful relations between states; transnational economic law is not exclusively domestic nor a matter of state relations, so it fits neither category; conventions and customs, which count as public international law, cover aspects of private international law topics.[14] "The truth," wrote a jurist in 1936, "is that it is difficult to make Private International Law fit any one single conception, whether municipal law or international law, for in fact it is a complex of both."[15] Another scholar at the time remarked, "There is no clear line of demarcation between [private] and public international law."[16] "Public international law, if regarded merely as applying only between sovereign states, will be eclipsed by the dire need of regulating and facilitating the mutual relations of peoples in trade, social intercourse, and other commerce."[17] Philip Jessup devoted his 1956 Storrs Lecture to advocating the label "transnational law," encompassing "all law which regulates actions or events that transcend national frontiers. Both public and private international law are included, as are other rules which do not wholly fit into such standard categories."[18]

---

[11] See Joel R. Paul, "The Isolation of Private International Law," 7 *Wisconsin International Law Journal* 149, 161 (1988).

[12] See John Westlake, *Treatise on Private International Law or the Conflict of Laws* (Philadelphia. PA: T. & J. W. Johnson & Co. 1859) (treating private international law "as a department of English law" v).

[13] Lassa Oppenheim, *International Law*, 7th ed., edited by H. Lauterpacht (London: Longmas, Green & Co. 1948) 6. The exception Oppenheim alludes to is when private international law matters are addressed in treaties.

[14] J. G. Starke, "Private and Public International Law," 52 *Law Quarterly Review* 395 (1936); John R. Stevenson, "The Relationship of Private International Law to Public International Law," 52 *Columbia L. Review* 561 (1952).

[15] Starke, "Private and Public International Law," supra 399.

[16] Philip Marshall Brown, "Private Versus Public International Law," 36 *American Journal of International Law*, 448, 450 (1942).

[17] Id. [18] Philip C. Jessup, *Transnational Law* (New Haven, CT: Yale University Press 1956) 2.

Once a label and corresponding conceptual implications take hold, however, they are hard to dislodge.[19] The very term "inter"-"national" law connotes relations between states, as Bentham intended. "International law is defined as 'inter-state' law," observed Anne-Marie Slaughter. "International society is a society of states; international law seeks to achieve the goals and values of that society; it does so primarily by regulating states."[20] International law texts typically repeat the standard divide, albeit acknowledging "the lines between international law and domestic law, as well as between public law and private law, have thus become blurred and somewhat artificial."[21]

Bentham's second negative impact came from his state law-based conception of law. "A law," he wrote, "may be defined as an assemblage of signs declarative of a volition conceived or adopted by the *sovereign* in a state, concerning the conduct to be observed in a certain case by a certain person or class of persons, who in the case in question are or are supposed to be subject to his power."[22] It follows from this definition "that a treaty made by one sovereign with another is not itself a law."[23] His disciple John Austin reiterated, "the law obtaining between nations is not positive law: for every positive law is set by a given sovereign to a person or persons in a state of subjection to its author."[24] International law "is not law properly so-called,"[25] but rather is a form of public morality, in Austin's view, because it does not issue from a sovereign and is not backed by a system of coercive enforcement. Also using state law as his standard, H. L. A. Hart reinforced the old legal positivist verdict that international law is not really law on the grounds that it lacks systematic unifying rules, though he allowed that it might someday become law.[26]

A separate set of theoretical consequences followed from Bentham's categorical distinction between state law and international law. Before this distinction had been drawn, many prominent judges and jurists saw the law of nations as part of law in general, with no separation.[27] Derived from "the law of nature and reason," Blackstone wrote, the law of nations is "held to be a part of the law of the land."[28] Thomas Jefferson

---

[19]   For contemporary critiques, see Joel P. Trachtman, "The International Economic Law Revolution," 17 *University of Pennsylvania Journal of International Economic Law* 33 (1996); Joel R. Paul, "The Isolation of Private International Law," 7 *Wisconsin International Law Journal* 149 (1988).

[20]   Anne-Marie Slaughter, "A Liberal Theory of International Law," 94 *Proceedings of the Annual Meeting* 240, 242 (2000).

[21]   Barry E. Carter, Philip R. Trimble, and Allen S. Weiner, *International Law*, 5th ed. (New York: Aspen 2006) 2.

[22]   Jeremy Bentham, *Of Laws in General*, edited by H. L. A. Hart (London: Athlone Press 1970) 1 (emphasis added).

[23]   Id. 16.

[24]   John Austin, *The Province of Jurisprudence Determined* (London: Weidenfeld and Nicolson 1954) 201.

[25]   Id.   [26]   H. L. A. Hart, *The Concept of Law*, 2nd ed. (Oxford: Clarendon Press 1994) chapter 10.

[27]   See James Brown Scott, "The Legal Nature of International Law," 1 *American Journal of International Law* 831, 851–63 (1907); William S. Dodge, "The *Charming Betsy* and *The Paquete Habana*," February 25, 2016, UC Davis Legal Studies Research Paper No. 485, http://papers.ssrn.com/sol3/papers.cfm?abstract_id=2738241.

[28]   Blackstone, *Commentaries*, supra 44.

wrote, "The law of nations makes an integral part . . . of the laws of the land."[29] Article I Section 8 of the U.S. Constitution, which empowers Congress "to define and punish piracies and felonies committed on the high seas, and offenses against the law of nations," reflects this understanding. An analytical scheme that requires something to be *either* state law *or* international law, and accords primacy to the former, results in the conclusion that international law is a source of law that becomes domestic law when recognized by national legislation or courts. When they were not seen as mutually exclusive categories, the issue of which system of law a given set of doctrines belongs to did not arise.

Bentham's ideas, supplemented by his jurisprudential successors, have the combined effect of substantially emptying international law. Private international law is domestic law. And public international law not enforced by state law does not count as "law." Hence, much of international law is neither "international" nor "law." International lawyers, who still take up the issue "Is international law really 'law'?"[30] have chafed against this dual dismissal ever since.

PART II. INTERNATIONAL LAW AS A SOCIAL-HISTORICAL TRADITION

European Origins and Spread

Hugo Grotius's *De jure belli ac pacis* (*On the Law of War and Peace*) (1625) is widely considered the founding classic of modern international law. It was not based on states and had no theory of sovereignty.[31] His account of international law was constructed on natural law, which imposed moral obligations directly on rulers as individuals.[32] Grotius's account drew on the Roman Christian tradition of law. As Oppenheim described, "it is in its origin essentially a product of Christian civilization, and began gradually to grow from the second half of the Middle Ages."[33] Before slowly morphing into secular international law, it was the international law of European *respublica Christiana*.[34] Natural law thinkers of the seventeenth and eighteenth centuries believed natural law was imposed by God's will, and "the values which they

---

[29] Quoted in Scott, "The Legal Nature of International Law," supra 860.

[30] See Anthony D'Amato, "Is International Law Really 'Law'?" 79 *Northwestern University Law Review* 1293 (1985); Carter, Trimble, and Weiner, *International Law*, supra 25.

[31] Benedict Kingsbury, "A Grotian Tradition of Theory and Practice: Grotius, Law, and Moral Skepticism in the Thought of Hedley Bull," 17 *Q.L.R.* 3, 13–15 (1996).

[32] Roscoe Pound, "Philosophical Theory and International Law," 1 *Bibliotheca Visseriana* 71, 76–77 (1923).

[33] Oppenheim, *International Law*, supra 5–6.

[34] See Heinhard Steiger, "From the International Law of Christianity to the International Law of the World Citizen – Reflections on the Formation of the Epochs of the History of International Law," 3 *Journal of the History of International Law* 180 (2001).

held to underlie [international] society were Christian."[35] Though a natural law skeptic himself, Oppenheim appreciated that natural law "supplied the crutches" international law leaned on in its infancy.[36] "The Modern Law of Nations in particular owes its very existence to the theory of the Law of Nature."[37]

The Treaty of Westphalia (1648) divided Europe between separate nations, recognizing the supremacy of sovereigns within national boundaries, projecting the image of separate states within a community of states. States came to be seen as independent, equal legal persons in international society.[38] An understanding gradually formed that "The law of nations was nothing more than the law of nature applied to nations in a state of natural liberty."[39]

With the nineteenth century rise of legal positivism, jurists abandoned the natural law grounding.[40] International law was reconceived as laws to which independent states consent, explicitly by treaties or implicitly through (claimed) universal customs.[41] Treaties meet legal positivist strictures as legal contracts binding on the parties, and customary international law is tacitly recognized as positive law binding on states (at least after it is authoritatively declared).[42] International law "was now regarded as a corpus of rules arising from, as it were, the bottom up, as the conscious creation of the States themselves, rather than as a pre-existing, eternal, all-enveloping framework, in the manner of natural law."[43] In this state-primacy scheme, individuals possess no pre-political natural rights: rights are civil rights granted to citizens within an organized polity.[44]

The cumulative labors of multiple generations of jurists literally created international law. "International law was born of juristic speculation," Roscoe Pound observed, "and became a reality because that speculation gave men something by which to make and shape international legal institutions and a belief that they could

---

[35] Hedley Bull, *The Anarchical Society: A Study of Order in World Politics* (New York: Macmillan 1977) 28; see also Michal Lobban, "Theory in History: Positivism, Natural Law and Conjectural History in Seventeenth- and Eighteenth-Century English Legal Thought," in Maksymillian Del Mar and Michael Lobban, eds., *Law in Theory and History: New Essays on a Neglected Dialogue* (Oxford: Hart Publishing 2016).

[36] Oppenheim, *International Law*, supra 89.   [37] Id.

[38] An informative description of the development of these ideas is provided in Stephane Beaulac, "Emer de Vattel and the Externalization of Sovereignty," 5 *Journal of the History of International Law* 237 (2003).

[39] Dickinson, "Changing Concepts and the Doctrine of Incorporation," supra 246.

[40] See Pound, "Philosophical Theory and International Law," supra 82–83.

[41] Oppenheim, *International Law*, supra 24–29.

[42] See Dickinson, "Changing Concepts and the Doctrine of Incorporation," supra 249–50.

[43] Stephen C. Neff, "A Short History of International Law," in *International Law*, 3rd ed., edited by Malcolm D. Evans (Oxford: Oxford University Press 2010) 15.

[44] These shifts are conveyed in Anthony Pagden, "Human Rights, Natural Rights, and Europe's Imperial Legacy," 31 *Political Theory* 171, 184 (2003).

shape them effectively."[45] A signal event was the founding of the Institute de droit international in 1873.[46]

Efforts to develop international law were not entirely idealistic juristic endeavors. International law was bound up with imperialism: providing justifications for securing land and seizing territory, entering unequal treaties, forcibly opening commerce and imposing trade monopolies, fighting wars, and more.[47] State status marked the difference between polities with international standing (civilized) and those without standing (uncivilized).[48] The nadir was when European powers met at the Berlin Conference (1884–85) to divide Africa among themselves, with no representation by African leaders. A private organization controlled by King Leopold II of Belgium was handed the Congo, ultimately leading to the deaths of millions of Africans.[49] International lawyers straddled contradictory positions that the absence of territorial sovereignty (*territorium nullius*) permitted takeover, but nevertheless, tribal leaders could cede land through treaties, although the capacity to enter treaties was tied to sovereignty, which they lacked.[50]

Differential treatment was justified under international law based on the level of political and moral development. Christian European and American nations were accorded full status; "barbarous humanity" (Asian nations) had partial

---

[45]   Pound, "Philosophical Theory and International Law," supra 88.

[46]   See in general Martti Koskenniemi, "A History of International Law Histories," in *The Oxford Handbook of the History of International Law*, edited by Bardo Fassbender and Anne Peters (Oxford: Oxford University Press 2012).

[47]   A leading work on this is Antony Anghie, *Imperialism, Sovereignty, and the Making of International Law* (Cambridge: Cambridge University Press 2005). See also Casper Sylvest, "'Our Passion for Legality': International Law and Imperialism in Late Nineteenth Century Britain," 34 *Review of International Studies* 403 (2008); Duncan S. A. Bell, "Empire and International Relations in Victorian Thought," 49 *Historical Journal* 281 (2006). It is not my position that international law was developed to serve colonial purposes. Core doctrines, particularly on natural law, were put in place earlier. These doctrines were then interpreted and utilized to serve the economic and political objectives of colonizing countries. See Ian Hunter, "On the Critical History of the Law of Nature and Nations," in *Law and Politics in British Colonial Thought: Transpositions of Empire*, edited by S. Dorsett and Ian Hunter (New York: Palgrave Macmillan 2010).

[48]   See Sylvest, "'Our Passion for Legality,'" supra.

[49]   On the Berlin Conference, see Andrew Fitzmaurice, "Liberalism and Empire in Nineteenth Century International Law," 117 *American Historical Review* 122 (2012).

[50]   See Fitzmaurice, "Liberalism and Empire in Nineteenth Century International Law," supra 131–32; Sylvest, "'Our Passion for Legality,'" supra 412. Travers Twiss was a prominent international jurist who advanced King Leopold's actions in the Congo. A less well-known example is Professor John Bassett Moore of Columbia, one of the founders of the American Society of International Law. Bassett successfully represented the New York and Bermudez Company (NY&B) in recovering property seized by Venezuela, despite the fact that NY&B had provided more than $100 million (in today's dollars) and munitions to a rebel force in an effort to overthrow the government. See Benjamin Coates, "Securing Hegemony through Law: Venezuela, the U.S. Asphalt Trust, and the Uses of International Law, 1904–1909," 102 *Journal of American History* 380, 388–92 (2015). Moore was also involved in other discreditable actions on behalf of American business interests in Latin America. See Carl Landauer, "The Ambivalences of Power: Launching the *American Journal of International Law* in an Era of Empire and Globalization," 20 *Leiden Journal of International Law* 325, 343–44 (2007).

recognition; and "savage humanity" (the rest) "stood beyond the pale of the society of states."[51] "Hunter-gatherers, or semi-nomadic peoples, peoples that is who did not live in what most Europeans, no matter what their religious attachments, would have accepted as a civil or political way of life, were necessarily excluded."[52] The British government invoked international law to operate extra-territorial courts proclaiming the exclusive right to try British citizens in civil and criminal matters in more than fifteen countries across Africa, the Middle East, and Asia, including advanced societies like Japan, Turkey, Iran, Egypt, and China, continuing well into the twentieth century in all but Japan.[53] Latin American countries avoided this humiliation because they counted as civilized owing to their Christian European heritage, though they were subjected to other depredations from American and European interests citing international law.[54] A notorious example of international law imperialism is the British-imposed Treaty of Nanking following the First Opium War, which required China to pay war reparations and cede Hong Kong, and forced open Chinese markets to opium brought by British merchants from India against an official Chinese ban. Historian Christopher Bayly noted the hypocrisy. "Here again, the British used the cry of 'free trade' and international law to justify a policy of economic penetration in the interests of an underlying monopoly."[55] Japan achieved equal sovereign status under international law following its victorious wars against China in 1894 and Russia in 1904, prompting a Japanese diplomat to comment bluntly: "We show ourselves equal to you in scientific butchery, and at once we are admitted to your council tables as civilized men."[56]

The extension of international law around the globe was not entirely by force. International law gained acceptance through general usage. National leaders appreciated its usefulness in consolidating their own rule. Any individual or group that seizes the reins of government, whether violently or peaceably, is a sovereign leader with the authority to act on behalf of the country. Weak countries also recognized that sovereignty could provide some defenses against Western impositions. By the late nineteenth century, jurists from South America, Asia, and the Middle East, many of whom studied in Europe, mastered

[51] Bull, *Anarchical Society*, supra 38. See generally Jennifer Pitts, "Empire and Legal Universalisms in the Eighteenth Century," 117 *American Historical Review* 92 (2012).

[52] Anthony Pagden, "Human Rights, Natural Rights, and Europe's Imperial Legacy," 31 *Political Theory* 171, 184 (2003).

[53] See Turan Kayaoglu, *Legal Imperialism: Sovereignty and Extraterritoriality in Japan, the Ottoman Empire, and China* (New York: Cambridge University Press 2010) 5.

[54] See Coates, "Securing Hegemony through Law," supra 393–94.

[55] C. A. Bayly, *The Birth of the Modern World, 1780–1914* (Oxford: Blackwell 2004) 138.

[56] Quoted in R. P. Anand, "Onuma Yasuaki's 'When Was the Law of International Society Born? An Inquiry of the History of International Law from an Intercivilizational Perspective,'" 6 *Journal of the History of International Law* 1, 9 (2004).

international law doctrines and invoked them against European powers, as well as in their dealings with neighboring countries.[57]

Through a cumulative process of extension backed by force, defensive invocation by countries subjected to this force, an increase in non-Western international jurists, and growing use globally to deal with interstate affairs, "European International law developed into world international law."[58] From its European beginnings, the international legal system spread around the globe in the name of advancing civilization.

A way to glimpse what transpired, suggested by Onuma Yasuaki, is to hearken back to the fifteenth century, when three (at least) major systems existed: European, Islamic, and Sinocentric.[59] All three applied to a substantial aggregation of polities and claimed universality. At that time, the Islamic and Sinocentric versions encompassed more territory, people, and wealth than did the European. Had either of these other universalistic traditions spread their influence around the globe in subsequent centuries, legal arrangements between and across polities would operate through a wholly different set of concepts, doctrines, and practices.

Historical abuses committed in the name of international law do not ineluctably dictate what international law is today or in the future. But echoes of this past reverberate in contemporary criticisms that international rules are made by and for wealthy countries. Objections about the American and Euro-centric tilt of international law include that legal mandates from good governance and structural adjustment programs infringe on self-governance of poor countries; intellectual property laws are detrimental to poor countries; international criminal courts target only people from weak countries (nine out ten full International Criminal Court investigations have been in Africa[60]); and human rights organizations focus on individualist rights while ignoring collective social and economic rights.[61]

---

57 Arnulf Becker Lorca, "Universal International Law: Nineteenth-Century Histories of Imposition and Appropriation," 51 *Harvard International Law Journal* 475 (2010). See Coates, "Securing Hegemony through Law: Venezuela, the U.S. Asphalt Trust, and the Uses of International Law," supra 388–92.

58 Wolfgang Preiser, "History of the Law of Nations: Basic Questions and Principles," 7 *Encyclopedia of Public International Law* 126, 128 (Amsterdam: Elsevier 1984).

59 Onuma Yasuaki, "When Was the Law of International Society Born? An Inquiry of the History of International Law from an Intercivilizational Perspective," 2 *Journal of the History of International Law* 1 (2000). Ian Hunter cautions that accounts of universalism – natural law theory especially – suppress that there were competing theories at the time, so painting them as single, coherent traditions flattens the reality. Ian Hunter, "On the Critical History of the Law of Nature and Nations," in *Law and Politics in British Colonial Thought: Transpositions of Empire*, edited by S. Dorsett and I. Hunter (New York: Palgrave Macmillan 2010).

60 Kate Cronin-Furman and Stephanie Schwartz, "Is This the End of the International Criminal Court?" *Washington Post*, October 21, 2016.

61 See Antony Anghie and B. S. Chimni, "Third World Approaches to International Law and Individual Responsibility in Internal Conflict," 36 *Studies in Transnational Legal Policy* 185 (2004). B. S. Chimni, "International Institutions Today: An Imperial Global State in the Making," 15 *European Journal of International Law* 1 (2004); Makau Mutua, "What Is TWAIL?" 94 *Proceedings of the Annual Meeting (American Society of International Law* 31 (2000); Emmanuelle Tourme-Jouannet, *What Is a Fair International Society?* (Oxford: Hart Publishing 2013) 66–80.

An indication of the continuing partiality of international law is that Asia, the most populous region of the world, participates at a much lower rate in international treaties and has less representation on important international bodies like the UN Security Council.[62] Proportionally fewer Asian states than any other region have accepted compulsory jurisdiction of the International Court of Justice or have agreed to the International Criminal Court; Asian states have repeatedly expressed reservations to human rights treaties; ASEAN is a bare regional association with few obligations and a small budget; and Asia belatedly developed an organization of international jurists in 2007.[63] International law is not genuinely international when a large region of the globe is not fully on board.

This should not obscure that international law has secured notable achievements with global application. "All states have accepted the humanitarian conventions on the laws of war which express customary international law. The multilateral regimes for the oceans, outer space, and key components of the environment (climate change, protection of the ozone layer, and biological diversity) are also widely accepted."[64] The World Trade Organization is an effective global legal body for trade regulation and dispute settlement.[65]

Changing Concept of Sovereignty

Social-political influences on international law are plainly visible in the evolving foundational concept of sovereignty. Grotius did not articulate a theory of sovereignty. States were in a nascent stage of development when he wrote, gradually establishing offices and transforming rulers into heads of state.[66] The shift from sovereign ruler to sovereign state depersonalized sovereignty,[67] rendering it an abstraction.[68] Theorists bulked up the demands of sovereignty to require internal supremacy within territorial borders and freedom from external intervention in domestic affairs. "A nation has the right of judging what her duty requires," Emerich de Vattel influentially wrote. "No other nation can compel her to act in such or such particular manner: for any attempt at such compulsion would be an

---

[62] See Simon Chesterman, "Asia's Ambivalence about International Law and Institutions: Past, Present, and Future," NUS Law Working Paper Series, 2015/014, December 2015, http://law.nus.edu.sg/wps.

[63] Id.

[64] Dina Shelton, "International Law and 'Relative Normativity,'" in Evans, ed., *International Law*, supra 148.

[65] See Neff, A Short History of International Law," supra 24–27.

[66] Pound, "Philosophical Theory and International Law," supra. 76–80; Edwin D. Dickinson, "Changing Concepts and the Doctrine of Incorporation," 26 *American Journal of International Law* 239, 247–48 (1932).

[67] Oppenheim, *International Law*, supra 76–80; Edwin D. Dickinson, "Changing Concepts and the Doctrine of Incorporation," 26 *American Journal of International Law* 239, 247–48 (1932).

[68] Heinz H. F. Eulau, "The Depersonalization of the Concept of Sovereignty," 4 *Journal of Politics* 3 (1942).

infringement on the liberty of nations."[69] The principle of non-interference became a cornerstone of international law, enshrined in the UN Charter, which explicitly disavows the power to "intervene in matters which are essentially within the domestic jurisdiction of any state."[70]

This combination of views has become descriptively and normatively problematic in modern times.[71] Descriptively it is inapt because, owing to greater interdependence and cross-border problems in matters like financial stability, environmental degradation, terrorism and crime, domestically applicable laws and regulations are being produced by international organizations either directly through promulgation or indirectly through diffusion of legal requirements.[72] These laws are generated by treaty-based organizations like the International Monetary Fund (IMF), the World Bank, and the UN Commission on International Trade Law (UNCITRAL), as well as non-treaty-based organizations like the Basel Committee on Banking Supervision, the International Organization of Securities Commissions, the International Association of Insurance Supervisors, and others.[73] Laws produced in these organizations can bind states without their specific consent, though sovereignty still operates to the extent that states can opt out entirely from these arrangements, giving up attendant benefits and suffering the consequences of nonparticipation (usually an unpalatable option).[74]

Notions of state sovereignty, furthermore, cannot be squared with the European Union. The European Union has many basic elements of statehood: a parliament, high court, a legal order, regulatory bodies, external borders, passport, free internal movement of persons and goods, a currency, a central bank, representation at the United Nations, international agreements with other countries. But the European

---

[69] Quoted in Beaulac, "Emer de Vattel and the Externalization of Sovereignty," supra 264. One indication of Vattel's influence is that he was cited in early U.S. Supreme Court opinions more times than all the other classical international law theorists (Grotius, Burlamaqui, etc.) combined. See Dickinson, "Changing Concepts and the Doctrine of Incorporation," supra 259 n. 132.

[70] UN Charter Art. 2, paragraph 7.

[71] An overview of the descriptive problems with sovereignty is Kal Raustiala, "Rethinking the Sovereignty Debate in International Economic Law," 6 *Journal of International Economic Law* 841 (2003).

[72] International financial organizations like the IMF and the World Bank create legal regimes by requiring domestic legal changes as conditions of loans, as well as through standard requirements in contracts on matters like corruption and environmental impact. An illustrative example in bankruptcy reforms is Terence C. Halliday, "Architects of the State: International Organizations and the Reconstruction of States in East Asia," in *Transnational Legal Ordering and State Change*, edited by Gregory Shaffer (New York: Cambridge University Press 2013); see also Benedict Kingsbury, "Global Administrative Law in the Institutional Practice of Global Regulatory Governance," 3 *World Bank Legal Review* 3 (2011).

[73] See David Zaring, "International Law by Other Means: The Twilight Existence of International Financial Regulatory Organizations," 33 *Texas International Law Journal* 281 (1998).

[74] See Kal Raustiala, "Rethinking the Sovereignty Debate in International Economic Law," 6 *Journal of International Economic Law* 841 (2003).

Union is not widely seen as a sovereign state. So what is it? Is the European Union a supranational organization or collection of organizations?[75] Is the European Union "a decentralized network that is owned by its member-states"?[76] Political scientists view the European Union from two perspectives – as an international organization, or a federation.[77] The European Union is more than an international organization, yet not a full-fledged state.[78] It defies standard theoretical categories.

Sovereignty misfits have always existed. In the past, private companies have acted as de facto political sovereigns. The Dutch East India Company fought wars, entered treaties, seized land, and administered territories.[79] The British East India Company operated similarly, seizing control of much of India from Mughal rule and imposing a trading monopoly.[80] Today, the Holy See, Taiwan, the Federated States of Micronesia, "First Nations" in North America, and a few other examples have certain aspects of sovereignty, but not others. Ill-fitting instances could be dismissed as historical anomalies or minor aberrations. But the European Union is too large and present to be brushed aside. Even if the European Union further unravels following the exit of the United Kingdom, the challenge it poses to traditional sovereignty stands.

Normative objections arise because sovereignty's non-interference principle immunizes leaders and states from accountability for egregious domestic conduct. The Nuremberg Trials, the International Criminal Tribunals for former Yugoslavia and for Rwanda, and the International Criminal Court all assert direct application to national officials, penetrating the sovereignty shield.[81] International lawyers and human rights activists in the past few decades have pounded a steady drumbeat to hold states and officials accountable for their actions.[82] Another normative objection is that the foregrounding of state sovereignty sends the message that what matters

[75]   See Heinhard Steiger, "From the International Law of Christianity to the International Law of the World Citizen – Reflections on the Formation of the Epochs of the History of International Law," 3 *Journal of the History of International Law* 180, 191 (2001).

[76]   This is Stephen Krasner's characterization, quoted in Anne-Marie Slaughter and William Burke-White, "The Future of International Law Is Domestic (or, The European Way of Law)," 47 *Harvard International Law Journal* 327, 337 (2006).

[77]   See Mark A. Pollack, "Theorizing the European Union: International Organization, Domestic Polity, or Experiment in New Governance?" 8 *Annual Review of Political Science* 357 (2005). A third perspective on the European Union discussed by Pollack is the new governance view of governance beyond government.

[78]   See James J. Sheehan, "The Problem of Sovereignty in European History," 111 *American Historical Review* 1, 14–15 (2006).

[79]   For a discussion of the issues raised by these commercial actors operating as states, see Emma Rothschild, "Global Commerce and the Question of Sovereignty in the Eighteenth Century Provinces," 1 *Modern Intellectual History* 3 (2004); Huw V. Bowen, "British Conceptions of Global Empire, 1756–83," 26 *Journal of Imperial and Commonwealth History* 1, 20 (1998).

[80]   Huw V. Bowen, "British Conceptions of Global Empire, 1756–83," supra 26.

[81]   See Slaughter, "A Liberal Theory of International Law," supra.

[82]   See Slaughter and Burke-White, "The Future of International Law Is Domestic (or, The European Way of Law)," supra 327. See generally Lawrence M. Friedman, *The Human Rights Culture: A Study in History and Context* (New Orleans. LA: Quid Pro Books 2011) 139–56.

above all else are the egoistic interests of individual states, implying the absence of any greater legal obligations to the international community and legal order.[83]

European theorists are formulating new accounts of sovereignty to account for these descriptive and normative issues. Notions of mixed or pooled or multilevel sovereignty have been proposed for the European Union.[84] A theorist has creatively argued that accountability for human rights is entailed within the very notion of sovereignty.[85] Courts and jurists are promoting *jus cogens* as peremptory binding legal obligations owed to the international community from which states may not derogate regardless of non-consent.[86]

Once again, Western theorists are taking the lead in modifying international law to suit their orientations and concerns. "In much of the rest of the world, however, sovereignty remains oriented around traditional concepts of non-intervention and domestic autonomy."[87] Asian nations in particular prefer non-interference sovereignty.[88] Leaders value sovereignty as armor against external impositions and meddling.

Theorists in the past have discussed sovereignty as a concept with an inherent nature and requirements, but that is no longer persuasive. It is a historically contingent, malleable notion that evolves in connection with surrounding political and power dynamics, material conditions and interests, ideologies, cultural beliefs, and other factors.

Three Slants in International Law

Owing to three intertwined factors, international law is tilted in ways that favor certain perspectives and nations over others. The first factor is historically grounded influences from the European origins of international law principles and customary international law. All the main doctrines were developed and shaped in the course of the nineteenth and twentieth centuries by Western jurists drawing from domestic bodies of legal knowledge and practices.[89] "Today's universal international law carries a strong European imprint – which is why, from a historic perspective, we may call it 'eurogenetic.'"[90]

---

[83] See Martti Koskenniemi, "What Is International Law For?" in Evan, ed., *International Law*, supra 36–37.

[84] See, e.g., Tanja A. Aalberts, "The Future of Sovereignty in Multilevel Governance of Europe – A Constructivist Reading," 42 *JCMS* 23 (2004).

[85] Patrick Macklem, *The Sovereignty of Human Rights* (New York: Oxford University Press 2015) 1–72.

[86] See Dina Shelton, "International Law and 'Relative Normativity,'" in Evans, ed., *International Law*, supra 146–57.

[87] Raustiala, "Rethinking the Sovereignty Debate in International Economic Law," supra 878.

[88] See Chesterman, "Asia's Ambivalence about International Law and Institutions," supra.

[89] See generally Yasuaki Onuma, *A Transcivilizational Perspective on International Law* (Leiden: Martinus Hijhoff 2010).

[90] Jorn Axel Kammerer and Paulina Starski, "Imperial Colonialism in the Genesis of International Law – Anomaly or Time of Transition?" Max Planck Institute Research Paper Series No. 2016–12, http://papers.ssrn.com/sol3/papers.cfm?abstract_id=2789595.

The second factor is Western jurists' continued dominance of the professional legal culture of international law as a field of knowledge, discourse, and practice. Europeans and Anglo-Americans heavily populate the ranks of international lawyers. The main journals in the field are in English, distantly followed by French and German; many prominent international law institutes and influential NGOs active on international law topics are European or Anglo-American. This dominance is reflected in Western-driven priorities, like free trade, intellectual property, the International Criminal Court, environmental protection, labor rights, and human rights. High on the agenda owing to Western jurists and activists, human rights is the only major topic of international law not directly grounded in interaction between and across polities.[91] Much of what is touted as human rights reflects Western liberal values: freedom of expression, right to privacy, equality between men and women, religious freedom, right to property, democracy, to mention a few examples from the Universal Declaration. Since they are Western derived, the critical import of human rights is mostly directed at non-Western countries.[92]

International law bears the marks of the professional legal culture of the jurists who produce it. If German jurists had exercised greater influence than Anglo-American jurists in the formulation of international doctrines, for example, it would be structured more in terms of public law than in contract terms.[93] If Latin American or Chinese jurists had played formative roles, it would be different in other ways.

The third slant lies in two structural factors beneath international law (elaborated in the next part): 1) polities are engaged in competition and cooperation with one another to secure wealth and national interests;[94] and 2) their interaction is marked by asymmetrical power relations. Economically and militarily powerful states and their commercial interests have greater influence in determining the contours of international legal regimes.[95] Developing countries have criticized international law regimes for favoring the economic interests of wealthy countries, like the TRIPS agreement on intellectual property rights, which imposes high costs on developing countries with few corresponding economic benefits. The Doha Round of trade negotiations intended to produce greater fairness for developing countries collapsed

---

[91] The other priorities mentioned do affect other polities: crimes against humanity often produce refugees and political instability, pollution affects neighboring countries, and labor rights affects transnational commerce.

[92] Onuma, A *Transcivilizational Perspective on International Law*, supra chapter V.

[93] I thank Jan Klabbers for this point.

[94] See Thomas Pogge, "The Role of International Law in Reproducing Massive Poverty," in *The Philosophy of International Law*, edited by Samantha Besson and John Tasioulas (Oxford: Oxford University Press 2010) 419–20.

[95] An exploration of this in multiple contexts is Walter Mattli and Ngaire Woods, *The Politics of Global Regulation* (Princeton, NJ: Princeton University Press 2009).

after fourteen years with no agreement.[96] The emerging international tax regime, Base Erosion and Profit Sharing (BEPS), was developed by the OECD and G20, which refused proposals by developing countries that it be formulated in the United Nations with more extensive international representation.[97] Climate change and environmental protection pit wealthy developed countries that consume disproportionally high amounts of fossil fuels against developing countries that need cheap energy. Developed countries want exacting labor standards, while developing countries prefer low regulations and low labor costs to attract TNCs. In these and other instances, economically powerful countries substantially shape international law,[98] though they do not always get their way.

These three factors are mutually reinforcing: the second descended from the first and both have historically aligned with results of the third.[99] The effects of the first slant arguably have diminished as international law principles, customs, doctrines, and practices came to be widely utilized and accepted. The second slant might diminish over time if jurists or NGOs from other traditions participate more actively.[100] People from countries around the world are calling for human rights, women's rights, trade, environmental protection, and labor rights. International law has become more general with the global extension of cosmopolitan culture and capitalism, though it is viewed differently from different national perspectives depending on historical and contemporary perceptions.[101]

There is no prospect the third slant will be eliminated: its source is structural. Competition between polities over the content and parameters of international law is inevitable, with leaders driven by the desire to advance their own perceived national and personal interests. Polities with greater power will exert more influence in shaping international legal regimes. "The global lawmakers today are the men who run the largest corporations, the U.S. and the EC."[102] What will change with

[96] See Editorial Board, "Global Trade after the Failure of the Doha Round," January 1, 2016, *New York Times*, www.nytimes.com/2016/01/01/opinion/global-trade-after-the-failure-of-the-doha-round.html?action=click&pgtype=Homepage&clickSource=story-heading&module=opinion-c-col-left-region&region=opinion-c-col-left-region&WT.nav=opinion-c-col-left-region&_r=o.

[97] See Itai Grinberg and Joost Pauwelyn, "The Emergence of a New International Tax Regime: The OECD's Package on Base Erosion and Profit Shifting (BEPS)," ASIL, www.asil.org/print/3382.

[98] See Jochen von Bernstorff, "International Law and Global Justice: On Recent Inquiries into the Dark Side of Economic Globalization," 26 *European Journal of International Law* 279 (2015); Eyal Benvenisti and George W. Downs, "The Empire's New Clothes: Political Economy and the Fragmentation of International Law," 60 *Stanford L. Rev.* 595 (2007).

[99] See Nico Krisch, "Internatoinal Law in Times of Hegemony: Unequal Power and the Shaping of the International Legal Order," 16 *European Journal of International Law* 369 (2005).

[100] Yasuaki Onuma advocates the latter in A *Transcivilizational Perspective on International Law*, supra; see also Anghie and Chimni, "Third World Approaches to International Law and Individual Responsibility in Internal Conflict," supra.

[101] Bull, *Anarchical Society*, supra 317.

[102] John Braithwaite and Peter Drahos, *Global Business Regulation* (Cambridge: Cambridge University Press 2000) 629.

time is the relative distribution of economic and military power, which in turn will alter the thrust of international law. The rise of China as a global economic behemoth promises to have an effect. Its currency is now among a handful of recognized elite currencies, and it has created a development bank that rivals the World Bank and the IMF.[103] As it flexes its economic heft, China will impact aspects of international law in ways yet unknown.

To mention these slants is not to dismiss international law as mere domination. Like other forms of law throughout history, it also offers functional benefits and restrains powerful states.[104] International law and organizations provide institutionalized settings within which contesting interests hash out arrangements, establish rules and institutions that help structure competition and cooperation between and across polities, and supply a shared discourse and body of knowledge and practices that help facilitate the process and carry through results. Reflecting power while also erecting constraints on power is common to state law as well as international law, as Hedley Bull describes:

> The special interests of the dominant elements in society are reflected in the way in which the rules are defined. Thus the particular kinds of limitations that are imposed on resort to violence, the kinds of agreements whose binding character is upheld, or the kinds of rights of property that are enforced, will bear the stamp of those dominant elements. But that there should be limits of some kind on resort to violence, an expectation in general that agreements will be carried out, and rules or property of some kind, is not a special interest of some members of society but a general interest of all of them.[105]

A corollary and consequence of these three slants is that there are different perceptions of international law around the globe depending on where one sits.[106] There is no single "African" or "Asian" or "Chinese" or "Russian" or "Third World" view of international law. Many societies have international jurists who are idealists, or realists, or pragmatists, or critical theorists. Still, there are broad differences in how international law is perceived as a function of local understandings of law in general and experiences of international law in particular. Jurists from countries that have been under the heel of international law understandably tend to view it skeptically. The domestic Chinese legal tradition is thoroughly legal instrumentalist, and the Treaty of Nanking is a bitter national humiliation, so it should not be surprising that Chinese jurists and officials exhibit a consummately instrumental

---

[103] Jane Perlez, "China Creates a World Bank of Its Own, and the U.S. Balks," December 4, 2015, *New York Times*, www.nytimes.com/2015/12/05/business/international/china-creates-an-asian-bank-as-the-us-stands-aloof.html?hp&action=click&pgtype=Homepage&clickSource=story-heading&module=first-column-region&region=top-news&WT.nav=top-news&_r=1.

[104] See Krisch, "International Law in Times of Hegemony," supra.

[105] Bull, *Anarchic Society*, supra 55.

[106] A nuanced essay on different perspectives of international law is Boris N. Mamlyuk and Ugo Mattei, "Comparative International Law," 36 *Brooklyn Journal of International Law* 385 (2011).

view of international law.[107] Western powers also exhibit an instrumental approach to international law,[108] it must be said, to the chagrin of their own idealistic internationalist jurists.

PART III. INTERACTION BETWEEN AND ACROSS POLITIES

Early History of Interaction

A style of world history popularized in recent decades emphasizes unceasing commercial, martial, and political interaction between human groups throughout history, increasing over time.[109] These histories teach that polities have always conducted relations with other polities and people have always been on the move, engaging in conquest or trade, relocating through forcible means, migrating for better opportunities, proselytizing a religion, fleeing threats, seeking adventure and fortune, and for other reasons.[110] A common theme is that throughout history, polities interact with other polities through competition (wars, conquest, wealth extraction) and cooperation (alliances, exchanges, trade).[111] Polities need commerce – directly or through private parties – to secure financial resources for rulers and the society.[112] Interaction is colored by asymmetry and unevenness across multiple dimensions. Polities and societies vary in their respective abilities to exert military and economic power, their technological and productive capabilities, their access to natural resources and fossil fuels, the functionality of their government institutions, their extent of urbanization, and other factors.

---

[107] See Orde F. Kittrie, *Lawfare: Law as a Weapon of War* (New York: Oxford University Press 2016) chapter 4.

[108] See Krisch, "International Law in Times of Hegemony," supra.

[109] See, e.g., J. R. McNeill and William H. McNeill, *The Human Web: A Bird's-Eye View of World History* (New York: W.W. Norton & Co. 2003); Clive Ponting, *World History: A New Perspective* (London: Chatto & Windus 2000); Bayly, *Birth of the Modern World*, supra. A theoretical account of interconnectedness is Justin Rosenberg, "Why Is There No International Historical Sociology?" 12 *European Journal of International Relations* 307 (2006).

[110] See especially Andrew Shryock, Timothy K. Earle, and Daniel Lord Smail, *Deep History: The Architecture of Past and Present* (Berkeley: University of California Press 2011) chapter 8, Migration. An overview of massive global migration in the past two centuries is Adam McKeown, "Global Migration, 1846–1940," 15 *Journal of World History* 155 (2004).

[111] My working definition for polities is societies organized as hierarchical political orders tied to a territory. I have extracted these points mainly though not exclusively from McNeill and McNeill, *The Human Web*, supra; Ian Morris, *Why the West Rules – For Now: The Patterns of History, and What They Reveal about the Future* (New York: Farrar, Straus and Giroux 2011); William J. Bernstein, *A Splendid Exchange: How Trade Shaped the World* (New York: Grove Press 2008); Shryock, Earle, and Smail, *Deep History*, supra; Robert Wright, *Nonzero: The Logic of Human Destiny* (New York: Vintage 2000).

[112] See especially Shryock, Earle, and Smail, *Deep History*, supra chapter 10.

Formal understandings of various kinds between polities extend back four millennia,[113] discovered among the earliest written records in existence.[114] A 4,000-year-old treaty from Elba in Syria, for instance, specifies which king has jurisdiction over particular cities, grants rights to merchants, and takes up taxation of foreign citizens, movement of emissaries, theft and damages to commodities, and other matters.[115] Hundreds of documents from 2000 to 1500 BC from this region detail diplomatic protections and rights and protections for foreign merchants, including residence and extraterritorial rights, and guarantees against losses from robbery.[116]

Evidence of long-distance trade likewise goes back millennia. Stone blades from Armenia were transported to Mesopotamia in 6000 BC; axe and chisel blades taken from quarries in the Balkans in 5000 BC made their way to the Baltic and North Seas; large quantities of copper from Turkey were transported to southern Iraq around 4000 BC; substantial copper–grain trade between Mesopotamia and the Persian Gulf took place in 3000 BC.[117] An extensive trading network between Africa, Arabia, and India operated 3,000 to 4,000 years ago, sending cattle, bananas, and yams west, and sorghum, millet, and donkeys east, dubbed "the first global economy."[118] "A ship wrecked at Ulubrun around 1316 BCE . . . was carrying enough copper and tin to make ten tons of bronze, as well as ebony and ivory from tropical Africa, cedar from Lebanon, glass from Syria, and weapons from Greece and what is now Israel; in short, a little of everything that might fetch a profit, probably gathered, a few objects at a time, in every port along the ship's route by a crew as mixed as its cargo."[119] At the height of the Roman Empire, Greek and Roman traders made their way to the Indian Ocean, prompting a "flourishing of large, ethnically diverse hubs such as Socotra and the Malabar ports – polyglot communities where trade diasporas of many nations and races mingled, managed cargoes, made fortunes, and satisfied an unquenchable Western (i.e. Roman) demand for such Oriental luxury goods as silk, cotton, spices, gems, and exotic animals."[120]

Several conditions facilitate long-distance trade. "Traders did not venture abroad without letters of introduction to expected business contacts, or without letters of safe conduct from the local rulers along their route."[121] Necessary were assurances that during transit and at trading centers, thieves and polities will not rob or kill traders or confiscate their goods or impose exorbitant taxes. Traders must have

---

[113] For an overview, see David J. Bederman, *International Law in Antiquity* (Cambridge: Cambridge University Press 2001).

[114] See Annon Altman, *Tracing the Earliest Recorded Concepts of International Law: The Ancient Near East* (Leiden: Brill 2012).

[115] Id. 37.   [116] Id. 77.   [117] See Bernstein, *A Splendid Exchange*, supra 20–42.

[118] Melinda A. Zeder, Eve Emshwiller, Bruce D. Smith, and Daniel G. Bradley, "Documenting Domestication: The Intersection of Genetics and Archaeology," 22 *Trends in Genetics* 139, 146 (2006); discussed in Shryock, Earle, and Smail, *Deep History*, supra 212.

[119] Morris, *Why the West Rules – For Now*, supra 200.

[120] Bernstein, *A Splendid Exchange*, supra 38–39.   [121] Id. 5–6.

reliable trading partners, mutually understood rules, and ways to resolve disputes. Shared currency (silver, gold, bills of exchange, or promissory notes) and methods of financing the journey are also essential. A contract on a clay tablet from around 2000 BC records an early financing agreement to repay a specified amount upon safe completion of a trading expedition.[122]

These conditions have been produced through two intermingled alternatives (in many variations).[123] The first involves an overarching political structure. A single polity or linked group of associated polities can establish political stability and shared rules over an extended territory encompassing many regions and peoples. Variations of these arrangements, listed from most to least politically consolidated, include the Qin Empire and the Roman Empire in the closing centuries BC,[124] the Mongol states across the Silk Road from the mid-1200s to the mid-1300s AD,[125] and the Hanseatic League of independent cities led by merchants who allied to monopolize trade across the Baltic and North Seas during the late Middle Ages.[126] Today, the European Union fits along this spectrum toward the relatively consolidated end.

The second alternative involves creating a trading network of relationships and common legal rules that spans multiple polities. One version of this, which is also a thin version of the political connections described earlier, was the great trading lane that opened in the medieval period across the expanse of Islam. The Sharia facilitated commerce because Muhammad himself was a trader and parts of the Sharia address trading and commercial law.[127] "The Muslim spice importer in Cairo or Tangier obeyed the same religious, ethical, and – most important – commercial code . . . as his Muslim supplier in Cambay or Malacca. The Muslim ruler, whether in Africa, Arabia, India, or Southeast Asia, observed the same basic rules regarding tax and customs rate."[128]

Another version of the second alternative (with shades of the first) is trade diaspora. "Trade diasporas are interregional exchange networks composed of spatially dispersed specialized merchant groups that are culturally distinct, organizationally cohesive, and socially independent from their host communities while maintaining a high level of economic and social ties with related communities who define themselves in terms of the same general cultural identity."[129] Many times

---

[122] Id. 30.   [123] See Shryock, Earle, and Smail, *Deep History,* supra 260.

[124] On the Qin and Roman Empires and trade, see Morris, *Why the West Rules – For Now,* supra 254–79, 292.

[125] Bernstein, *A Splendid Exchange,* supra 91, 117.

[126] For a description, see Rhiman A. Rotz, "The Lubeck Uprising of 1408 and the Decline of the Hanseatic League," 121 *Proceedings of the American Philosophical Society* 1 (1977).

[127] See Bernstein, *A Splendid Exchange,* supra 69–76, 90–108; McNeill and McNeill, *The Human Web,* supra 88–99.

[128] Bernstein, *A Splendid Exchange,* supra 97.

[129] Gil J. Stein, "From Passive Periphery to Active Agents: Emerging Perspectives in the Archaeology of Interregional Interaction," 104 *American Anthropologist* 903, 908 (2002).

in history have trade diasporas organized by polities or merchant groups established trading posts or expatriate enclaves in distant lands. Greek and Phoenician city-states traded across the Mediterranean in the first millennium BC by establishing colonies on multiple lands.[130] In some cases, what started as trade diasporas matured into a common political structure (the first alternative), as occurred with the Hanseatic League.[131]

There are also commercial networks with shared practices and procedures where overarching political ties are lacking. During Islamic dominance of the Mediterranean, Jewish traders across the western Mediterranean conducted trade through relationships and reputations with a common merchants' law, operating within local formal legal institutions.[132] The *lex mercatoria* existed at medieval markets, fairs, and seaports across European polities, interacting with local courts and regulations.[133] Fair courts or merchant guild tribunals were staffed or aided by merchants providing guidance or serving as jurors, with decisions based on common practices (banking, insurance, bills and notes, insurance, suretyship, and agency), usages, and equity.[134]

A theoretical clarification about this historical sketch bears emphasis. This is not about the history of international law.[135] International law is a historically specific tradition that emerged in Europe and spread in the past few centuries to mainly address interaction between polities. This discussion is about the ecology or social space of competitive-cooperative interaction among political and economic actors between and across polities pursuing power, wealth, and security. Interaction in this

[130] Shryock, Earle, and Smail, *Deep History*, supra 215–16.
[131] Philip D. Curtin, *Cross-Cultural Trade in World History* (Cambridge: Cambridge University Press 1984) 7–8.
[132] Avner Greif, "Contract Enforceability and Economic Institutions in Early Trade: The Maghribi Traders' Coalition," 83 *American Economic Review* 525 (1993). Subsequent research has brought into question Greif's emphasis on informal coalitions. A more complete picture is that they relied on formal legal mechanisms as well as informal relationships. Jeremy Edwards and Sheilagh Ogilvie, "Contract Enforcement, Institutions, and Social Capital: The Maghribi Traders Reappraised," 65 *Economic History Review* 421 (2012).
[133] See W. Mitchell, *An Essay on the Early History of the Law Merchant* (Cambridge: Cambridge University Press 1904); see also Harold J. Berman and Colin Kaufman, "The Law of International Commercial Transactions (Lex Mercatoria)," 19 *Harvard International Law Journal* 221, 224–29 (1978).
[134] Recent historical work has cast significant doubts on claims by historians and economists that *lex mercatoria* was a transnational law of sales that operated independently of local authorities. Even skeptics acknowledge, however, that *lex mercatoria* was mentioned in medieval documents in connection with jurisdiction, procedure, and shared commercial practices, and merchants played significant roles in dispute resolution. For an excellent revisionist account, see Emily Kadens, "The Medieval Law Merchant: The Tyranny of a Construct," 7 *Journal of Legal Analysis* 251, 254–55, 261, 270 (2015).
[135] It is possible that one stream of ancient practices is historically part of the international law tradition. Based on striking similarities in treaty terminology and formalities, as well as diplomatic practices, a few scholars have argued there is a continuous tradition of international law and diplomacy stretching from Mesopotamian civilizations to classical Greece and Rome, forward to the present. See Raymond Cohen, "The Great Tradition: The Spread of Diplomacy in the Ancient World," 12 *Diplomacy & Statecraft* 23 (2001).

space is a constant of human history. And it gives rise to functional necessities that are filled through various common mechanisms, independently arrived at or copied. Interaction between polities is facilitated through use of formal understandings on an array of matters, which take many forms, including treaties or covenants, concessions, executive agreements, capitulations, declarations, unilateral oaths or commitments, and memoranda of understanding, among others. Commerce across polities is facilitated by assurances of personal safety, protection of property, enforcement of agreements, common rules, reliable credit and payment methods, opportunities for exchange (regular gatherings or markets), acceptable dispute resolution mechanisms, and restrained taxation, fees, or customs that allow the retention of sufficient profits. These basic political, economic, and legal arrangements have been constructed time and again throughout history.

Interaction Today

Interaction between and across polities has reached unimagined heights. People are moving, communicating, transacting, and despoiling the environment across borders in incalculable volumes. Transnational corporations (TNCs) play a significant role in this interaction, crossing multiple national borders within a single organization. TNCs locate production facilities in the Global South to take advantage of low-wage labor, while banking, accounting, legal services, and corporate headquarters are located in financial centers.[136] Products made in low-wage factories are shipped to consumers in cities around the globe.[137] Transnational banks, foreign investment firms, and currency traders are involved in a vast global flow of money and finance beyond state control.[138] Transnational corporations handle "a quarter of all industrial production" in advanced economies."[139] By the 1980s, "a third of all world trade took place as transactions *within* TNCs."[140] TNCs now rival states in wealth and influence. "By the end of the twentieth century half of the 100 largest economic entities in the world were states and half were corporations."[141]

---

[136] See Peter J. Taylor, "World Cities and Territorial States under Conditions of Contemporary Globalization," 19 *Political Geography* 5 (2000); Peter J. Taylor, "Leading World Cities: Empirical Evaluations of Urban Nodes in Multiple Networks," 42 *Urban Studies* 1593 (2005); J. R. Short, Y Kim, and H. Wells, "The Dirty Little Secret of World Cities Research: Data Problems in Comparative Analysis," 20 *International Journal of Urban & Regional Research* 697 (1996); Neil Brenner, "Global Cities, Glocal States: Global City Formation and State Territorial Restructuring in Contemporary Europe," 5 *Review of International Political Economy* 1, 5–6 (1998); Jonathan V. Beaverstock, "Re-thinking Skilled International Labor Migration: World Cities and Banking Organizations," 25 *Geoforum* 323 (1995). See Taylor, "World Cities and Territorial States Under Conditions of Contemporary Globalization," supra 15; Peter J. Taylor, "Specification of the World City Network," 33 *Geographical Analysis* 181 (2001).

[137] See Wouter Jacobs, Cesar Ducruet, and Peter de Langen, "Integrating World Cities in Production Networks: The Case of Port Cities," 10 *Global Networks* (2010).

[138] See Paul L. Know, "World Cities in a World-System," in *World Cities in a World-System*, edited by Paul L. Knox and Peter J. Taylor (Cambridge: Cambridge University Press 1995) 5.

[139] Ponting, *World History*, supra 811.   [140] Id. (emphasis added).   [141] Id.

Competition for wealth and power takes place among states, among transnational (and national) corporations, and between corporations and states. Polities compete with one another to attract TNCs for employment and revenues through favorable tax benefits and desirable regulatory regimes (minimal safety and pollution standards, minimal labor standards).[142] Tax havens welcome TNCs to domicile in their jurisdictions subject to minimal taxes although they do scant business in these countries.[143] Even within a single overarching polity like the European Union, states construct tax shelters or offer preferential tax deals to attract corporations while depriving fellow member states of their share of revenues.[144] TNCs manipulate their abstract legal existence to relocate through "corporate inversions," whereby a large company buys a small company in a foreign nation with a lower tax rate, which it then claims as its domicile.[145] Thus do transnational corporations utilize their mobility to take advantage of and influence domestic and transnational regulatory regimes.[146]

Nation-states went from centuries of battling one another for control over territory and natural resources to now battling for bigger shares of export markets, more jobs for citizens, and tax revenues.[147] Currently emerging is "a new type of 'competition state' whose central priority is to create a favorable investment climate for transnational capital."[148] And on the field taking advantage of and participating in the battle are TNCs, savvy economic entities relentlessly pursuing wealth with little national allegiance.

Increase of International Organizations

In the same period that organizations dramatically multiplied in society, a multitude of organizations emerged to manage competitive-cooperative interactions between and

[142] See Trachtman, "The International Economic Law Revolution," supra 50.

[143] Adam H. Rosenzweig, "Why There Are Tax Havens," 52 *William & Mary L. Rev.* 923 (2010).

[144] See James Kanter, "EU Orders Two Nations to Recover Taxes from Starbucks and Fiat," October 21, 2015, *New York Times*, www.nytimes.com/2015/10/22/business/international/starbucks-fiat-eu-tax-netherlands-luxembourg.html?_r=1; Edward Kleinbard, "U.S. Treasury Publishes White Paper in Support of Tax Avoiders," August 29, 2016, *The Hill*, http://thehill.com/blogs/pundits-blog/economy-budget/293642-us-treasury-rallies-in-support-of-tax-avoiders. Tax avoidance is also arranged through administrative techniques, see Omri Marian, "The State Administration of International Tax Avoidance," http://papers.ssrn.com/sol3/papers.cfm?abstract_id=2685642.

[145] Fifty American corporations have altered their tax homes through corporate inversions in the past decade. Alexandra Thornton, "The Skinny on Corporate Inversions," September 25, 2014, *Center for American Progress*, www.americanprogress.org/issues/tax-reform/report/2014/09/25/97827/the-skinny-on-corporate-inversions/.

[146] See generally David Vogel, "The Private Regulation of Global Corporate Conduct," in Mattli and Woods, *The Politics of Global Regulation*, supra.

[147] This has been described as the transformation of nation-states to the market state; see Philip Bobbitt, *The Shield of Achilles: War, Peace, and the Course of History* (New York: Anchor 2002).

[148] Neil Brenner, "Beyond State-Centrism? Space, Territoriality, and Geographical Scale in Globalization Studies," 28 *Theory and Society* 39, 65 (1999).

across polities. Early examples are the International Committee of the Red Cross (1863), International Telegraph Union (1868) (now the International Telecommunications Union), the Universal Postal Union (1874), to name a few, with numerous additional organizations created in the twentieth century, prominently including the United Nations, World Trade Organization, Organization for Economic Cooperation and Development, World Health Organization, World Bank, and many more.[149] The defining features of international governmental organizations are they 1) institutionalize state decision making, 2) constitute stable bureaucracies, and 3) exercise a degree of autonomy from states in carrying out their designated tasks.[150] In furtherance of their objectives, organizations manage and coordinate collective activities, gather information and utilize expertise, establish binding rules, monitor circumstances, act on a case-by-case basis, change policies and rules when necessary, facilitate collaboration, pool resources, provide dispute resolution forums, and carry out enforcement actions.[151] International organizations have a dual existence: they serve as arenas for contests among competing interests to shape objectives and rules, which they subsequently carry out.[152]

There are more than 7,000 active intergovernmental organizations and 60,000 nongovernmental international organizations (excluding for-profit corporations).[153] An overwhelming proportion of international organizations, including many with significant regulatory powers, is not constituted through international law. Roughly 265 formal intergovernmental organizations with permanent structures, rules, and procedures have been created by treaties between states; thirty-three of these have universal reach, while the rest are regional organizations.[154] Befitting the emphasis of globalization on cross-border economic interaction, about two-thirds of formal international governmental organizations are oriented to economic purposes.[155]

---

[149] See C. F. Amerasinghe, *Principles of the Institutional Law of International Organizations*, 2nd ed. (Cambridge: Cambridge University Press 2005) 3–4. See David Kennedy, "The Move to Institutions," 8 *Cardozo Law Review* 841 (1987).

[150] See Thomas J. Volgy, Elizabeth Fausett, Keith A. Grant, and Stuart Rodgers, "Identifying Formal Intergovernmental Organizations," in *The Politics of Global Governance: International Organizations in an Interdependent World*, 4th ed., edited by Paul F. Diehl and Brian Frederking (Boulder, CO: Lynne Rienner Publishers 2010) 16.

[151] See generally Kenneth W. Abbott and Duncan Sindal, "Why States Act Through Formal International Organizations," in Diehl and Frederking, *The Politics of Global Governance*, supra 27–65.

[152] This dual existence is emphasized in Susan Block-Lieb and Terence C. Halliday, *Global Legislators: How International Organizations Make Commercial Law for the World* (New York: Cambridge University Press forthcoming 2017).

[153] Union of International Organizations, Yearbook of International Organizations, www.uia.org /yearbook.

[154] See Richard Woodward and Michael Davies, "How Many International Organizations Are There? The Yearbook of International Organizations and Its Shortcomings," October 11, 2015, *Political Insight*, www.psa.ac.uk/insight-plus/blog/how-many-international-organisations-are-there-yearbook -international.

[155] Volgy et al., "Identifying Formal Intergovernmental Organizations," supra 20.

The increase of organizations in the modern period is an organic response to problems between and across polities that utilize the superior capacity of informal and formal organizations to formulate and coordinate action.[156] International jurists have observed that a great deal of international law is now produced in international organizations and multilateral forums.[157] Another notable point is that many organizations dealing with transnational regulatory matters are not international law organizations.

Transnational Law and Regulation

The necessity to deal with intercourse between and across polities far outstrips the capacity, mechanisms, and scope of international law. Growing talk of transnational law and governance reflects this. Four closely overlapping theoretical strands simultaneously emerged out of and broke away from international law theory at the turn of the twenty-first century.[158] One strand, referred to as *transgovernmental networks*,[159] prominently developed by Anne-Marie Slaughter and Kal Raustiala, emphasizes the growth of arrangements between government bureaucrats across liberal countries constructing institutions and regulations to deal with transnational problems, "networking with their counterparts abroad, creating a dense web of relations that constitutes a new, transgovernmental order."[160] The officials in this arena are representatives from disaggregated functional subunits at national levels who interact with colleagues abroad (legislators, judges, police, environmental regulators, bank regulators, etc.). "Today's international problems – terrorism, organized crime, environmental degradation, money

[156] See Felicity Vabulas and Duncan Sindal, "Organizations without Delegation: Informal Intergovernmental Organizations (IIGO) and the Spectrum of Intergovernmental Arrangements," 8 *Review of International Organizations* 193 (2013).

[157] Jonathan I. Charney, "Universal International Law," 87 *American Journal of International Law* 529, 551 (1993).

[158] This is not a comprehensive survey of international theories, but a discussion of theories directly relevant to my analysis. Other theoretical perspectives have emerged, including critical theory and Third World approaches to international law, which I do not systematically cover.

[159] For an overview of networks, see France S Berry, Ralph S. Brower, Sang Ok Choi, Wendy Xinfang Goa, HeeSoun Jang, Myungjung Kwon, and Jessica Ward, "Three Traditions of Network Research: What the Public Management Research Agenda Can Learn from Other Research Communities," 64 *Public Administration Review* 539 (2004).

[160] Anne-Marie Slaughter, "The Real New World Order," 76 *Foreign Affairs* 183, 184 (1997); Anne-Marie Slaughter, "International Law in a World of Liberal States," 6 *European Journal of International Law* 503 (1995); Kal Raustiala, "Architecture of International Cooperation: Transgovernmentalism and the Future of International Law," 43 *Virginia International Law Review* 1 (2002); Anne-Marie Slaughter, Andrew S. Tulumello, and Stephan Wood, "International Law and International Relations Theory: A New Generation of Interdisciplinary Scholarship," 92 *American Journal of International Law* 367, 371 (1998). The focus on networks of actors is part of a more general trend also occurring in history and sociology. See Paul A. Kramer, "Power and Connection: Imperial Histories of the United States in the World," 116 *American Historical Review* 1348, 1383–85 (2011).

laundering, bank failure, and securities fraud – created and sustain these relations."[161] National regulators come together to exchange information and agree on shared standards and mutual assistance, leading to harmonization of domestic law and enforcement coordination.

A second strand, *global administrative law* (GAL), identified with Benedict Kingsbury, Nico Krisch, Richard Stewart, and Sabino Cassese, "begins from the twin ideas that much global governance can be understood as administration, and that such administration is often organized and shaped by principles of an administrative law character."[162] Their focus is international organizations "that perform administrative functions but are not directly subject to control by national governments or domestic legal systems or, in the case of treaty-based regimes, the states party to the treaty."[163] These regulatory organizations include public as well as private or hybrid public-private bodies that consider input from governments, NGOs, experts, and affected parties.[164] This represents "the emergence of a 'global administrative space': a space in which the strict dichotomy between domestic and international has largely broken down, in which administrative functions are performed in often complex interplays between officials and institutions on different levels, and in which regulation may be highly effective despite its predominantly non-binding forms."[165] Many of these international organizations, GAL scholars assert, are developing uniformity along procedural lines in providing greater transparency, more participation by affected parties, and review of legality by judicial bodies.

A third strand, labeled *international economic law* or *transnational commercial law*, prominently discussed by John Jackson and Ernst-Ulrich Petersmann, encompasses "the law of economic transactions; government regulation of economic matters; and related legal relations including litigation and international institutions for economic relations. Indeed, it is plausible to suggest that 90 percent of international law work is in reality international economic law in some form or another."[166] International economic law includes two perspectives: private parties engaged in transnational

---

[161] Slaughter, "The Real New World Order," supra 184.

[162] Nico Krisch and Benedict Kingsbury, "Introduction: Global Governance and Global Administrative Law in the International Legal Order," 17 *European Journal of International Law* 1, 2 (2006). See Sabino Cassese, "Is There a Global Administrative Law?" in *Exercise of Public Authority by International Organizations*, edited by Armin von Bogdandy, Rudiger Wolfrum, and Jochen Bernstorff (Berlin: Springer 2010).

[163] Id.

[164] Benedict Kingsbury, Nico Krisch, and Richard B. Stewart, "The Emergence of Global Administrative Law," 68 *Law and Contemporary Problems* 15, 16 (2005).

[165] Krisch and Kingsbury, "Introduction: Global Governance and Global Administrative Law in the International Legal Order," supra 1.

[166] John H. Jackson, "Global Economics and International Economic Law," 1 *Journal of International Economic Law* 1, 8 (1998); Ross Cranston, "Theorizing Transnational Commercial Law," 42 *Texas International Law Journal* 597 (2007); Ernst-Ulrich Petersmann, *International Economic Law in the 21st Century* (Oxford: Hart Publishing 2012).

commerce, and regulatory regimes with a direct or indirect impact on transnational commerce.[167] The former includes private legal regimes like the new *lex mercatoria*, private arbitration, model contract terms, commercial usages, and more; the latter includes the WTO, intellectual property rights (TRIPs), international banking standards, domestic anticorruption laws, labor laws, tax laws, and more.[168] A subset of this strand emphasizes sector-specific transnational private regulation or voluntary codes created by companies, trade associations, and NGOs, sometimes in conjunction with intergovernmental organizations.[169]

A fourth strand, *global legal pluralism*, developed by Francis Snyder, Guenther Teubner, Paul Berman, and others,[170] paints transnational law as a host of institutions, norms, and dispute-processing organizations located at various sites and levels.[171] These "sites may be hierarchically organized, autonomous or even independent, mutually constitutive, competing or overlapping, part of the same or different regimes, or converging or diverging in terms of institutions, norms or processes of dispute resolution."[172] Pluralist theorists accept that a unified global order is unlikely, so the wiser approach is to aim at strengthening coordination and normative consistency between international institutions.[173]

These closely related strands have much in common and are distinct mainly in their angle of emphasis. They highlight many of the same organizations, including the WTO, OECD, World Bank, IMF, and the Basel Committee on Banking Supervisions. The Basel Committee consists of a group of central bankers from Europe, Japan, and the United States who meet four times a year to exchange information and work out policies and banking requirements, which they thereafter implement at national levels.[174] Bank capital adequacy requirements devised by the group have been adopted by more than 100 countries.[175] They also agreed on a set of

[167] Jackson, "Global Economics and International Economic Law," supra 9.

[168] For this broader perspective, see Joel P. Trachtman, "The International Economic Law Revolution," 17 *University of Pennsylvania Journal of International Economic Law* 33, 49 (1996).

[169] A superb introduction to this perspective is Colin Scott, Fabrizio Cafaggi, and Linda Senden, *The Challenge of Transnational Private Regulation: Conceptual and Constitutional Debates* (Oxford: Wiley-Blackwell 2011).

[170] See Francis Snyder, "Governing Economic Globalization: Global Legal Pluralism and European Union Law," 5 *European Law Journal* 334 (1999); Gunther Teubner, "Global Bukowina: Legal Pluralism in the World Society," in Gunther Teubner, ed., *Global Law Without a State* (Aldershot: Dartmouth 1997); Andreas Fischer-Lescano and Gunther Teubner, "Regime-Collisions: The Vain Search for Legal Unity in the Fragmentation of Global Law," 25 *Michigan Journal of International Law* 999 (2004). See also Paul Schiff Berman, *Global Legal Pluralism: A Jurisprudence of Law Beyond Borders* (New York: Cambridge University Press 2012); Peer Zumbansen, "Transnational Legal Pluralism," 1 *Transnational Legal Theory* 141 (2010).

[171] Snyder, "Governing Economic Globalization: Global Legal Pluralism and European Union Law," supra.

[172] Francis Snyder, *The EU, the WTO and China: Legal Pluralism and International Trade Regulation* (Oxford: Hart 2010) 32.

[173] Id. 32–34.   [174] See Slaughter, "The Real New World Order," supra 190–91.

[175] See Michael S. Barr and Geoffrey P. Miller, "Global Administrative Law: The View from Basel," 17 *European Journal of International Law* 15, 17 (2006).

principles bank supervisors use to regulate transnational banks and they coordinate supervision of these banks.[176] The first strand presents the Basel Committee as the locus of a network of relationships between national bank regulators; the second strand presents it as an administrative agency that follows procedures, receives comments, and applies expertise to adopt and implement rules; the third and fourth strands describe it as an important element of transnational financial law that helps maintain global financial stability.[177]

All four approaches cross over domestic and international law, public and private international law, as well as public and private actors. They emphasize the combined actions of NGOs, national bureaucrats, commercial entities, trade associations, and national and international jurists in creating regulatory activities. They take expansive views of law, including privately produced legal regimes, and "soft law" like standards, codes of conduct, and best practices. And, with the exception of global legal pluralism, which emphasizes diversity, they present these legal orderings as emergent coalescing or loosely connected global systems of law.

All four stands leave international law behind in the sense that significant elements of the legal phenomena they focus on lie outside the conventional domain of international law.[178] Much of it is grounded in domestic law and in the actions of private or quasi-private organizations, and much of it does not count as "law" by traditional criteria. The Basel Committee is not an international law organization, though it undeniably engages in regulatory actions with global significance. Recall the point made earlier, that Bentham's conceptualization substantially emptied "international law." These new theoretical strands do not empty "international law," but instead completely overrun its parameters.

By moving in this direction, international law theorists have come to occupy the same ground as political scientists, legal sociologists, and others focused on globalization, capitalism, and regulation.[179] No single label is used for this burgeoning field of study, variously referred to as "transnational legal ordering," "global governance," or "global regulation," among others.[180] This focus overlaps with the new governance perspective on decentralized regulation through networks of public and private actors, first applied to analyze national governance, then extended to transnational governance.[181] Private firms, trade associations, and advocacy NGOs are

---

[176] Id. 21–22.   [177] See Cranston, "Theorizing Transnational Commercial Law," supra 597–98.

[178] John Murphy notes this departure in *The Evolving Dimensions of International Law: Hard Choices for the World Community* (New York: Cambridge University Press 2010).

[179] The political science perspective is represented in Mattli and Woods, *The Politics of Global Regulation*, supra.

[180] See Gregory Shaffer, "Transnational Legal Ordering and State Change," supra; Benedict Kingsbury, "Global Administrative Law in the Institutional Practice of Global Regulatory Governance," 3 *World Bank Legal Review* 3 (2011).

[181] See Kenneth W. Abbott and Duncan Snidal, "Strengthening International Regulation through Transnational New Governance: Overcoming the Orchestration Deficit," 42 *Vanderbilt Journal of Transnational Law* 501 (2009).

central participants. The "most striking feature" of transnational new governance "is the decentralization of regulatory authority from the state to private and public-private schemes."[182] It is characterized by a substantial role for private actors in producing rules, voluntary acceptance of the rules, and private monitoring and enforcement efforts. Two leading social legal theorists, Gregory Shaffer and Terrence Halliday, draw together these themes to construct a sophisticated account of transnational law as a burgeoning realm of legal ordering that operates with the state and beyond the state, involving public and private actors, at different levels and contexts (international organizations, networks, governmental institutions, trade associations, NGOs, etc.).[183]

Jurists favor the term transnational law to cover these phenomena, first coined by Jessup to cover all legal matters not purely domestic.[184] The massive increase in political, economic, and social interaction between and across polities in the past century, impelled especially by the global expansion of capitalism, is behind these developments: more people, more polities, more movement, more commerce, new technology (transportation, communication, energy extraction and exploitation), more cross-border consequences (financial instability, ecological degradation, terrorism, crime, migration, internet), more complexity, more, more, more. A mass of organizations, networks, agreements, and regulatory regimes and actions is being produced by public and private actors to address a myriad of matters in a problem- or sector-specific fashion in the social space of competitive-cooperative interaction between and across polities.

PART IV. THEORETICAL CLARIFICATIONS OF INTERNATIONAL LAW

Confusion of Category and System

Caught in Bentham's framework, theorists and international jurists routinely present international law and state law as parallel categories – but they are fundamentally different in two overlooked respects. For one, the state law category is filled with multiple versions of the same thing (state legal systems), but the international law category is not like that. Many varied examples fall in the state law category at various levels of generality, for instance, the legal systems of Japan, of South Africa, of

---

[182] Id. 542.

[183] See Terrence C. Halliday and Gregory Shaffer, "Transnational Legal Orders," in *Transnational Legal Orders*, edited by Terence C. Halliday and Gregory Shaffer (New York: Cambridge University Press 2015); Gregory Shaffer, "Theorizing Transnational Legal Ordering," 12 *Annual Review of Law and Social Science* 231 (2016). An illuminating case study of lawmaking in UNCITRAL is Susan Block-Lieb and Terence C. Halliday, *Global Legislators: How International Organizations Make Trade Law for the World* (New York: Cambridge University Press, 2017). An illuminating account of these developments focusing on the emergence of legal regimes with global aspirations is Neil Walker, *Intimations of Global Law* (Cambridge: Cambridge University Press 2015).

[184] Craig Scott, "'Transnational Law' as Proto-Concept: Three Conceptions," 10 *German Law Journal* 859, 871 (2009).

France, of the United States, of Massachusetts. Members of the state law category share a set of defining features, typically including institutions that declare, enforce, and apply law within a specified territory.

The category of international law, in contrast, does not consist of multiple versions of a thing with shared core features, but instead is filled with whatever counts as international law. Since international law has several criteria for inclusion, it is filled with a grab bag of particulars: specific treaties, organizations produced by treaties, recognized customs and principles, human rights, international courts, and more. What the particulars in this category share is that they meet the criteria of inclusion – qualifying as instances of international law – though they do not all possess the same basic form and function characteristics.

The second difference is state law is an abstraction that is not a particular member of its own category, whereas international law frequently is treated as a category and as a comprehensive whole that exhausts that category. When international law is portrayed as a global legal system consisting of a complex of principles, doctrines, and institutions, everything in the category put together amounts to an international legal system. International law, then, is a category and the international legal system is the all-encompassing member of that category.

Generations of international jurists have presented international law as "the present world international law."[185] What underwrites this depiction is the belief that international law is evolving toward a more systematic form (perpetually on the horizon). "The time will come when international law will have evolved into a legal system capable of meeting the needs of the international community in the modern world."[186]

Sometimes it is described more strongly as an "international constitutional order,"[187] largely by European jurists who project the model of the European Union on the global stage.[188] The international legal system, in their account, has achieved unified characteristics: a basic charter (UN Charter) and key functional charters (World Trade Organization, World Health Organization, International Criminal Court, UN Convention on the Law of the Sea, etc.), lawmaking bodies (UN), a high court (International Court of Justice) and separate functional courts

---

[185] Wolfgang Preiser, "History of the Law of Nations: Basic Questions and Principles," 7 *Encyclopedia of Public International Law* 126, 128 (Amsterdam: Elsevier 1984); see, e.g., James Crawford, *International Law as an Open System* (London: Cameron May 2002).

[186] Yoram Dinstein, "International Law as a Primitive System," 19 *N.Y.U. International Law & Policy* 1, 32 (1986).

[187] See Erika de Wet, "The International Constitutional Order," 55 *International and Comparative Law Quarterly* 51 (2006); Andreas L. Paulus, "The International Legal System as a Constitution," in *Ruling the World? Constitutionalism, International Law, and Global Governance*, edited by Jeffrey L. Dunoff and Joel P. Trachtman (New York: Cambridge University Press 2009). An aspirational account is Jurgen Habermas, "The Constitutionalization of International Law and the Legitimation Problems of a Constitution for World Society," 15 *Constellations* 444 (2008).

[188] See Mattias Kumm, "The Legitimacy of International Law: A Constitutionalist Framework of Analysis," 15 *European Journal of International Law* 907, 930 (2004).

(WTO), a recognized set of shared values (Universal Declaration of Human Rights, Covenant on Civil and Political Rights, and Covenant on Economic, Social and Cultural Rights), and a shared commitment to the rule of law.[189] Proponents acknowledge weaknesses and inconsistencies within the system, but contend this no different from all legal systems in early stages of development. "In the increasingly integrated international legal order there is a co-existence of national, regional, and sectoral (functional) constitutional orders that complement one another in order to constitute an embryonic international constitutional order."[190]

To repeat, state law and international law are not parallel categories for two reasons. First, the state law category is filled with individual members that possess the same core features (lots of versions of the same thing), whereas the international law category is filled with whatever meets international law's validity requirements (lots of different things). Second, state law is not a member of its own category, whereas international law is both a category and the all-encompassing member of the category. Theorists and international jurists who posit them as parallel categories unwittingly compare an abstraction (state law) against concrete institutions (recognized international law). International law is a particular social-historical legal tradition – like French law – not an abstraction like state law.

Transnational law as a category differs from both. Unlike state law, it does not consist of multiple versions of the same thing, and unlike international law, its members are not identified through a common pedigree test, but in spatial terms. Transnational law encompasses the forms of law and regulation that exist in the space between and across polities, including aspects of state law, international law in its entirety, and other bodies of law like new *lex mercatoria*.

Why International Law Is "Law"

Hart articulated several compelling reasons to believe international law is a form of law. For "the last 150 years," Hart wrote (five decades ago), common "usage" has identified international law as "law."[191] He also recognized that courts – the quintessential legal institution – function at the international level, issuing legal rulings "that have been duly carried out by the parties."[192] Furthermore, although organized coercive sanctions are lacking, Hart (who did not require coercive force as an element of law) acknowledged international law consists of rule-based regimes generally considered binding: "what these rules require is thought and spoken of as obligatory; there is general pressure for conformity to the rules; claims and admissions are based on them and their breach is held to justify not

---

[189]   See de Wet, "The International Constitutional Order," supra; Paulus, "The International Legal System as a Constitution," supra.

[190]   De Wet, "The International Constitutional Order," supra 75.

[191]   Hart, *Concept of Law*, supra 214.   [192]   Id. 232.

only insistent demands for compensation, but reprisals and counter-measures."[193]

Additional characteristics of legality are the prototypically legalistic aspects of international law: legal analysis based on principles, doctrines, precedents, treaties, and juristic writings.[194] Hart acknowledged, "many of its concepts, methods, and techniques are the same as those of modern municipal law,"[195] which makes "the lawyers' technique freely transferable from the one to the other."[196] International law is steeped in legal "formalities" and "artificial distinctions."[197] These aspects of international law, he noted, are law's characteristic features. "Regard for forms and detail carried to excess has earned for law the reproaches of 'formalism' and 'legalism'; yet it is important to remember that these vices are exaggerations of some of the law's distinctive qualities,"[198] he observed. Jurists engaged with international law are trained lawyers performing classic legal activities.

After considering these factors, Hart nevertheless concluded that although international law has the "function and content" of municipal law, it lacks systematic form, and therefore is not quite law.[199] Jeremy Waldron chastised Hart for holding international law to an unduly high standard by exaggerating the actual systematicity of state legal systems.[200] Though he does not put it in these terms, Waldron's criticism exposes the error of comparing state law as an abstract category with international law as a particular. Hart did not compare international law with particular state legal systems, which exhibit a great range of systematic unity or lack thereof (unsettled contestation is common, particularly in the Global South). Instead, he evaluated international law against an idealized abstraction of the core features of state law.

Hart made another error when he conflated system with category. International law, in his analysis, was either a simple set of rules or a unified system.[201] Finding international law unsystematic and not unified, he concluded it is a bare set of primary rules like primitive law. Hart in effect adopted the vision of international jurists that international law in the aggregate constitutes a system, putting it to a test that it inevitably failed because many treaties are mutually disconnected. If he had instead taken up specific international legal institutions, like the International Court of Justice (ICJ) and the Law of the Sea, several are systematic on their own terms (with additional examples today, like the World Trade Organization).[202]

---

[193] Id. 220, 226, 231.   [194] Hart, *Concept of Law*, supra 229.   [195] Id. 227.   [196] Id. 237.
[197] Id. 239.   [198] Id. 229.   [199] Id. 237.
[200] See Jeremy Waldron, "International Law: 'A Relatively Small and Unimportant' Part of Jurisprudence?" (2013), http://papers.ssrn.com/sol3/papers.cfm?abstract_id=2326758.
[201] Hart, *Concept of Law*, supra 234.
[202] A sophisticated argument applying legal positivist strictures to show legal elements of global administrative law is Benedict Kingsbury, "The Concept of 'Law' in Global Administrative Law," 20 *European Journal of International Law*, 23 (2009).

Another unjustified assumption Hart made was international law must satisfy criteria set by state law. He did not contemplate the possibility of various forms of law, each with its own features. A critic of Austin protested, "Is it not possible that two systems of law, municipal and international, may co-exist, and that each may be enforced in a different way corresponding to the nature of one and the other?"[203] This was recently echoed in Waldron's objection that Hart was "unwilling to consider how different our philosophical analysis would be if both of these were treated as paradigms instead of only one."[204]

Nothing requires that every and all forms of law must be unified and systematic. Noting that lawyers learn it as law and nations consider it law, Oliver Wendell Holmes criticized Austin's assertion that international law is not law. "Why does it so much matter that they are not prescribed by a sovereign to a political inferior?" he asked.[205] Citing the same legalistic qualities Hart identified, English jurisprudent Frederick Pollock concluded against Austin that international law is indeed law. "If therefore we find that our definition of law does not include the law of nations, the proper conclusion is ... that our definition is inadequate."[206]

Notwithstanding the flaws in his analysis, Hart hit on a deeper insight that merits repeating. International law draws on terminology, doctrines, procedures, processes, and legal formality utilized in domestic law. Though coming from separate common law and civil law traditions, international jurists share broad bodies of legal knowledge, practices, and an overlapping culture of legality that extends from the domestic to the international law realms. Domestic and international law have simultaneously been influenced by the same theoretical streams: natural law, legal positivism, legal realism, critical theory, and economic analysis of law. Jurists trained in domestic law can with effort master and engage in international law and practices. A century ago, it was not unusual for lawyers to work in domestic and international law, as did Travers Twiss and Elihu Root. Today, corporate law firms with branches around the world house lawyers who practice domestic and/or international law, collaborating when called on.

International law is a genuine form of law conventionally recognized as law and constructed in legalistic terms by jurists. The professional culture of lawyers – including legal education and law firms – suffuses international law.[207] There is

---

[203]   James Brown Scott, "The Legal Nature of International Law," 1 *American Journal of International Law* 831, 845 (1907).

[204]   Waldron, "International Law: 'A Relatively Small and Unimportant' Part of Jurisprudence?" supra 210.

[205]   Oliver Wendell Holmes, "Codes, and the Arrangement of the Law," 5 *American Law Review* 1, 5 (1870).

[206]   Frederick Pollock, "The Methods of Jurisprudence," 8 *Law Magazine and Review of Jurisprudence Quarterly* 25, 39 (1882).

[207]   See Walker, *Intimations of Global Law*, supra 29–54. The empirically informed theoretical perspective of transnational law as a process that Walker develops is consistent with the realistic theory I articulate herein.

a shared corpus of legal knowledge and sources, modes of lawmaking, legal interpretation, legal practices, and international courts and law declaring and applying
organizations.[208] International law fills prototypical legal functions of establishing
binding rules that are generally followed,[209] which state and international courts and
other tribunals apply to resolve disputes. Though international law lacks overarching
unity and a systematic apparatus for coercive sanctions, it possesses distinctively legal
qualities.

Not a Unified, Hierarchical System

When international jurists see international law as a system comprised of everything
that falls in the international law category – conflating system with category – another
set of theoretical puzzles arises.[210] Current worries about the fragmentation of international law are encouraged by this conflation of system with category. International
jurists are concerned that the multiplication of specialized legal regimes – trade, law of
the sea, crimes, intellectual property, human rights, etc. – and regional regimes
increase the risk of forum shopping and inconsistent outcomes, threatening the
unity of the international legal system.[211] "What must be avoided," one jurist writes,
"is this fragmentation leading to self-contained islands of international law, de-linked
from other branches of international law."[212] Another international jurist comments,
"The variations among tribunals deciding questions of international law are not so
significant as to challenge the coherence of international law and its legitimacy as
a system of law."[213]

As these statements reflect, discussions about fragmentation presuppose that
international law generally hangs together as a system of law. What provides the
appearance of a system are common sources of law (customs, treaties, principles,
court decisions[214]), accepted norms (*jus cogens, pacta sunt servanda, opinio juris,*
equal sovereignty of states, good faith fulfillment of obligations, etc.), common

---

[208] Julius Stone pointed to the same factors to assert international law is a social fact. See Julius Stone, "Problems Confronting Sociological Enquiries Concerning International Law," 89 *Recueil Des Cours* 61, 68, 116 (1957).

[209] Jessup, *A Modern Law of Nations*, supra 7–8.

[210] Many international jurists do not make this mistake, but it is common.

[211] See Gilbert Guillaume, "The Future of International Judicial Institutions," 44 *International and Comparative Law Quarterly* 848, 862 (1995).

[212] Joost Pauwelyn, "Bridging Fragmentation and Unity: International Law as a Universe of Interconnected Islands," 25 *Michigan Journal International Law* 903, 904 (2004).

[213] Jonathan I. Charney, "The Impact on the International Legal System of the Growth of International Courts and Tribunals," 31 *N.Y.U. International Law and Policy* 697, 706 (1999).

[214] Article 38(1) of the Statute of the International Court of Justice identifies international conventions, international custom, general principles of law recognized by civilized nations, and "judicial decisions and the teachings of the most highly qualified publicists ... as subsidiary means for the determination of rules of law." A concise account is Bederman, "Constructivism, Positivism, and Empiricism," supra 485–92. See also Murphy, *Evolving Dimensions of International Law*, supra.

interpretive doctrines and practices (preeminently the Vienna Convention on the Law of Treaties), recognized doctrines developed by jurists and courts, and legal institutions like the International Court of Justice – constituting a common international juristic tradition, culture, and complex of institutions.

The idealized notion of a legal system, however, also entails overarching unity, hierarchical authority, and substantial internal coherence. International law is not a legal system in this sense. The International Law Commission made this explicit in a 2002 report, finding international law should not be analogized to state legal systems because "the concept of hierarchy" is "not present on the international level," there is "no well-developed and authoritative hierarchy of values," and there is "no hierarchy of systems represented by the final body to resolve conflicts."[215] As Samantha Besson remarked, "There is no such hierarchy to date given the fragmentation of the international legal order between different legal matters and regions, and what one may refer to as (internal) horizontal legal pluralism."[216] Judge Bruno Simma, a member of the International Court of Justice, observed, "While international law certainly is systematic, it does not necessarily constitute a comprehensive and organized legal order."[217]

Unity and hierarchy are absent and unlikely to be achieved.[218] What stands in the way is the political reality that leaders of powerful states and states in general overwhelmingly do not want to construct international law as an overarching, unified system because they do not consider it in their national and personal interest, and nationalist sentiments remain powerful. In the competitive-cooperative relations between polities, the competitive side is more compelling, with states always striving for an advantage.

On top of this (though it is enough in itself), international law is not a unified legal system because among the four sources of international law, treaties are dominant, and the dynamics underlying treaties point away from overarching unity. Two of these sources are limited at the outset: general principles are few in number, vague, and sparingly invoked;[219] judicial decisions develop law incrementally and interstitially. That leaves customary international law and treaties.

---

[215] Paragraph 506, Report of the International Law Commission on the Work of Its Fifty-Fourth Session (2002), p. 98, http://legal.un.org/docs/?path=../ilc/reports/2002/english/chp9.pdf&lang=EFSRAC.

[216] Samantha Besson, "Sources of International Law," in Besson and Tasioulas, *The Philosophy of International Law*, supra 183.

[217] Bruno Simma and Dirk Pulkowski, "Of Planets and the Universe: Self-Contained Regimes in International Law," 17 *European Journal of International Law* 483, 500 (2006).

[218] For doubts about the unity of international law, see Martti Koskenniemi and Paivi Leino, "Fragmentation of International Law? Postmodern Anxieties," 15 *Leiden Journal of International Law* 553 (2002); Andreas Fischer-Lescano and Gunther Teubner, "Regime-Collisions: The Vain Search for Legal Unity in the Fragmentation of Global Law," 25 *Michigan Journal of International Law* 999 (2004).

[219] See generally Giorgio Gaja, "General Principles of Law," *Max Plank Encyclopedia of Public International Law* (Oxford: Oxford University Press 2014) at http://iusgentium.ufsc.br/wp-content/uploads/2014/10/General-Principles-of-Law-Giorgio-Gaja-2.pdf.

Customary international law (CIL) has endured withering attacks by critics.[220] "Some scholars complain that it is incoherent, others assert that it is irrelevant or a fiction, and virtually everyone agrees that the theory and doctrine of CIL is a mess."[221] To obtain recognition, a custom must be a general and consistent state practice backed with a subjective sense of obligation (*opinio juris*). Key issues remain unsettled: What proportion of state conformity is enough (it need not be universal) and for how long, what counts as evidence of state practice, how is subjective obligation established, why are customs binding, which customs are binding, what does their content consist of, how are state objectors treated? There is also skepticism about whether custom truly reflects universal consent. "Traditionally, customary law has been made by a few interested states for all."[222] Even a staunch defender of CIL acknowledges "many of the criticisms are powerful because they are correct."[223] Despite these flaws, CIL is entrenched within international law discourse,[224] with newly recognized CIL mainly used to fill gaps in treaties or to extend treaties to non-signatories.

By default, then, treaties are the main generative source for what counts as international law. Every treaty arrangement is based on a unique cluster of states and mix of factors involving a specific set of problems, aimed at achieving particular objectives. States come to agreement through political compromises, side deals, temporary alliances, vote trading, and other situation-specific arrangements, with no necessary relationship to other problems and agreements.[225] States form different alignments on different issues depending on interests at stake. States engaging in this process pursue their perceived national interests in the competition for wealth and power – which at times is advanced through cooperation and at times not. Powerful states can mold treaty regimes to their liking, or scuttle treaties. Treaties are congeries of political calculations and power. The result is a hodgepodge of deals.

The requirements for valid treaty making do not include achieving substantive consistency and coherence with all other existing treaties, and adding these requirements would impossibly burden an already fraught process. Agreements are

---

[220] J. Patrick Kelly, "The Twilight of Customary International Law," 40 *Virginia Journal of International Law* 449 (2000).

[221] Andrew T. Guzman, "Saving Customary International Law," 9 27 *Michigan Journal of International Law* 115, 116–17 (2005).

[222] Jonathan I. Charney, "Universal International Law," 87 *American Journal of International Law* 529, 538 (1993).

[223] Guzman, "Saving Customary International Law," supra 118.

[224] A lively critique of the flaws in CIL doctrines and the commitment of international jurists to preserve it is Jean d'Aspremont, "The Decay of Modern Customary International Law in Spite of Scholarly Heroism," *Global Community: Yearbook of International Law and Jurisprudence 2015* (Oxford: Oxford University Press 2016).

[225] Gunther Teubner and Andreas Fischer-Lescano argue that the sources of fragmentation are at a deeper level than these factors, located in the different rationalities operative in different sectors of global society. Andreas Fischer-Lescano and Gunther Teubner, "Regime-Collisions: The Vain Search for Legal Unity in the Fragmentation of Global Law," 25 *Michigan Journal of International Law* 999 (2004).

formulated on specific matters – environment, trade, aviation, telecommunications, labor rights, intellectual property rights, human rights, etc. – without ensuring that no conflicts arise and all gaps are filled. The desire for unified systematic coherence dear to internationalists is external to the concerns of parties hashing out a deal on particular matters.

Confusion arises when international lawyers treat as treaties as *constitutive* of the international law system. Based on this understanding, international law texts commonly discuss regional entities like the European Union, the North American Free Trade Agreement (NAFTA), the Association of Southeast Asian Nations (ASEAN), the Common Market of the South Cone (MERCOSUR), as well as regional courts, like the European Court of Justice, the European Court of Human Rights, and the Inter-American Court of Human Rights, and treaty-based organizations like the World Trade Organization, the International Labor Organization, and the World Health Organization.[226] All of this is stitched together as elements of the international law system because they were created by treaties, despite inconsistencies in purposes and orientations among them.

A better understanding is that treaties in general are *products* of international law mechanisms that create legal obligations – not automatically constitutive aspects of an international legal system.[227] Like contracts, treaties are formal agreements between parties on specific matters. Contracts are legal products created through legally recognized means. Jurists do not think all contracts are part of the legal system or suggest they comprise a unified and coherent legal system in the aggregate. What they share is they meet the criteria for valid contracts and are interpreted and enforced through shared legal doctrines and institutions. The same observations hold for treaties. Just as one would not say all contracts are part of a legal system, it is senseless to assert that all treaties are part of the international legal system.

Only a subset of treaties is constitutive of international law – those that create international organizations engaged in lawmaking, law enforcement, and law application, involving truly international legal regimes. The UN Charter is a constitutive treaty. The Law of the Sea Treaty and the Rome Statute of the International Criminal Court are also examples. Bilateral treaties, regional treaties, regional organizations, and more generally treaties not truly international in scope are not constitutive of international law – only products.

Even if the focus is limited to constitutive treaties, however, international law is not a unified system of law. Separate international regimes on different substantive issues do not cohere in the aggregate, as mentioned earlier, because multilateral agreement on each subject matter is a unique combination of calculations and

---

[226] See, e.g., Carter, Trimble, and Weiner, *International Law*, supra 13–14.
[227] See Philip Allott, "Language, Method, and the Nature of International Law," 45 *British Yearbook of International Law* 79, 132–33 (1971).

power. Absent are hierarchically structured legal institutions with system-wide authority, which state officials do not want to be subject to.[228] International law is not breaking down through greater fragmentation. It has never existed as a unified, hierarchical system. Disjunctions and inconsistencies among separate treaty regimes and the legal actions of intergovernmental organizations are more evident today because more of them exist.[229] Whether an overarching international legal system will one day be created is a political choice for future generations of political leaders. Until that occurs, if it does, uniformity is brought by the labors of international jurists perpetuating international legal knowledge and practices.

Not Separate Systems

International law is widely seen as parallel to and separate from state law. Ever since Bentham set them apart, this impression has held fast. As Slaughter and Burke-White declare, "International law has traditionally been just that – international. Consisting of a largely separate set of legal rules and institutions, international law has long governed relationships among states."[230] This common perception distorts the actual intertwined relationship between state law and international law.

Two centuries ago, they were not seen as separate legal orders. As Edwin Dickinson observed, "The law of nations was necessarily and literally a part of national law in the 18th century, since the two systems were assumed to rest in their respective spheres upon the same immutable principles of natural justice."[231] Even Dickinson slipped to the modern position in this description, calling it "two systems," which they were not. Law of Nations referred to laws recognized by all ("civilized") nations, not a separate system, but a collection of doctrines addressing diplomatic matters between states, the high seas, transactions between merchants from different countries, and so on. It was only after legal positivist views became dominant in the course of the nineteenth century that "law of nations became a source, rather than an integral part, of the national system."[232]

Theorists of international law have construed the relationship between international law and state law in either dualistic or monistic terms, both of which perpetuate the distortion. Dualists present them as mutually independent systems of law with different sources and subject matters. "International law is a law between

228 Richard Collins argues that the decentralized structure of international law is a virtue that suits its purpose of providing a framework for coexistence and cooperation among states. Richard Collins, *The Institutional Problem in Modern International Law* (Oxford: Hart Publishing 2016).

229 See Marti Koskenniemi, Chairman, *Fragmentation of International Law: Difficulties Arising from the Diversification and Expansion of International Law*, April 13, 2006, pp. 11, 14–15, http://repositoriocdpd .net:8080/bitstream/handle/123456789/676/Inf_KoskenniemiM_FragmentationInternationalLaw_2006 .pdf?sequence=1.

230 See Slaughter and Burke-White, "The Future of International Law Is Domestic (or European Way of Law)," supra 327. The authors insist on maintaining the conceptual separation between domestic and international law at 349.

231 Dickinson, "Changing Concepts and the Doctrine of Incorporation," supra 259.   232 Id. 260.

sovereign states: municipal law applies within a state and regulates the relations of its citizens with each other and with the executive."[233] Oppenheim explained dualism: "Law of Nations can neither as a body nor in parts be *per se* a part of Municipal Law. Just as Municipal Law lacks the power of altering or creating rules of International Law, so the latter lacks absolutely the power of altering or creating rules of Municipal Law."[234]

Monists see a unified system of law based on an overarching international law system with state legal systems as subsystems. "The main reason for the essential identity of the two spheres of law is, it is maintained, that some of the fundamental notions of International Law cannot be comprehended without the assumption of a superior legal order from which the various systems of Municipal Law are, in a sense, derived by way of delegation."[235] Hans Kelsen, the most prominent philosophical proponent of monism, points out that "the international legal order determines the territorial, personal, and temporal spheres of validity of the national legal orders, thus making possible the coexistence of a multitude of States."[236]

Both theories maintain a distinction between domestic and international law as separate systems or orders, differing in how relations between the two are construed. From a dualist perspective, when international law is recognized by domestic legal institutions, this occurs through the operation of state law. From a monist perspective, state law functions in these contexts as an organ or agent of international law.[237]

The "dualism versus monism" divide has served as the main theoretical framework for international law theory for more than a century, though jurists have objected for decades that "both theories conflict with the way in which international and national organs and courts behave."[238] Dualism is descriptively inapt because aspects of international law, like principles and customary international law, directly apply within national systems, and monism is hard to reconcile with how domestic law conditions the creation and application of international law. Long-standing criticisms of the public–private international law division are another manifestation of this misfit. Private international law has domestic

[233] Ian Brownlie, *Principles of Public International Law*, 7th ed. (Oxford: Oxford University Press 2008) 31–32.

[234] Oppenheim, *International Law*, supra 35.

[235] Id. 36. See also J. G. Stark, "Monism and Dualism in the Theory of International Law," 17 *British Yearbook of International Law* 66 (1936).

[236] Hans Kelsen, *General Theory of Law and State* (Cambridge, MA: Harvard University Press 1945) 363. In Kelsen's early account, it is logically possible for monism to be under primacy of either state law or international law. But only primacy of international law can explain the international legal order. For an explanation, see Paul Gragl, "In Defense of Kelsenian Monism: Countering Hart and Raz," available at http://papers.ssrn.com/sol3/papers.cfm?abstract_id=2828191.

[237] See Starke, "Monism and Dualism in the Theory of International Law," supra 71. William Dodge argues that the United States began as monist, with international law integrated within domestic law (unless explicitly superseded by statute), but shifted to dualist by the end of the nineteenth century, with international law part of domestic law only if adopted. Dodge, "The Charming Betsy and The Paquete Habana," supra. This understanding of monist-dualist differs from Starke's.

[238] Brownlie, *Principles of Public International Law*, supra 33.

qualities as well as international qualities. Because a categorical separation requires that it be one or the other, it was deemed domestic, suppressing its international law aspects. Certain transnational legal regimes, furthermore, are generated in international forums and have international reach but are enacted by domestic means – to call them purely international or purely domestic is ill-fitting either way. [239]

Earlier, I articulated why international law is not a unified, hierarchical legal system. Here, I further argue, it is a mistake to think of international law and state law as separate systems, though it seems natural to see them as separate because they have long been viewed as such.

They have always been intermingled. Prior to the modern era, there were no international courts, so admiralty law, diplomatic immunity, rights of foreign citizens, enforcement of foreign judgments, and so on were secured within state institutions. International law has always relied heavily on state legal regimes.[240] From 1979 to 2004, for instance, 88 percent of criminal trials for human rights violations were held in domestic courts, and only 4 percent in international courts (the remaining 8 percent were tried in a foreign domestic court).[241] While the number of international courts has multiplied in recent decades, their caseloads are small. The International Court of Justice averages fewer than ten decisions annually, with similarly low numbers of cases for other international courts as well.[242] The only high-volume courts are the EU Court of Justice and the European Court of Human Rights, but this is a reflection of advanced institutional capacities of the European Union, not international law generally.

International courts regularly cite domestic legal decisions on international law issues, and domestic courts regularly take up international law matters. Lord Bingham remarked in 2005, "To an extent almost unimaginable even thirty years ago, national courts in this and other countries are called upon to consider and resolve issues turning on the correct understanding and application of international law, not on an occasional basis, now and then, but routinely, and often in cases of great importance."[243] Domestic courts also "play an extremely important role in the

---

[239] See, e.g., Slaughter and Burke-White, "The Future of International Law Is Domestic (or, The European Way of Law)," supra.

[240] Although they maintain a conceptual separation between the two, Slaughter and White list multiple examples of international law reliance on state law. "The Future of International Law Is Domestic (or, the European Way of Law)," supra 339–43.

[241] Kathryn Sikkink, "From State Responsibility to Individual Criminal Accountability: A New Regulatory Model for Core Human Rights Violations," in Mattli and Woods, *The Politics of Global Regulation*, supra 125–30.

[242] See Karen J. Alter, *The New Terrain of International Law: Courts, Politics, Rights* (Princeton, NJ: Princeton University Press 2014) 72–75.

[243] Tom Bingham, quoted in Antonios Tzanakopoulos and Christian J. Tams, "Introduction: Domestic Courts as Agents of Development of International Law," 26 *Leiden Journal of International Law* 531 (2013).

identification and formation of international law."[244] Domestic judicial decisions are looked to as sources of state practice on international customs. Domestic judicial decisions produce interpretations of international law that introduce limitations, extensions, and exceptions.[245] When followed by other courts, domestic and international, these domestic judicial decisions create international law. International tribunals, on their part, regularly survey national law and adopt approaches generated at the national law.[246]

The frequent involvement by domestic courts in international law produces mixed international-national law, whereby domestic legal doctrines and modes of analysis are fused with international law interpretations. An example involves the U.S. Alien Tort Claims Act, which provides jurisdiction in U.S. courts for tort claims involving violations of the law of nations or a treaty. A commentator noted, "Far from merely enforcing existing international law, U.S. courts acting under the ATCA are staking out an aggressive (and depending on one's viewpoint a progressive or regressive) position on universal civil jurisdiction, and applying an eclectic mix of domestic and international standards in the process."[247] Other scholars speak of the "Europeanization of international law" owing to the heavy use of international law in European courts.[248]

Another kind of mix is found in the creation of special tribunals dealing with international crimes in East Timor, Kosovo, and Sierra Leone.[249] "They were usually situated within the targeted state; were staffed by international and domestic personnel (judges, prosecutors, investigators, defense counsel, administrators, and support staff) working in tandem; and applied a mixture of international and domestic criminal law and procedures."[250] These hybrid tribunals exist on a continuum with both domestic and international qualities, which is likely to continue because it is less costly than standalone international law institutions and helps bolster weak domestic legal institutions.

All efforts to categorically separate domestic and international law inevitably fail because they are thoroughly enmeshed. When state law (in legislative, executive,

---

[244] Anthea Roberts, "Comparative International Law? The Role of National Courts in Creating and Enforcing International Law," 60 *International and Comparative Law Quarterly* 59, 63 (2011).

[245] See Id. See also Tzanakopoulos and Tams, "Introduction: Domestic Courts as Agents of Development of International Law," supra 538.

[246] For extensive examples taken from international criminal law, see James G. Stewart and Asad Kiyani, "The Ahistoricism of Legal Pluralism in International Criminal Law," January 4, 2016, http://papers .ssrn.com/sol3/papers.cfm?abstract_id=2710899; see especially pages 4–6, notes 3 and 4. The authors point out that the International Criminal Court has adopted German principles of attribution, and various international criminal tribunals survey national laws when adopting criminal law and procedure.

[247] Roberts, "Comparative International Law," supra 77.   [248] Id. 79–80.

[249] See "Hybrid Courts," Project on International Courts and Tribunals, www.pict-pcti.org/courts/ hybrid.html.

[250] Beth van Schaack, "The Building Blocks of Hybrid Justice," 3, December 17, 2015, http://papers.ssrn .com/sol3/papers.cfm?abstract_id=2705110.

judicial, and administrative settings) recognizes international law, *both* are operating. They are doctrinal streams, not separate systems or categories, and their status is not categorically determined, but rather depends on a given context and the questions at issue. Sovereignty is a doctrine within both domestic and international law, as are admiralty doctrines, diplomatic immunity, treaty interpretations, and so forth. One might ask, are EU laws domestic law or international law? They can be seen as either or both depending on the inquiry. Would the proposed "Treaty Establishing a Constitution for Europe" (if ratification were to occur) be an international law product or domestic law? As the inclusion of "treaty" and "constitution" in its title suggests, the answer is both.

Domestic legal systems and international law are coincident social-institutional traditions drawing from a shared pool of legal knowledge and practices that have never been separate systems. International law consists of anything constructed in "international law" terms, consistent with recognized rules of validity, in whatever context they might arise. Recognition of international law occurs in domestic legal contexts and within regional and international legal institutions and organizations. International law operates within, alongside, interconnects with, interacts with, and sometimes competes and conflicts with state legal regimes. International law is substantially imbricated within domestic legal institutions, and also exists in a number of institutional contexts apart from domestic law. It is a field of discourse, practices, and institutions conducted in the name of "international law" operating across domestic, transnational, and international contexts.

To say that state law and international law are not separate, mutually exclusive systems is not to say that they cannot be distinguished, analyzed, compared, and taught as separate bodies of doctrines and complexes of institutions. They are separable for many purposes. But the impression that a categorical separation exists is misleading.

International Law and Transnational Law and Regulation

A final theoretical clarification situates international law vis-à-vis transnational law and governance. The key distinction is that international law is a *particular social-historical legal tradition* comprised of doctrines, practices, and institutions that emerged in Europe and spread over time, whereas the labels transnational or transgovernmental law refer to regulatory phenomena operating in the *social space* of cooperative-competitive intercourse between and across polities. Jessup's proposal to substitute transnational law for international law did more than go from a narrower to a more encompassing framework. It involves a qualitative shift from a specific juristic tradition to all regulatory activities that transcend national boundaries – an immense space with an extraordinary number and variety of arrangements. Transnational law is a category that encompasses all forms of law within this space, whether domestic, international, or some other form.

Competitive-cooperative intercourse between and across polities is a constant of recorded human history, now occurring at unprecedented levels, as detailed earlier. International law developed in connection with a narrow though visible slice of this intercourse, but it never occupied the entire social space. No single system could take up more than a small piece of this vast arena. The bulk of coordination and regulation is managed through countless separate functionally oriented organizations and networks, as occurs throughout modern society generally. International jurists who see the domain of intercourse between and across polities as theirs to wholly occupy or dominate do not appreciate that the unfathomable volume and variety of activities within this arena renders this impossible.

In addition, the treaty apparatus is cumbersome and problematic. Though they serve important functions, treaties can be undesirable for national officials, particularly when domestic approval or cooperation must be secured. The international deal on Iranian nuclear development is not a treaty or executive agreement, but a "joint plan of action" by Iran, the United States, the United Kingdom, France, Germany, Russia, and China.[251] The BEPS tax regime is not a treaty, but a commitment by G20 countries consisting mainly of soft law provisions to be incorporated at the domestic level.[252] The governing body of the internet, ICANN, with participation by public and private stakeholders, has been structured to avoid governance under a multilateral treaty.[253] These are just three recent examples of major international arrangements that intentionally bypassed treaties. Important treaties are still enacted, though even then the limits of treaties show. The celebrated Paris Agreement on Climate Change was reached on the condition that no mandatory legal obligations were imposed on the reduction of carbon emissions.[254]

Regulation of matters between and across polities – the arena of transnational law – is not an emerging legal order as such, but incalculable separate instances of reglementary activity in the social space of intercourse between and across polities. The parallels and commonalities scholars identify in the ongoing proliferation of transnational regulation – like transgovernmental networks or administrative practices – are attributable to similarities in institutional arrangements that have become common in the age of organizations owing to their functional utility. Tying these innumerable regulatory arrangements together to constitute a global ordering is a theoretical projection on what are in reality separate, repeated instances of common institutional arrangements. Keeping this in mind will make it easier to

---

[251] See Letter to U.S. Representative Mike Pompeo, from Julia Frifield, Assistant Secretary of Legislative Affairs, U.S. Department of State, November 19, 2015, http://pompeo.house.gov/uploadedfiles/151124_-_reply_from_state_regarding_jcpoa.pdf.

[252] See Grinberg and Pauwelyn, "The Emergence of a New International Tax Regime," supra.

[253] Kal Raustiala, "Governing the Internet," 110 *American Journal of International Law* 491 (2016).

[254] See Marty Lederman, "The Constitutionally Critical, Last-Minute Correction to the Paris Climate Change Accord," December 13, 2015, *Balkinization*, http://balkin.blogspot.com/2015/12/the-last-minute-correction-to-paris.html.

recognize when genuine instances of global regulatory regimes actually develop, as may occur.[255]

International law is best discarded as an abstract category, instead seen as a specific legal tradition and complex of doctrines and institutions that operates within state law as well as beyond. Transnational law, as Jessup proposed, encompasses international law (public and private), maritime and admiralty, transnational legal regimes like the new *lex mercatoria*, coordinated actions agreed to in international forums and implemented at the domestic level like the Basil Committee, and much else mentioned in this chapter. This reconstruction takes us back conceptually to where things stood before Bentham's unfortunate theoretical intervention.

Three standard distinctions have been questioned in this exploration: between state law and international law as separate systems and parallel categories; between public and private international law; between monism and dualism. Also, the distinction between public and private actors is less stark in this arena, as both assume legal functions. The extraordinary multiplication of intercourse between and across polities has given rise to an intensification of regulatory activities that construct whatever arrangement is most likely to work, paying no heed to these distinctions.

[255] See Walker, *Intimations of Global Law*, supra.

Conclusion

A Realistic Theory of Law

This conclusion articulates several basic propositions of the realistic theory of law. These are summary statements, leaving details and support to preceding pages or remaining work.

Law (and translations thereof) *is* whatever social groups conventionally attach the label "law" to. Though state law is a familiar form of law today, the territorial state with a unified, hierarchical system of law is only a few centuries old. Other commonly identified forms of law in the past and present include bodies of customary law, religious law, natural law, international law, merchants' law, and other forms of transnational law. When looking to the distant past, early forms of law can be identified by tracing backward from what is conventionally recognized as law today to locate phenomena that bear core similarities (a genealogical approach).

Long-standing folk concepts of law in the Western tradition contain deeply entrenched connotations revolving around 1) fundamental rules of social intercourse, addressing property rights, personal injuries, enforceable obligations, control over labor, and rights and responsibilities with respect to family unions and children; 2) institutionalized rule systems administered by a polity backed by coercion; and 3) justice, fairness, and right. Conventional identifications of law usually attach to phenomena with one or more of these three connotations; because they are weighty, the label "law" is not easily attached conventionally to new phenomena. Theories of law typically center on and abstract from one or more of these three connotations. They are often invoked in debates over law.

Forms of law are constituted and evolve in connection with surrounding circumstances. Starting with basic rules of social intercourse among hunter-gatherers, I have highlighted four transformations that ushered in new social-legal arrangements. First, the formation of polities within large social groups (complex chiefdoms, early states) brought, alongside maintaining basic rules of social intercourse, coercive legal enforcement of social, economic, and political hierarchies and legal backing of the polity itself. Second, following several thousand years of social development, law declared at will by modern state legal institutions became a multifunctional tool utilized by government organizations to carry out tasks.

Third, owing to the proliferation of organizations and networks that structure relationships through law and to voluminous instrumental uses of law by government to achieve social objectives, a relatively fixed legal fabric has come into existence in advanced capitalist societies. A fourth transformation, currently under way, involves regulatory arrangements being constructed to deal with intercourse between and across polities.

These transformations are linked to law's involvement in increasing social complexity. Human social groups must cooperate and must manage conflict. Greater numbers of people living in settled residential centers produce more social, economic, and political interaction and common tasks that are coordinated through functionally differentiated organizations relying on legal mechanisms. When combined with advances in transportation and communication, population growth also leads to greater interaction between and across polities, producing an increase in regulatory mechanisms to deal with issues that extend beyond individual polities. This process began several millennia ago and has massively increased with the global extension of capitalism.

Natural necessity owing to human nature and requirements and tendencies within social groups appears to be behind fundamental aspects of law. Scientific evidence presently is thin,[1] so these assertions are speculative. The universality of family units and universal reactions that property of others should not be taken, deceptive exchanges are wrong, and intentional injuries are wrong suggest there is a naturalistic basis for basic rules of social intercourse (although the content of the rules vary across societies) – the first connotation of law.[2] The apparent necessity for large social groups to use hierarchical organizations to manage cooperation and conflict, which operate more effectively when backed by organized coercive force, is behind the second connotation of law. Another apparently universal trait within social groups is a strong sense of justice and fairness (again with much variation),[3] which underlies the third connotation of law.

[1] I have not engaged with these issues in the text because scientific findings are too limited and tentative to say much with confidence. For an overview, see Joshua Green, *Moral Tribes: Emotion, Reason and the Gap between Us and Them* (New York: Penguin Press 2013).

[2] See Paul H. Robinson and Robert Kurzban, "Concordance and Conflict in Intuitions of Justice," 91 *Minnesota L. Rev.* 1829, 1848 (2007); Paul H. Robinson, Owen D. Jones, and Robert Kurzban, "Realism, Punishment, and Reform," 77 *Chicago L. Rev.* 1611, 1617–18 (2010). On the naturalistic basis for responses to battery, see John Mikhail, "Any Animal Whatever? Harmful Battery and Its Elements as Building Blocks of Moral Cognition," 124 *Ethics* 750 (2014). Tempering claims about universality, there is also much variation. See Donald Braman, Dan M. Kahan, and David A. Hoffman, "Some Realism about Punishment Naturalism," 77 *Chicago L. Rev.* 1531 (2010).

[3] See Laura Nader and Andree Sursock, "Anthropology and Justice," in *Justice: Views from the Social Sciences*, edited by Ronald L. Cohen (New York: Plenum Press 1986) 205; Ken Binmore, "The Origins of Fair Play," 151 *Proceedings of the British Academy* 151 (2007); Marc D. Hauser, *Moral Minds: How Nature Designed Our Universal Sense of Right and Wrong* (New York: Harper 2006) chapter 2; Paul H. Robinson, Robert Kurzban, and Owen D. Jones, "The Origins of Shared Intuitions of Justice," 60 *Vanderbilt L. Rev.* 1633 (2007). An evolutionary account of justice is articulated in Ken Binmore, "Justice as a Natural Phenomenon," available at http://discovery.ucl.ac.uk/14995/1/14995.pdf.

Naturalistic tendencies also explain the close association between law and domination. The common human pursuits of material comfort and seeking to better one's relative position generates efforts by individuals and groups to use the normative and coercive powers of law to their advantage. Powerful groups are more successful in controlling and enlisting law to support their agendas – law is a constitutive aspect of their social, economic, and political power.

All forms of law operate in social space alongside and dependent on other norms, rules, institutions, and modes of ordering – customs, morals, etiquette, habits, practices, institutional structures, language, shared concepts and ideologies. The thick social normative stew has many ingredients, law one among others, which often exert greater immediate influence than law. Formal legal institutions are influenced by and rely on supportive social beliefs and institutions.

Attention must be paid to three levels of social recognition of law. The first level is when a community recognizes the existence of legal rules like property rights, marriage, etc. Conventionally recognized beliefs and actions oriented to these rules make them real. This is how customary law operates through community recognition, notwithstanding the absence of an organized legal system. A second level is conventional recognition of legal officials – recognition that certain people or positions possess legal authority to create, enforce, and apply legal norms. A third level, emergent out of the second, is legal officials' recognition of what counts as valid legal rules and actions. The coordinated conduct of legal officials produces institutional legal actions and facts.

In the standard legal theory image, these three levels coincide. Legal norms collectively recognized by the community match legal norms collectively recognized by legal officials, constituting a mutually supportive social construction of law. This is not the only arrangement, however. The legal norms members of the community recognize may diverge from legal norms legal officials recognize. And a legal system can exist without support from the community, when only the legal officials themselves recognize and coordinate their legal actions, though conflicts will arise with the community and the social efficacy of the legal system will suffer. In these situations, multiple forms of law coexist.

Society and law are constantly evolving, reflecting new social, cultural, economic, political, ecological, and technological circumstances. Increases in population and social complexity, new religions or political ideologies, changes in distributions of economic and political power, significant alterations in the ecosystem, natural disasters, conquest or interference from external threats, new discoveries, economic and technological changes – these are just a few of innumerable social developments reflected in legal changes. Over time, social arrangements build through, on top of, and around legal arrangements, interconnecting law within the whole culture, economy, and polity, mutually supporting and anchoring one another. Legal changes typically occur piecemeal, with selected alterations absorbed and fitted within preexisting legal arrangements, in turn affecting related social arrangements. People may alter their actions to conform to new legal requirements – responding to the costs, benefits, or normative authority attached to the law – or people may be unaware of, disregard, or circumvent legal requirements.

Social forces influence law via officials exercising legal powers and through the daily activities of jurists tailoring law to meet objectives. Officials with legislative power enact laws that reflect prevailing ideologies and cultural, religious, or moral views, the interests and goals of powerful sectors, the outcomes of battles between competing social groups, the backgrounds and personal interests of lawmakers, their perceptions of what promotes the social welfare, and in other ways. Executives who utilize law, administrative regulators who carry out policies, judges who decide legal cases, jurists who develop legal knowledge, and lawyers who represent clients are subconsciously and consciously affected in the same ways. Social, cultural, economic, and political influences thereby ooze into law, obtaining legal recognition and support. When incorporated into law, they are fitted into the body of legal knowledge, institutions, and practices maintained by the professional legal culture.

Legal professionals and their collectively produced legal culture have secured pivotal positions within state legal systems. The production of law is processed through these specialized legal cultures. Legal knowledge and practices are cultural complexes in two distinct senses: 1) legal knowledge incorporates surrounding social-cultural-economic-political-ecological-and-technological ideas and influences; and 2) legal terminology, knowledge, doctrines, modes of analysis, and practices collectively constitute a professional legal culture into which jurists are indoctrinated – the legal tradition. The professional legal cultures of advanced capitalist societies emphasize formal legality, coherent bodies of legal knowledge, and rational legal regimes (evidence-based, means-ends rationality, efficient operation, etc.). The professional legal culture has its own imperatives as a semiautonomous body of specialized knowledge, institutions, and practices that absorb and incorporate social influences. What results from this combination are unique bodies of law within societies. European and Anglo-American professional legal cultures also developed (and extended to) the international legal culture.

Decision makers in legal disputes (judges, elders, community) range in orientation along a spectrum from rule-bound decisions to outcome-oriented decisions. The former pole involves reasoning from applicable rules to legal consequences. The latter pole aims at achieving a result. Common examples of result orientations are doing justice or equity; reaching an acceptable consensus among the parties; achieving the purposes behind the legal rules; or reaching the most socially beneficial result. These orientations draw on social views as they bear on the decision makers. Between these two poles are various other decision orientations, including balancing, proportionality, and rule-oriented instrumental rationality (combining rule application with attention to outcomes). Modern rule of law systems explicitly identify with formal legality at the rule-bound end, but outcomes also matter to decision makers, at least when the consequences are compelling enough, and a range of other orientations come into play as well. In small communities with long-term face-to-face relations (rural villages, business communities, disputes between neighbors, etc.), decisions makers tend to be result-oriented more so than rule-bound (though norms and rules matter), striving to achieve an acceptable outcome.

The ongoing production of law involves a constant interplay between enacted laws reflecting contesting social interests, doctrinal coherence rooted in the legal tradition, considerations of future social utility or welfare, and social norms of justice and fairness, all within broader social-cultural-economic-political surroundings.

A significant factor in the functionality of state legal systems is whether substantial aspects of law are homegrown over a long period of time – the ideal relationship postulated by Montesquieu – or whether they have been transplanted from elsewhere. (All legal systems have elements of both.) In the later context, law that developed in connection with one cultural, social, economic, political context is transplanted to another context, plopped into an arena already suffused with established indigenous cultural, social, economic, political, and legal institutions. Transplanted law inevitably functions differently and has different social consequences because it is placed in a wholly different social milieu that it may conflict with, and it is deprived of supportive informal norms and social attitudes that undergirded its functioning at home. With the passage of time, surrounding social arrangements develop in response to and in connection with the transplanted law, sometimes entrenching dysfunctionality, sometimes developing new ways of working.

These propositions provide a bare sketch of aspects of law covered in this book. Additional propositions can be added. Different angles on law within society will produce different theoretical insights. There can be no final theoretical statement since law and its relations within society continue to evolve.

Index